HOME OF MODEL T

Here at his Highland Park Plant, Henry Ford in 1913 began the mass production of automobiles on a moving assembly line. By 1915 Ford built a million Model T's. In 1925 over 9,000 were assembled in a single day. Mass production soon moved from here to all phases of American industry and set the pattern of abundance for 20th Century living.

MICHIGAN HISTORICAL COMMISSION REGISTERED SITE NO. 8

Monument outside Ford's Highland Park Plant, Detroit
(in operation 1910–1927, now in disrepair)

HOME ECONOMICS

The economic news is bleak. On Friday, Americans learned that 651,000 jobs vanished in February, bringing the total number lost in this recession to a staggering 4.4 million. The stock market continues to crater. Banks, despite an almost trillion-dollar bailout, continue to falter. The Op-Ed editors asked four writers from around the country to provide quarterly snapshots of their local economies. Here are their first dispatches.

For Sale: The $100 House

By Toby Barlow

DETROIT

RECENTLY, at a dinner party, a friend mentioned that he'd never seen so many outsiders moving into town. This struck me as a highly suspect statement. After all, we were talking about Detroit, home of corrupt former mayor Kwame Kilpatrick, beleaguered General Motors and the 0-16 Lions. Compared with other cities' buzzing, glittering skylines, ours sits largely abandoned, like some hulking beehive devastated by colony collapse. Who on earth would move here?

Then again, I myself had moved to Detroit, from Brooklyn. For $100,000, I bought a town house that sits downtown in the largest and arguably the most

Toby Barlow is the author of "Sharp Teeth."

ILLUSTRATIONS BY SOPHIA MARTINECK

beautiful Mies van der Rohe development ever built, an island of perfect modernism forgotten by the rest of the world.

Two other guests that night, a couple in from Chicago, had also just invested in some Detroit real estate. That weekend Jon and Sara Brumit bought a house for $100.

Ah, the mythical $100 home. We hear about these low-priced "opportunities" in down-on-their-luck cities like Detroit, Baltimore and Cleveland, but we never meet anyone who has taken the plunge. Understandable really, for if they were actually worth anything then they would cost real money, right? Who would do such a preposterous thing?

A local couple, Mitch Cope and Gina Reichert, started the ball rolling. An artist and an architect, they recently became the proud owners of a one-bedroom house in East Detroit for just $1,900. Buying it wasn't the craziest idea. The neighborhood is almost, sort of, half-decent.

Yes, the occasional crack addict still commutes in from the suburbs but a large, stable Bangladeshi community has also been moving in.

So what did $1,900 buy? The run-down bungalow had already been stripped of

Filling Detroit's desolate neighborhoods with starving artists.

its appliances and wiring by the city's voracious scrappers. But for Mitch that only added to its appeal, because he now had the opportunity to renovate it with solar heating, solar electricity and low-cost, high-efficiency appliances.

Buying that first house had a snowball effect. Almost immediately, Mitch and Gina bought two adjacent lots for even less and, with the help of friends and local youngsters, dug in a garden. Then they bought the house next door for $500, reselling it to a pair of local artists for a $50 profit. When they heard about the $100 place down the street, they called their friends Jon and Sarah.

Admittedly, the $100 home needed some work, a hole patched, some windows replaced. But Mitch plans to connect their home to his mini-green grid and a neighborhood is slowly coming together.

Now, three homes and a garden may not sound like much, but others have been quick to see the potential. A group of architects and city planners in Amsterdam started a project called the "Detroit Unreal Estate Agency" and, with Mitch's help, found a property around the corner. The director of a Dutch museum, Van Abbemuseum, has called it "a new way of shaping the urban environment." He's particularly intrigued by the luxury of artists having little to no housing costs. Like the unemployed Chinese factory workers flowing en masse back to their villages, artists in today's economy need somewhere to flee.

But the city offers a much greater attraction for artists than $100 houses. Detroit right now is just this vast, enormous canvas where anything imaginable can be accomplished. From Tyree Guyton's Heidelberg Project (think of a neighborhood covered in shoes and stuffed animals and you're close) to Matthew Barney's "Ancient Evenings" project (think Egyptian gods reincarnated as Ford Mustangs and you're kind of close), local and international artists are already leveraging Detroit's complex textures and landscapes to their own surreal ends.

In a way, a strange, new American dream can be found here, amid the crumbling, semi-majestic ruins of a half-century's industrial decline. The good news is that, almost magically, dreamers are already showing up. Mitch and Gina have already been approached by some Germans who want to build a giant two-story-tall beehive. Mitch thinks he knows just the spot for it. ◻

Toby Barlow, *The New York Times* Sunday Op-Ed section, 28 March, 2009

Detroit's daily newspapers cut back on their home distribution on Monday. Jason Watson, 24, handing out free copies of truncated print versions of the two papers.

FABRIZIO COSTANTINI FOR THE NEW YORK TIMES

DETROIT JOURNAL

In a Grand Experiment, 2 Daily Newspapers Now Not So Daily

By MARY M. CHAPMAN
and RICHARD PÉREZ-PÉNA

DETROIT — Maybe once a year, a city has a news day as heavy as the one that just hit Detroit: The White House forced out the chairman of General Motors, word leaked that the administration wanted Chrysler to hitch its fortunes to Fiat, and Michigan State University's men's basketball team reached the Final Four, which will be held in Detroit.

All of this news would have landed on hundreds of thousands of Motor City doorsteps and driveways on Monday morning, in the form of The Detroit Free Press and The Detroit News.

Would have, that is, except that Monday — of all days — was the long-planned first day of the newspapers' new strategy for surviving the economic crisis by ending home delivery on Mondays, Tuesdays, Wednesdays and Saturdays. Instead, on those days, they are directing readers to their Web sites and offering a truncated print version at stores, newsstands and street boxes.

"This morning, I felt like something was missing," said Nancy Nester, 51, a program coordinator at a traumatic brain injury center who is from West Bloomfield and has subscribed to both papers for four years. "There was this feeling of emptiness."

She did not even bother to pick up the condensed print versions that were offered free on Monday. "I don't have time to stop at the store," she said. "That's why I have home delivery."

Mary M. Chapman reported from Detroit, and Richard Pérez-Péna from New York.

To Carol Banas, a retired city planner and longtime Free Press reader, the idea of not having a printed paper is unimaginable. "I'm at the age where I like my newspapers in hand," said Ms. Banas, 56, who read a hard copy of Monday's abbreviated Free Press in an Einstein Brothers Bagels shop in Royal Oak. "I know that's English online, but it's not the same."

On Monday, The News and The Free Press, which share business functions under a joint operating agreement, distributed more than half a million free copies of their condensed print editions, but they will begin charging (50 cents, as always) on Tuesday. The Free Press, the larger of the papers, will still make home deliveries on Thursdays, Fridays and Sundays, and The News, which does not have a Sunday issue, will deliver on Thursdays and Fridays.

They have been heavily promoting not just their Web sites, but also online "e-editions" that look just like the printed papers. The e-editions have been open to everyone, but executives say that soon, only paying customers will be able to see them. For a day, at least, there was no doubt about the demand: the computers delivering the e-editions could not keep up on Monday morning, and many people were unable to load them.

"We had an overwhelming — literally overwhelming — number of people trying to get onto the e-edition site this morning, and it's gratifying on one hand, but it slowed things down," said Jonathan Wolman, editor and publisher of The News, which is owned by MediaNews Group.

The papers went to great effort to prepare readers, printing warnings and guides to the new

PHOTOGRAPHS BY ROBERT STOLARIK FOR THE NEW YORK TIMES

Delivery boxes stood idle Monday as newspaper readers in the Detroit area were directed to the smaller, free publications.

format, but not everyone got the message. "A lot of people were prepped for it, and yet we've also been hearing from folks who were surprised that today was the day," Mr. Wolman said.

With profits shrinking fast, newspapers are grasping for the formula that will ensure survival, and a few have decided to save on printing and distribution by publishing only on the most profitable days of the week — potentially a step toward an all-digital future. The Detroit papers are not going quite that far, but clearly the impetus is the same. Executives have called it a calculated gamble, but they say that Thursdays, Fridays and Sundays account for more than 80 percent of their advertising revenue.

About 50,000 people tried to click on the e-editions Monday, five times as many as usual, said David Hunke, chief executive of the Detroit Media Partnership. And squeezing all of the day's news into a 32-page print edition "certainly tested our theories on design and editing."

In a speech to the Detroit Economic Club on Monday, Mr. Hunke presented a strategy for winning readers electronically. The papers will soon be available on Amazon's Kindle reader and, possibly by early next year, on another device from a company called Plastic Logic, said Mr. Hunke, who is also the publisher of The Free Press, which is owned by the Gannett Company.

Despite the added demand and confusion, it probably worked to the papers' benefit that the new strategy began with a crush of news, said Bob Giles, who held Mr. Wolman's posts in the 1990s and is now curator of the Nieman Foundation for Journalism at Harvard University. "It reminds people how valuable their newspapers are, even if it's online," he said.

The future no doubt lies in that direction, but for now, it is a tough sell for some readers of a certain age.

Howard Waxer, 60, dropped his longtime Free Press subscription in anticipation of losing seven-day delivery and said he would not read online. He leafed through The Free Press while eating a club sandwich at Country Oven Family Dining restaurant in Berkley and said this would be his approach from now on — pick up a copy and read it over lunch.

"There's always going to be this," he said, holding up the paper. "I can't picture this city without a paper coming out."

Mary M. Chapman and Richard Pérez-Péna, *The New York Times* National section, 31 March, 2009

Still from *Farewell etaoin shrdlu*, a 1980 documentary about the last days of hot metal typesetting at the *New York Times* directed by David Loeb Weiss (a proofreader at the newspaper)

EITHER OR OR OR: HOW I GOT RELIGION

by Domenick Ammarati

Is there a word for something that exists only in its self-negation? A Möbius strip comes to mind; to exist it destroys its two constituent parts, back and front.

———

On 23 October, 2008, I attended a public memorial for the writer David Foster Wallace. This essay, meager as it is, I dedicate to him. He was a hero of my youth.

The service was large: closer to 200 attendees than 100, a dozen speakers. It lasted a little over two hours and was extremely moving. It took place in a theatre at New York University that struck me as both solemn and stylish, vaguely Scandinavian in design—brownish-blond wood with dynamic patterns inset into the wall panels, with a broad expanse of seating rising up from the stage. Before the ceremony began, a still projection of a beaming Wallace resided where the perspectives converged, like a jewel ensconced in a cool yet tender jewel box.

Among the speakers, near the end, was a woman whose identity I could not remember afterward. It was Zadie Smith, I later discovered, someone who I'd never have guessed to be friends with Wallace. She told a story about his recommending to her Kierkegaard's *Fear and Trembling*, and proceeded to read from his essay about being caught in a tornado as an adolescent. Or was that someone else? Overall my recollection of the event is fish-eyed, much out of focus but a few details, by contrast, even sharper—Don DeLillo's wild hair, Donald Antrim's chilling confession of his depression. Perhaps the theatre was less grand than I have described. In memory the whole experience feels extra large and I quite small; it somehow etched itself on the scale of memories from childhood.

After the memorial was over, I walked to the nearby bookstore Shakespeare & Company, which I was relieved to find still existed, as I hadn't set foot inside it for a couple of years. Books are doomed, bookstores dependent for their survival on greeting cards and children's playrooms, and independent bookstores deserving of federal protection. The shop was quiet, with more staff than customers; but marvelously, in the basement, they had a healthy selection from the oeuvre of Søren Kierkegaard. I'd never read a word of it, though he'd been recommended to me on more than one occasion. Judging from my perusing, *Fear and Trembling* retold and interpreted the story of Abraham and Isaac in a way that seemed to have to do with the idea of embracing or even claiming one's fate. While its approach surprised me—I had been expecting something 'philosophical', whatever that might mean, more abstract and resistant to narrative, I suppose—the style seemed thick, and the allegory exhausting.

On the shelf next to *Fear and Trembling* stood *Either/Or*. Unlike the former, which contained itself within a compact volume, *Either/Or* was fat. The bulk was daunting but the subtitle intriguing: *A Fragment of Life*. Like any creature of the contemporary art world, which I find myself to be, somewhat unexpectedly at age 37, I am a sucker for the blending of art and life. Too, I am a sucker for direct entreaties to the reader, such as Kierkegaard (whom I soon came to think of as 'K') makes in the book's opening passage, not to mention for the themes he summarily introduces: mystery, melancholy, and alienation: 'Perhaps it has sometimes occurred to you, dear reader, to doubt the correctness of the familiar philosophical proposition that the outward is the inward, the inward the outward. You yourself have perhaps nursed a secret which, in its joy or pain, you felt was too precious for you to be able to initiate others into it.' A few minutes of inspection (with help from the back-cover copy) revealed that the book's gist is the conflict between the quote aesthetic and the quote ethical ways of being, and that it was divided against itself into two sections, with two different 'authors', both of course K. With his recommendation of *Fear and Trembling*, Wallace had been wanting perhaps to communicate to fellow prodigy Smith something about his own grappling with his senses of fate and talent —with greatness—or doling out a bit of advice to a peer, or simply propagating a book he loved. In my reading of *Either/Or*, however, which quickly ensued, I identified with the sprawling book's internal conflict, with its mixed-upness. My sense of internal division is a problem I alternately frame as a disease of our culture and ascribe to my own personal weakness. It's an uncertain perspective not so different from what emerges from *Either/Or*, or from Wallace's oeuvre.

The Penguin Classics edition of *Either/Or* costs $18. Unlike many versions of the book, it comes in a single volume, of which the main text (including footnotes) occupies 632 pages, abridged, translated, and with an introduction and notes by a well-known Kierkegaard scholar, Alastair Hannay.

For the Uninitiated

I'm going to assume, dear reader, that you have not read

Kierkegaard, or not much of it, or not for some time. You may have glanced at a little here or there, in particular 'The Seducer's Diary', an essay of some 140 pages that is often sold as its own work; or perhaps, in the peregrinations of your soul, you, like Wallace, read *Fear and Trembling*, or else, *The Sickness unto Death*. For the record, I skipped parts of *Either/Or*, and so have only read about 80% of the book. Given the abridgement of the Hannay edition, the true figure is probably closer to 70.

Either/Or is a bastard work of post-Hegelian, post-Romantic philosophy delivered primarily by two fictional characters. The book's first half comprises essays and musings by a young, but not too young, early 19th century version of a decadent, mildly construed. Known to us only as 'A', he moons about despair and fixates on girls and the cold voids of loneliness and death; he also pens elaborate, vivid, insightful, and often fannish criticism. Part two of the book comprises longer philosophical texts-cum-letters authored by an older, but not too much older, judge named Vilhelm, who is a friend of the anonymous first character. Vilhelm advocates explicitly to A that he should get a job, marry, and behave like a normal citizen, and offers lengthy disquisitions to prove he's right about it all. The entire thing is introduced by yet a third character, a seeming bystander by the name of Victor Eremita who claims to have discovered the book's contents as two sets of manuscripts stuffed inside an escritoire he purchased from a second-hand furniture dealer. It is he who sets up the works according to the back cover's ready schematic: 'A's papers contain a variety of attempts at an aesthetic view of life ... [Vilhelm's] papers contain an ethical life-view.' In the end, Kierkegaard advances through Eremita a strange and teasing hypothesis: yes, the two sets of papers are clearly in two different hands, but they 'could yield a new

aspect if regarded as the work of one man'—an aspect of progression through, or at least reflection on, the various stages of life.

Before the book is over, two more authorial voices will have been introduced, one for the last section of each half, including that of 'The Seducer's Diary', whose existence Eremita describes in another tease as 'an old short-story writer's trick'. Plunging into the book, then, is a bit like waking up in that favourite locale of essay writers, the hall of mirrors. It's hard to know how to find one's bearings with various narrators of unclear agenda, parodic name, and likely unreliability. And as in the hall of mirrors, one sees oneself, if distorted, no matter which way one turns.

K as Aphorist: Overture

To one discovering Kierkegaard —or perhaps I should just say, 'to me'—what strikes first is what a good writer he is. The badge of this ability, and to a certain degree, what constitutes it, is his ability to turn a phrase. The book begins with a series of epigrammatic entries titled 'Diapsalmata', which means 'refrains' in Greek, and the section brims with one provocative, newly minted adage after the next: 'One should be an enigma not just to others but to oneself too'; 'The door of fortune does not open inwards so that one can force it by charging at it'; 'How the world will come to an end: to general applause from wits who believe it's a joke'; and so on. They pepper 'Either' throughout:

'The unhappy man is always absent from himself.'

'The future is nearer the present than is the past.'

'A person's resilience can really be measured by the power to forget.'

'A bad conscience can make life interesting.'

And so on. Of course an aphorist is only as good as his translator, which limits judging too firmly. And it's easy to forget, particularly on the first go-round with the book, that an entire, often plodding rebuttal, waits at the end of 300 pages: it's not a given that K will write in a sharp style. But his ability and his willingness to do so underscores his strong interest in rhetoric that sets him apart from your Hegels, your Kants; he's less interested in the production of knowledge per se than in the promulgation of a point of view. Hence his readability and relative popularity, particularly in the 20th century, when he influenced Sartre, et al.

K as Critic

In another surprise, I soon found that the essays in 'Either' contain a wealth of writing about various art forms. 'The Immediate Erotic Stages, or The Musical Erotic' kicks off A's general obsession with Mozart, and in particular *Don Giovanni*; other of his pets include *The Magic Flute* and Faust. 'Shadowgraphs' discusses Goethe's *Clavigo* and *Faust* as well as *Don Giovanni*. 'Ancient Tragedy's Reflection in the Modern' is, basically, about how the moderns will always fall short of Sophocles, et al. because today we believe that people are in some sense responsible for themselves and their fate in ways that the Greeks did not conceive, and so we cannot reach their tragic heights.

Throughout, K practices critical methods that we would call unorthodox. Some of these appear so simply because of changes over the years in what we think criticism should be. In 'The Immediate Erotic Stages', for example, he seeks to create grandiose hierarchies of greatness: 'With his *Don Giovanni*,' he writes, 'Mozart enters that small, immortal band of men whose names, whose works, time will not forget, for they are remembered in eternity.' He ranks not only artists but also art forms, with music's gaining an easy primacy thanks to its high degrees of abstraction of medium and idea. Such impulses stand out as archaic in context of so much else in *Either/Or* that seems fresh—and perhaps this element is an aspect of parody of A's pompousness and naïveté; one cannot say for sure.

Other of Kierkegaard's approaches are, however, just plain odd. Most notably, he explicitly re-imagines artworks, entering into them and re-jiggering plot and character to see what the implication would have been if the author had done such-and-such—an implication that connects to whatever lesson he, A, would like to impart. 'Ancient Tragedy' provides the best example, in the form of a vivisection of *Antigone*. K's basic point, as noted, is as follows: 'the more the subjectivity becomes reflected, the more one sees the individual … left to himself, the more guilt becomes ethical … [and] the tragic collision loses its power.' Rather than find examples from actual ancient works, let alone modern ones, he declares that he is going to re-fictionalize Antigone's character. He leaves the set-up of Sophocles's *Antigone* the same; it's the Oedipus story—Sphinx's prophecy, killing dad, fucking mom. But like a theatre director liberally adapting a classic, K imagines new psyches for the characters, new situations, whole new acts. The new Antigone knows her father's horrible secret, and as a result she suffers from a modern ailment *par excellence*, anxiety. As a result, even with her youth in full bloom, 'Antigone's life is … essentially over.' She takes pride in keeping her secret 'to save in so remarkable a manner the honor and esteem of the house of Oedipus.' Sorrow becomes her *élan vital*; 'her sorrow is her love.'

K then leaps forward in the story. Oedipus dies, circumstances unspecified, and Antigone is left not having even spoken to her father about his secret. Thus she does not know if he knew the truth about himself. Now she is completely

isolated, and her misery is sealed within her like 'an arrow which life has driven constantly in deeper and deeper, without depriving her of life … but the moment it is drawn out she must die.' The final act of the tragedy is honor's collision with love: she falls for a guy. Of course she cannot tell her beloved of her secret. He senses her reserve and, misunderstanding, spends his life trying to convince her that he loves her. She cannot marry, since marrying would shift her loyalty from father to husband; death will be her only relief. How this occurs, and whether the beloved ever succeeds, even at the moment of Antigone's death, in wresting the fatal arrow from her, K leaves us to imagine.

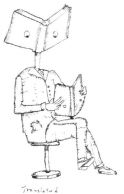

Translated

While this kind of revisionist fantasy—recasting the work under consideration—is not pervasive, the impulse rears up elsewhere; see 'Shadowgraphs', for example ('The individual traits Goethe has emphasized are naturally of great value, yet I believe that for the sake of completeness we must imagine a little modification.') And, significantly, the impulse to overread, if not exactly rewrite, extends to the book's second half, despite the fact that the character authoring the 'Or' writes nary a word on a work of art. Rather, Vilhelm's fodder for overinterpretation, wish fulfillment, and projection is the psyche and personality of his friend A, which he defines frequently and variously. 'You are a hater of activity in life', he writes. 'You are an observer'; 'You train yourself in the art of

being a riddle to everyone'; 'You are living in an illusion and you accomplish nothing'. He compares A to a jellyfish, a figure of 'complete receptivity'; he imagines in detail A's hypothetical path through first love and his refusal to convert it into marriage. If you got letters like these, you would likely be both impressed at your friend's perspicacity and irritated at his telling you so monotonously—and with such accuracy—who you were.

———

I should note here that when I discovered *Either/Or*, I was having a bit of an identity crisis. Or a midlife crisis; having never experienced the latter, I was familiar with its symptoms only from popular culture—second wives and convertible red sports cars. I haven't the means for either, which troubles diagnosis. But I was experiencing a vivid bewilderment, an incessant asking of the question, 'How did I get to this unsatisfactory place with so few of my years left to live?' Kierkegaard died at 42, published *Either/Or* when he was 30. Wallace hanged himself at 46.

The only answer, unfortunately, was that I had spent my adulthood 'iffing'—proliferating options, fantasizing, pretending, half-doing, all with the hubristic idea lying behind it that, hey, I'm smart, I can do anything I want. I suppose that, having escaped the comfortable but inert context of my childhood and adolescence, and the barren social milieu surrounding it, I assumed I could do no wrong, and that a positive outcome was preordained. Certainly I could, and it was not. The mental disorder I'd been suffering was a variation on the Hamlet problem, with indecision trumping action; with Antigone's anxiety and isolation, it forms the modernity trinity, the tripartite god we worship and fear. Of course in 2009 we are beyond modernity, and to be still suffering from its most clichéd discontents when others have moved on to god knows what makes one feel even more obsolete.

I should also note, if you hadn't surmised, that I am a critic, one who sometimes has trouble figuring out where the subject at hand stops and where I begin. 'You have become what you despise most of all—a critic,' Vilhelm writes to A, 'a universal critic in all departments ... It is sad that your truly excellent intellectual gifts are dissipated in this way.' You can see how *Either/Or* might get me hooked.

K as Novelist

So he turns a phrase like a motherfucker. But does Kierkegaard rate as a novelist? Novels are inescapably rooted in character and plot, and all but the most radical examples of the genre preserve these elements in some form. With regard to plot, *Either/Or* accomplishes little; there is no *Pale Fire*-ish nesting of story within the commentary here, and the scenario develops with little more detail than what I have outlined. With regard to character, however, K's peculiar persona-based philosophizing comes closer to crossing over. The young, moony dilettante and the older, responsible householder form a vivid odd couple, neither as extreme in their positions as their rhetoric might suggest, well able to remain friends. Their relationship is left vague: they seem to eat dinner together sometimes, but beyond that? One suspects that Vilhelm is a bit obsessed with his young friend; perhaps they are not so much friends at all. In an extreme interpretation, one wonders whether A even exists, or is solely a fictive opposite number Vilhelm has conjured, an alter ego symbolizing possibilities he has either left behind or never had at all. All these possibilities are enhanced by the fact that, in 'Either', A displays no awareness of, let alone interest in, his counterpart. When Vilhelm describes A as 'the epitome of all possibility', the line reads less like a compliment and more like an

inadvertent double entendre. The indistinction on K's part about the pair's relationship is a stratagem, luring the reader to fill in the large gaps and engage in the kind of overinterpretation, or outright invention, that *Either/Or*'s protagonists do in their 'critical' analyses.

op

A Reconsideration of the Newspaper Industry in 5 Easy Illusions (1)

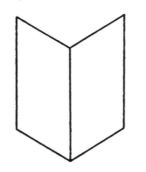

As you stare at this form, watch your perspective flip back and forth.

K's use of fake authorial personages is hardly limited to *Either/Or*: he used pseudonyms extensively. His other works are 'written' by kookily named personages including Johannes Climacus, Anti-Climacus, Johannes de Silentio, H.H., and Constantin Constantius. Historically, pseudonyms reflect practical/political concerns: the Bronte sisters' Currer, Ellis, and Acton Bell come to mind; Brian O'Nolan created two personæ, Myles na Gopaleen and Flann O'Brian, because his job as a civil servant muzzled him. Kierkegaard, however, had no clear reason to avoid publishing under his own name—he published under it often—and he was generally known to have been the author of his books. The use of the pseudonym then becomes a distinctly literary concern, a textual effect. The book-within-book conceit produces dramatic irony and elicits extra labour on the part of the reader who seeks to determine what substrate exists

'below' the book's fictional worlds. Too, the interplay between the various levels of fictionality might have intriguing thematic aspects —about the nature of reality, to cite the broadest possible example— and the juxtaposition of elements in counterpoint and variation can open up rich veins of reflection, not to mention pleasure.

In *Either/Or*, however, these effects are all a bit muted. Not much of a world exists 'outside' the two sets of manuscripts Eremita has found. The couple of winks he throws at the reader do little to advance any thematic ends or greater 'novelistic' ones, and he never reappears. Nor do the intertextual games grow any more intricate, despite their remaining elusive in terms of overall import. The research I did—admittedly limited—suggests that there is no definitive interpretation of the book and its nesting of philosophy within multiple characters. There's only to decide for oneself—which is of course in keeping with the book's motifs of self-extension and projection.

———

As a writer of fiction, the only novel I ever came close to finishing failed because it was too sketchy: I wanted to test the limits of the reader's ability and willingness to fill in what's absent from the text. I was heavily under the influence of Donald Barthelme at the time, and other 1970s experimentalists. Apparently my stratagems resulted only in frustration and boredom on the part of the reader. I quit the book after a woman I was wooing told me it sucked. It was only the first time she would break my heart.

On October 12, 1968, Barthelme, or 'Don B.' published in *The New Yorker* the story 'Kierkegaard Unfair to Schlegel'. I had forgotten completely about it until I began writing this essay. It's a form I've tried many times myself, the fake interview, or self-interview: two voices in a void,

8

talking about sex and books, including Kirkegaard's *The Concept of Irony*. Wallace used a similar structure in the titular pieces in *Brief Interviews with Hideous Men*, the book for which he was touring on the only time he and I ever spoke. It was a telephone interview, me goldbricking at my day-job office in SoHo, him implausibly parked at the Chateau Marmont in LA. He was at the height of his name-recognition then—fame, if you prefer—and I was calling on behalf of the quarterly book supplement of a Philadelphia alternative weekly. While he was patient, he was also combative, and the interview was bizarrely interrupted by a telephone outage, but in the end, thanks to a good editor, the small piece turned out reasonably well. As usual, I got tangled in a couple of needless metaphors: Wallace 'pokes around the fence that separates conventional narrative from "experimental" writing', I declared. What was he supposed to be, a dog? But I also got in some nice analysis and managed to elicit the following from the author: 'What this kind of fiction needs to do is not just be difficult and weird but to be seductive and kind of fun enough to seduce the reader into doing the weird work.'

At the time of the interview, ten years ago this summer, Wallace was the age I am today.

K as Lover

I didn't finish reading 'The Seducer's Diary', didn't even come close. By the time I got to it, at the end of A's half of the book, I was a little sick of the guy—sick of the pretension, sick of the obsessiveness, sick of the all-talk-no-action programme. I was sick, obviously, of a certain version of myself.

K as Post-Modernist & Anti-Modernist

As is the way with most nonspecialists, I've lavished more attention on 'Either', with its virtuosic writing

and its tantalizing contemporaneaity. As the book's translator points out in his introduction, Kierkegaard himself anticipated such a focus and rejected it: 'If someone starts by saying "either" … you owe it to him either to ask him not to begin or to listen also to his "or".' And in fact I did spend more or less equal amounts of time reading and thinking about the 'Or', wending through its sometimes apt, sometimes convoluted arguments in favour of marriage and in favour of choosing a course in life and acting on it. *Either/Or* is nothing without the internal contradiction this second half of the book provides—its dramatic irony, its irresolution.

A component of this irresolution, and a kind of lens the book interposes between reader and text, is Kierkegaard's use of the fragment. This figure of disunion is branded on *Either/Or* by its subtitle and its introductory selection of fragments, the diapsalmata. Only a little further on, in a passage in 'Ancient Tragedy's Reflection in the Modern', K propounds 'the fragmentary endeavour' and links it to his theory that all writing should be done as if left unfinished by the author's death: 'A fully completed work has no relation to the poetic personality; with posthumous papers one constantly feels, because of their broken-off, desultory character, a need to imagine the personality as being a part.' K's imagining of a reader's imagining an author remarkably ties together not only mortality—parcel of K's typical gloom—and a bit of phenomenology but also his theatricality and his love of contradiction ('The art is to produce an enjoyment which never actually becomes present, but always has in it an element of the past, so that it is present in the past'). Together with the other effects of personae, these elements form a foundation for K's ultimate desire for heightened engagement by the reader. Certainly this book, composed a bit like a collage, follows K's own

prescripts. Even Vilhelm, who praises unity as a virtue (in opposition to the scattered behaviour that results from embracing both this and that, from not choosing), tacitly endorses the disjunctive in his ventriloquizing A's objections to his arguments in favour of marriage, in his flights into allegory, and in the 'Or' section's inclusion of yet another voice to close the entire work.

The fragment is, of course, a hallmark meme of poststructuralism, and K's advocacy of it made a plum if modest place for him at the intellectual banquet in the second half of the 20th century. It marks his opposition to the emergent modernism of his time. Indeed, while the two main authors of *Either/Or* disagree on much, they share a discontent with modernity. Vilhelm, the traditionalist conservative, makes explicit complaints about the times, on points large—the pernicious effects of the contemporary interpretation of romantic love, for example—and small: 'Have you noticed that … [t]here are people so weak that they need proper noise and distracting surroundings to be able to work?' In a characteristically cranky jab at Hegel—which sounds an awful lot like conservatives as current as the 21st century—Vilhelm attacks the idea that conflict between opposites can actually be resolved, seeing the idea of agreement as a construct of history or philosophy and nothing real. Kids nowadays, he goes on, have taken book learnin' and applied it to living their lives, with paralyzing effects: 'In our age it is part of the order of the day to be confronted with the distasteful sight of young men able to mediate Christianity and paganism … yet who are unable to tell a plain man what he has to do here in life, and who do not know any better what they themselves have to do.' Hence recourse to that ultimate know-it-all, God, in an aspect of K's writing that, nascent in *Either/Or*, ends up causing the most problems for his cachet in recent intellectual history. At the banquet, he slides a few seats away from the head of the table.

A, meanwhile, embodies the tack seen full bloom later in the 19th century in the dandy: he vacillates, ruminates, critiques, champions despair, plunges himself into that odd existence known as the aesthetic life. As a tactic for resisting the de-individualizing aspects of modernity, it retains currency to this day. A's way of being, and the form and content of his writings, protest against the modern even if at times he wallows in what he deplores: drama fallen to a low state, eroticism reduced to voyeurism with sadistic overtones, all of us Antigones wracked and isolated by our inability to communicate. He rejects life in favour of art, rejects hidebound and flagging institutions of church and societal tradition. In one of the book's most famous passages, itself titled 'Either/Or: An Ecstatic Lecture', A embraces rejection as a life axiom: 'If you marry, you will regret it; if you do not marry, you will also regret it; if you marry or if you do not marry, you will regret both; whether you marry or you do not marry, you will regret both. Laugh at the world's follies and you will regret it; weep over them, you will also regret it ...' and so it goes, through sex ('Believe a girl, you will regret it') and death ('If you hang yourself, you will regret it'). The passage recalls Samuel Beckett; but the significant difference between them is that Beckett draws on an inexplicable power to persist in the creative act—I can't go on, I'll go on; or, if you prefer, Fail again, fail better —whereas K's A gets stricken with a paradigmatic modern affliction, indecision, and the only escape route for the author is the aforementioned peculiar Christianity.

———

To a reader in 2009—and to this one in particular—the book feels extravagant, perhaps more so than it did at the time, beholden as we can be in Anglo-American circles

to concision, and used as we are to the idea that, in literature, donning mask after mask is a kind of experimentation, a snatching away of our safety-blanket identity. K wrote during the emergence of codified rules for both identity as we know it and for novelistic realism. But the book undeniably feels mad and manic at times—the writing varying between the stunning and the unedited, strong on phrasing and sometimes wobbly when it comes to structure, the micro often winning out over the macro. Of course the overall structure is what makes the book remarkable: the two halves do truly refuse to resolve into one thing with one coherent message.

Even this set-up I can imagine as more or less incidental, in the way that many good ideas are. One wee hour of a jag, stars peeking through clouds peeking through greasy windowpane, K spread out his blotted reams of foolscap to see what he'd been doing for the past few weeks and decided that he sounded like a caricature of himself, fucking idiot, a teenager. Someone should have talked some sense to him. And so he sat down and did it himself. The result is uncommonly effective. No, it's not as if you feel you're reading two or three or five different

writers; but neither the aesthetic nor the ethical carries the day, nor is there a synthetic, Hegelian third term to which *Either/Or* clearly resolves. The book is permanently wedged open: you can rest there but not stay, there's always a breeze blowing through it.

Exit

In a coincidence notable to no one but me, Wallace cites *Either/Or* in *The Pale King*, the novel he was working on when he died. 'Strange that boredom, in itself so staid and solid, should have such power to set in motion', he quotes, in an excerpt that appeared posthumously in *The New Yorker* magazine. The line is from an essay in 'Either' titled 'Crop Rotation', which shows author A at his most caustic, advocating that one never marry or take a job, joking that Denmark ransom the Persian Shah to fund the Copenhagen arts scene. In *The Pale King* it appears in a pocket etymology of boredom, which the book takes as its subject. The plot, such as it seems to be, tracks the struggles of a group of IRS agents with their soul-crushing work.

Boredom, of course, is another modern problem, the benumbed flipside of entertaining ourselves to death, which Wallace famously anatomized in *Infinite Jest*. In *The Pale King*, he seems to propound that the solution to modernity's excess of disorderly stimulation is to dissolve one's consciousness: to approach, in a meditative way, the infinite. We turn to the infinite in times of crisis, personal or societal, the first inklings of modernity and what feel like the last. Kierkegaard's narrators find it in the lofty: God and art. I've tried to find it in a few thick books. Wallace, by contrast, remembered that the infinite lies not just in the grandiose but in the little things. Bogged down in *The Pale King*, he wrote to a friend about quitting writing and opening a dog shelter. 'Who knows?' he said. 'Life sure is short though.' *The Pale King*, left in

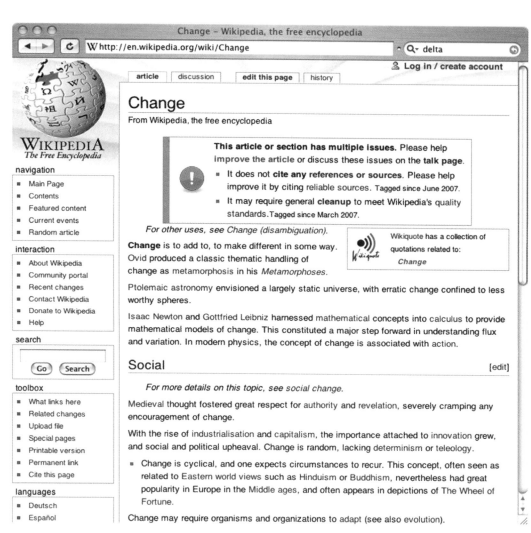

W http://en.wikipedia.org/wiki/Change

Q▾ delta

 Log in / create account

article   discussion   edit this page   history

Change

From Wikipedia, the free encyclopedia

> **This article or section has multiple issues.** Please help
> improve the article or discuss these issues on the **talk page**.
> - It does not **cite any references or sources**. Please help
>   improve it by citing reliable sources. Tagged since June 2007.
> - It may require general **cleanup** to meet Wikipedia's quality
>   standards. Tagged since March 2007.

For other uses, see Change (disambiguation).

Change is to add to, to make different in some way.
Ovid produced a classic thematic handling of
change as metamorphosis in his *Metamorphoses*.

Wikiquote has a collection of quotations related to:

Change

Ptolemaic astronomy envisioned a largely static universe, with erratic change confined to less
worthy spheres.

Isaac Newton and Gottfried Leibniz harnessed mathematical concepts into calculus to provide
mathematical models of change. This constituted a major step forward in understanding flux
and variation. In modern physics, the concept of change is associated with action.

Social [edit]

For more details on this topic, see social change.

Medieval thought fostered great respect for authority and revelation, severely cramping any
encouragement of change.

With the rise of industrialisation and capitalism, the importance attached to innovation grew,
and social and political upheaval. Change is random, lacking determinism or teleology.

- Change is cyclical, and one expects circumstances to recur. This concept, often seen as
  related to Eastern world views such as Hinduism or Buddhism, nevertheless had great
  popularity in Europe in the Middle ages, and often appears in depictions of The Wheel of
  Fortune.

Change may require organisms and organizations to adapt (see also evolution).

navigation
- Main Page
- Contents
- Featured content
- Current events
- Random article

interaction
- About Wikipedia
- Community portal
- Recent changes
- Contact Wikipedia
- Donate to Wikipedia
- Help

search

Go   Search

toolbox
- What links here
- Related changes
- Upload file
- Special pages
- Printable version
- Permanent link
- Cite this page

languages
- Deutsch
- Español

CHANGE PAGE

Wikipedia is meant to be a collaboratively authored,
continuously updated encyclopedia. For this reason,
one might look to the main 'Change' page for a demonstration as much as for a definition of the term.
Indeed, if coincidentally, the first item on the page
emphatically calls out for changes. Relative to when
I am writing this, the page was last changed by
someone three days ago. Yet the warning box says
the page was 'tagged' about thirteen months ago.

Of course the warning box is not there to alert
us to the absence of change, or to a lack of engagement by individuals in the collective enterprise;
rather, it is to indicate a need for particular kinds
of change. These are itemized as a need for more
—and more reliable—sources, as well as 'general
cleanup', including corrections of 'spelling, grammar,
tone, and sourcing'. Together, these amount to,
on the one hand, the removal of factual impurities,
political or ideological biases, and extraneous
informational clutter, and, on the other, the insertion
of more accurate statements and helpful interpretations. The first would seem to specify a minimum
condition, meant to correct an existing negative
state, while the second seems more like a desire
for the future, to move toward an increasingly
positive state (of neutrality, reliability, and/or
consensus).

This procedure entails well-qualified individuals
stepping in to remove any statements made by
authors who are less informed or who inappropriately
express vested interests. These experts collectively
excise any information that is not widely supported.
This methodology is, of course, a general feature of
the 'informational contract' at Wikipedia, and not
specific to the 'Change' page. Yet the content of the
page speaks quite specifically back to the two-part
improvement procedure called forth in the headline
box. Regarding the first point, the organizers' call
for assembling reliable sources has a faintly medieval
ring to it, and points toward an implicit alignment
between consensus (truth?) and stasis, or at least
equilibrium within the Wikipedia model. The rest
of the discussion mentions some of the things—
revolutions and paradigm shifts—that can puncture
any established equilibrium, or introduce a new one.
But within any given historical moment and any
given Wikipedia page, the drive toward democratic
consensus is underwritten by a valorization of stasis.
Even in the modern scientific paradigm, which
privileges change more than any previous confluence
of epistemology and culture, it seems that certain

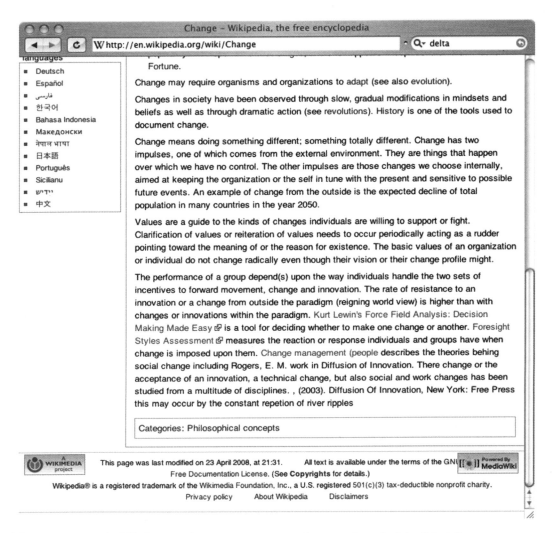

languages
- Deutsch
- Español
- فارسی
- 한국어
- Bahasa Indonesia
- Македонски
- नेपाल भाषा
- 日本語
- Português
- Sicilianu
- ייִדיש
- 中文

Fortune.

Change may require organisms and organizations to adapt (see also evolution).

Changes in society have been observed through slow, gradual modifications in mindsets and beliefs as well as through dramatic action (see revolutions). History is one of the tools used to document change.

Change means doing something different; something totally different. Change has two impulses, one of which comes from the external environment. They are things that happen over which we have no control. The other impulses are those changes we choose internally, aimed at keeping the organization or the self in tune with the present and sensitive to possible future events. An example of change from the outside is the expected decline of total population in many countries in the year 2050.

Values are a guide to the kinds of changes individuals are willing to support or fight. Clarification of values or reiteration of values needs to occur periodically acting as a rudder pointing toward the meaning of or the reason for existence. The basic values of an organization or individual do not change radically even though their vision or their change profile might.

The performance of a group depend(s) upon the way individuals handle the two sets of incentives to forward movement, change and innovation. The rate of resistance to an innovation or a change from outside the paradigm (reigning world view) is higher than with changes or innovations within the paradigm. Kurt Lewin's Force Field Analysis: Decision Making Made Easy ☞ is a tool for deciding whether to make one change or another. Foresight Styles Assessment ☞ measures the reaction or response individuals and groups have when change is imposed upon them. Change management (people describes the theories behing social change including Rogers, E. M. work in Diffusion of Innovation. There change or the acceptance of an innovation, a technical change, but also social and work changes has been studied from a multitude of disciplines. , (2003). Diffusion Of Innovation, New York: Free Press this may occur by the constant repetion of river ripples

Categories: Philosophical concepts

stabilities are assumed within its procedures: minimally, only one variable may be changed at a time; new results and propositions must remain stable enough to be tested and repeated by independent experimenters; and finally, the group with the authority to corroborate or deny cannot change overnight. Perhaps these features are true of any epistemological, cultural, or political system.

While others more qualified and less biased pick the foregoing statements apart, it is worth considering the second point, and how errors of fact and language function to effect change. In the narrow context of Wikipedia, the organizers hope such impurities and obstacles will prompt users to change the afflicted pages, and by so doing improve the quality of the reporting of the ideas and facts of the world. The larger question is whether any function or value might be assigned to error or excess in the world itself. Sometimes for good and often for ill, history is riddled with examples of error, excess, and idiosyncratic conviction that understood itself to be both counter to the status quo, and truth. But what about the deliberate impurity or intentional obstacle placed within the system by one of its own advocates?

A culture that puts a premium on change might welcome such a principle of deviation, a source of novelty, a difference agent or operator (e.g., the cultural discourse of the avant-garde, the valorization of individual expression, the means of market expansion). Alternatively, as espoused here by Wikipedia, a culture of consensual truth would count a deliberate error negatively (as malicious corruption or sabotage) and attempt to exclude it.

But in a culture which claims to value both change and consensus, what does one make of the known and knowing 'mistake'? How is it accounted for? Is there any place from which it can even be considered as such, or must it always fall into either the camp of revolution or the cave of ignorance? We can toggle between these sites and their competing privileging of change and stasis (we resolve contradictions by channel surfing all the time) but is it possible to sidestep this competition completely? Staking such a position would mean divesting change of the idea of teleology and consensus of the notion of a moral high ground. In whose interest would this be? Who would co-opt it first? Could it produce more than the staging of self-reflexivity? And anyway, isn't self-reflexivity one person's tactic for change, and another person's tactic for truth?

Dave Hullfish Bailey

12

THE RELATIONS

Clémentine Deliss in conversation with Michelangelo Pistoletto
Biella, Autumn 2004

A minor glossary is prerequisite to this discussion, which circles around contemporary art education: METRONOME is an artists' and writers' organ conceived in 1996 by Clémentine Deliss as both a collective artwork and a research methodology; FUTURE ACADEMY is a form of inquiry also directed by Clémentine from Edinburgh College of Art since 2002 which investigates unorthodox art practices, educational models, and particularly how they might usefully affect each other; CITADELLARTE is a pedagogical foundation established in 1996 by the Italian artist Michelangelo Pistoletto in a disused textile factory in Biella which works with a broad range of outside professions towards socially constructive ends; UNIDEE is a compression of 'The University of Ideas', a branch of Citadellarte which operates an international residency programme; and BICEPHALOUS means 'having two heads'.

––––––––

Michelangelo Pistoletto: What has changed since the last time we saw each other? Has something changed for you, is something different, have you gone into something, or turned somewhere else? Have you divided yourself? What happened to you since we met last five years ago? Many things have happened here over the last five years. I'm curious to know what has happened to you. Have you moved on since five years or did you go further inside, up or down, left or right? What is the drawing you would do to describe this?

Clémentine Deliss: At the moment I would do a bicephalous drawing.

MP: Okay ...

CD: Over the last few years I have become quite academic.

MP: So you went in?

CD: Yes, I went in.

MP: Bringing the two poles in one?

CD: No, I put *Metronome* to the back of my work, and went deeper into the whole question of the institution, of independent research, independent thinking, and independent production, and where one can do these today. Now I'm slowly coming back to *Metronome*.

MP: But one does not function without the other?

CD: It does but differently.

MP: *Metronome* can be very functional too. But now you have the idea of the academy as a centre?

CD: I have brought together young artists, designers, and architects to question the future of the art academy. In April we held a large symposium in India to which 45 artists and students came: 17 from Edinburgh all of very different nationalities rather like you have here at the Cittadellarte; five from a very good architecture school called KRVIA in Mumbai; 11 from Srishti School of Art, Design & Technology in Bangalore and who were also the hosts; and finally five from Senegal. They came together once I had worked with them in their different locations. They came to meet and together develop propositions for the art college or art academy of the future. These included economic propositions,

questions about mobility, architecture, and about the kinds of things one might teach and research in the future.

Here I think I have been very influenced by you, influenced by your interest in lawyers, economists, ecologists, those people who are forecasting the way the world will develop and how artists can engage with these changes. When you invite experts to the Cittadellarte, you don't invite classic experts in the arts, in other words, you don't invite floods of artists and curators, you invite other researchers ...

MP: Ignorants not experts! [laughter]

CD: You do call them experts though!

MP: I'm teasing you. We call them experts but it's difficult to define what an expert can be. It all depends on whether you're an expert in creating ideas or just an expert in something you can reproduce forever. We find it increasingly a problem to work with really well formed professionals. They cannot switch. That's why we prefer to work mainly with people who are on the inside and who are looking for research that emerges from new ideas. Of course, you have to know where you are coming from in the first place. One always has to know that in order to look for something new.

CD: Do the experts correspond to the different departments at the University of Ideas, such as your Department of Economics, for instance?

MP: We have departments of economics, of politics, of education, of work, of production and of art, of course. Art is connected to everything, it is everywhere in the University of Ideas.

CD: But if you invite an expert economist to come and work with you, do they get involved in the Department of Economics?

MP: We know how economists think because we see the work that they produce. What we are trying to do here is to find different ways of driving forward activities and perspectives in order to produce values that can give another meaning to economics. We need to find human values and not just economic values. Therefore we must not engage with economics but engage with human values. And to find out what it is that human values actually means is the real job! We have to know how to render these values evident and practicable. Economics has to serve these values, not to spend them. We don't need experts who say that if you spend more on this or that then you shall increase your money in this or that way. They know only one way of going forward, in the direction of making more money, of accumulation. We are not looking for accumulation but for ways of participating in those possibilities that are changing reality. Money is not the goal but the necessity. We look for money to make that same money clean rather than dirty.

CD: In the development of Future Academy, the Senegalese team worked on the 'Tontine', a system devised by Lorenzo Tonti, the Neapolitan who invented the rotating savings association in the 17th century.

MP: Ah …

CD: A basic example would be that you have ten people in a room who place ten Euros in a pot each month. Each month one person can make use of the total sum of 100 Euros. You have a budget that rotates around a group of people. It is not about accumulation but about a rotating responsibility. Each person has a partner who is chosen arbitrarily from within the group. If a person doesn't put in their money one month, then the

partner is responsible for them. The duty is to make sure that they contribute to the common pool, and failing this the partner takes on the responsibility of their absence. It is very powerful because it creates trust and solidarity within a group and acts as an alternative to the banking system. The Tontine is also called micro credit and it exists in many different parts of the world including Senegal and India.

MP: It's good to know that this kind of experiment takes place. We need to know how it works and if it doesn't work, why that is. It reminds me of the theatre group we had in 1969 in Cornelia. Everyday another member of the team became the *metteur en scene* or the director. They had to think of how to organize scenes for everyone, give them roles that again could not be static but had to participate in this creativity. That was theatre, but what you are describing here is similar. It's another game.

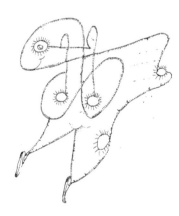

CD: It is a game but also it offers serious possibilities. If you have a group of ten students, ten Euros every week for several months leads to quite a large amount of money. As it functions on a monthly basis it means that every month a certain sum is made available for one participant, and that person has the ability to use this money as they wish. I think this is important because it is not about a group electing what it is that one

person should do with the budget. Each person has the right to do something with that money that is right for him or for her. I think the relative autonomy this creates within the group that nevertheless has a sense of solidarity built into through the Tontine is healthy.

The students at Edinburgh College of Art adopted the Senegalese Future Academy system and organized their own Tontine with their own money. They set it up before they came to India for a think-tank called 'Synchronisations', and thereby managed to bring lots of presents to their hosts. The Tontine can even provide funds for vital activities, such as inviting people from abroad. The Senegalese used the system in order to raise money for their Indian and French visas.

MP: There is something in what you are saying. Again, it's similar to what we did in Cornelia where we were free on a daily basis to reorganize and recreate individual decisions for ourselves and for the group. This means that there's no final decision but a daily decision! The decision changes, and in the case of the theatre group we had, we passed effectively from director to actor each day.

But what did we do for money? Well, we all worked for a period of time every week. With 12 people all doing this we easily had enough to cover one day. We did not save our money but instead we pooled it together. That's fantastic because the needs you have when you spend in a collective way are much less than the accumulation that each person can produce individually. You gain time for freedom. If you organize your creativity you can make practical things happen such as an exchange with someone who produces food. In a certain way, society is already organized like this. Everybody is doing something in society and here we are not talking about twelve people but about millions. However, if you are more astute, more aggressive and more powerful, you can accumulate money and the others won't have any. This is possible because we place importance on money and not on life. The prize becomes money not life. Money should be used to enhance the quality of life but the quality of life is not related to the quantity of money. This is a distortion. You can never know if it is good to have an enormous amount of cars or palaces or something else in order to become happy.

CD: What makes you happy is unpredictable ...

MP: It is unpredictable. But what I see in the Cittadellarte is a vision, and a common goal. Here everybody understands that what makes him or her rich is to pursue that common goal and enrich yourself with others. This is a real participation in the economy. You gain more if you participate with others than if you just take for yourself.

CD: You referred to the theatre group in which roles rotated and someone who was a director then became an actor. Does this relationship take place between the experts, the residents and the different departments at the University of Ideas?

MP: No I don't think so. That was an experiment of the 1960s.

CD: When I worked at Unidee five years ago, I felt at the time that if one were to create a university then one would have to have people researching and working on every level.

MP: When a professor from the university comes to visit us and says interesting things they are nonetheless repeating the school system. For that to work you have to be there for four years, with the same concept continuing, and everyone listening. But here we don't have the time. We have to move fast.

CD: But you don't bring in lawyers or economists to work at Unidee for four months as you do the residents?

MP: No, because if we did it would really become like a normal college. We consider that the people who come here have already done all this kind of schooling already.

CD: I did not see these people as being involved in teaching, but in doing research in parallel with the residents.

MP: Researching, yes, but you can't do that for four months either. You need to do that for years, as you would do in a university. In four months we want to elaborate ideas and create situations. This has to be very productive and less the result of a long-term study. We try to reach some kind of project or something practical as quickly as possible. It is more like the concept of an art laboratory than that of a long-term study. When I taught at the Academy of Fine Arts in Vienna it took four years to reach a certain result with a student and few of them reached that point. The majority were dispersed. Here in four months we do more than we could do in four years in Vienna. Here 80–90% of the residents reach a practical and a good result because they are constantly creating. We have a strict selection process. To come here, they have to be prepared to take a step forward.

CD: The selection of residents is determined by foundations who send people to you.

MP: Some institutions select for us but we try to set up a second selection process. Sometimes we have problems because people have been less selective than we would like. Little by little the information gets through that if you're not specifically interested in the dimensions of Unidee then don't go.

CD: How does the Italian art school establishment see you? Do you have any contact with it? Is there interest in what you do?

MP: In five years we've only had three Italian residents. We had two this year and we had one the year before. We receive a lot of applications from Italy but we don't find interesting people for what we are looking into. That's strange isn't it?

CD: What about staff from the art colleges in Rome and Milan? Do they come to visit you?

MP: Yes of course, there are always people coming down from the academies to visit us. But it is very hard work to make them understand what it is that we are looking for, and that we are not just looking for art works, but for methods. We are interested in methods rather than works, something that goes back into society and begins to exist like a body, an animal, something that can grow.

CD: That produces a value and a currency, and a form of exchange?

MP: Yes. We have completely lost any sense of the currency of human value, of what it means to be human. To reconstruct this is a big job. We don't have any good teachers to do this. So we have to create these teachers of humanity. We live in a moment when conflict, economical, spiritual and humanist is very extreme. It has never been so intense and yet so evident. What we don't have is the only thing we should have, we don't have anything that is able to create a new energy.

CD: Your idea of the 'Living Library' is interesting. I've been thinking a lot about the future library of the art school. What would it contain, who it would contain, who these teachers of humanity would be? Would they be books or people?

MP: I wanted to have an exhibition of selected books directed towards transformation and engagement because I was tired of making installations that had to talk about something yet without talking directly on the subject, that had to be a second or third step removed. I think what is necessary today is to create a culture not only out of practical considerations—and we are working on these—but to create another mentality, a mentality with which to really understand what is going on, and what the real problems are of different races and different cultures. What does religion mean today? I see two types of religion: on one hand all religions are mixed up into the powerful religion of consumerism, which we cannot escape from—it goes so far as to create its own war. There is also the terrible problem of consuming nature, of absorbing nature, and of producing pollution. On the one hand we have so-called underdeveloped countries that appear to be much less dangerous than the developed countries. Yet China is becoming very dangerous. If Africa were to become similar then it would be dangerous too. If all the world reaches the same level of artificial life based on artificial necessities, then the world will be self-consumed in a minute and we will explode. We cannot go on in this direction. But the other direction we have is religious fighting. These are the two terrible polarities we face.

This is why culture is so important. Culture helps us to imagine something between these two extremes, so that we can combine them in a different way. And this sensibility has to be taught. That is why I liked the idea of exhibiting the books of people who are writing. They spend their lives looking and writing and expressing problems in order to create a new myth of the mind.

CD: When Srishti School of Art, Design & Technology hosted 'Synchronisations' in April in Bangalore, I came across something I did not expect. That the cost of bringing 17 people from Edinburgh to Bangalore was the same as that of bringing five people from Senegal to India. The hardest thing I've ever done has been to find that person or foundation who would be responsible for paying for the Senegalese travel costs. It's not common for people from West Africa to go down to Southern India. It's not the accepted trade route; it's not the imperial route, nor the colonial route. That would go from East Africa to India but not from West Africa. Léopold Sédar Senghor, the late poet and president of Senegal, knew that there were connections between Senegal and Southern India in terms of aesthetics, spirituality and even linguistics. But today I couldn't find any political, economic or cultural responsibility for this from the obvious foundations. So together with the Indian Ambassador to Senegal we worked to create a bilateral cultural agreement between the two countries. Yet even when I spoke to the head of cultural industries at Unesco, for example, and presented her with the situation, of wanting to bring young cultural engineers from India and Senegal together, she asked me: what will they produce? She was imagining perhaps pots, ceramics, mats, cloth, and all those things that these continents are being pushed to produce. I answered 'relations', and she looked at me blankly and didn't understand.

So I see it as a political move to get the younger generation together who are in a post-manufacturing frame of thought with regard to the cultural values of their countries and who have a strongly developed social consciousness. Students may not be educated in art in the same way, and in this case they did not see their work in isolation, produced in the studio, and about becoming a famous artist. They are articulate and flexible. It makes me think about what actually constitutes an international group today, and that it has nothing to do with nationality. To be international is a state of mind, an openness and a readiness.

MP: That which is new for me today is Internet and scientific research into DNA. DNA research has completely changed the direction of science. Until now science had been seen in terms of progress and always moving in one direction. When I did my first mirror paintings in the early 1960s, I realized that I could see my back too and that therefore perspective did not only go outwards from myself. It could be turned in the opposite direction. In order to enter it, I had to move to the other side, to try to go into life in a different way, by looking back too. Modern art has always been directed towards forgetting about the past and going towards the new. What did it mean when Mondrian put a wall between the art of today and the perspective of yesterday? Science was doing that too. But finally ten years ago we began to see that science was looking backwards. When you look into DNA you look into a map, you look backwards in order to go forwards. What is the memory of the body, in other words DNA, if not the mirror of the past?

Now it's about looking back and knowing that you are made of that memory, and that you can put a new message into that memory.

CD: But isn't that a deterministic way of analysing memory?

MP: Of course, but until now science didn't look back, it just looked ahead. This is another scientific way of saying something new. Before we just thought about producing new visions, of going higher and further. With this we know that we can go back, back and further back and reach the origins. And there is memory, the mirror painting. It is the combination of memory and the process of the future that gives you a vision.

The other important issue is the Internet because it creates the possibility for one thing to be in different places at the same time. We have mobility that is not physical but that is a mental mobility. You can be in Africa or in Norway at the same time.

CD: I agree but I'm not convinced by it. At the end of the 'Synchronisations' project, we set up a virtual studio for 60 people. They had met for two weeks and it was a very intense time. They wanted to continue working together. So we created a communal 'studio' on the net. As far as I can see, it hasn't been used. I think that the difficulty remains of understanding how to keep communications going, and in particular with regard to those relationships that exist over vast distances. I'm not talking about people who meet at art biennials in between and say 'Hello', but what happens when you attempt to stretch the map even further.

MP: I'm not talking about that, but of the real acquisition of something that never existed before —and that is ubiquity, how we can be in one place and in another at the same time. And with Internet you have that. If you have a book in the library and someone comes and takes it, the book's not there any more. If you put the book on the Internet it's there for everybody. Everybody can have it at the same time. Practically speaking, this is incredible. It creates a rapport between a spiritual imagination and a practical realization.

The problem lies in the way these things are used, as it does with how you use money, science, and everything really. This is where the school becomes important: to help one to understand how to think, develop and, at the same time, participate in these fantastic possibilities. We mustn't stop what is already going on, but we also mustn't think that the work operates only in one sense. The work is double-sensed. We have to

reunite the brain—you said you were bicephalous [laughter]—we have to create a complexity of the mind and produce another way of considering life. We can't say that we don't wish to know how science is developing. If science just carries on producing things in the context of the economy, then that's not what we want.

Science has become technology. There's no invention that can enable the participation of people without the use of technology. You can invent penicillin but if you can't produce it it's worth nothing. You have to produce from an idea, but you need to know what the consequence of the idea is within the life of many people, and what direction this idea will take. Because everything we do is carried out through technology, you need to know how this idea will be used. We have science, but then we have the participation and application of the idea. You can make a fantastic painting, but it doesn't exist without a system that brings this painting into communication, and that system is technology. Otherwise it's just a painting and what's that good for? The biggest invention was the atomic bomb, and it was fantastic but it was used to kill millions of people.

CD: In order to work out what the future academy might be, the

students in Dakar first tried to forecast what a future society might become. So they created a backdrop, a conceit. Although it may not be possible, they spoke of a condition in 50 years from now of 'zero degree mendicité', that is to say, zero degree begging. We'll work on the basis that there will be no more begging in Dakar, they said. Then they looked at the beggars and realized that these were predominantly children who attended Coranic schools. They also saw that there was a link between the pots used by the children to collect money and advertising. The empty pots of tomato purée were produced by a corporate company, in other words, the beggars were advertising this company's identity and at the same time bringing back the money they gathered to give to the marabouts or spiritual leaders.

But what also came out of their questioning of begging within society was the scholastic method. They began to look more closely at the Coranic schools for which there is a training based on memorization. A child between the ages of four and nine learns the Coran off by heart. The actual teaching alongside begging is training in memorization. This interests me: I can't remember a basic bank code!

You were talking earlier about the consumer world and another religious world, and what I find interesting at the moment is to think of memorization as a method, and why it is that we're becoming incapable of remembering things. Some artists tell me that when collectors come to pick up works they've bought, they can't remember what they saw. Today people have no system, no techne for remembering. So the Senegalese Future Academy group proposed that a future academy might have learning by memory, not by coding, not by writing, or even the Internet, but instead through the memory of relations.

MP: We're passing through different steps. The first step was memory, we had no books and people told stories. Everything in the old times was transmitted by words. It was necessary to have your brain filled with knowledge. Then we began to put everything into the book, and finally we put everything onto the Internet. So we start to forget.

CD: Or in consumerism?

MP: Yes, but we still start to forget. Memory needs experience in order to correct mistakes little by little. If you don't have memory you don't have responsibility. You have to look back and see that which was done, recognize that it was terrible, and say, 'I don't want to repeat that. I want to change.' Memory is useful in order to create in a better and new way. But today we have a new form of analphabeticism. People are becoming less and less able to write and conceive a phrase, a way of expressing themselves, of having a complete connection between words in order be able to write and express themselves. Everything is more simplified and language is changing. Firstly we are losing memory, and secondly we are losing the capacity of writing and thinking in a complex way. We simplify, simplify, and simplify further. Looking back becomes very important in order to move forward.

When you mention the Coran, that's also something that needs to be reconceived. Because what's terrible is when the Coran becomes a limitation, the only word, the only law. We need to have a view backwards and a view forwards. We mustn't forget the importance of science in looking at new possibilities of organizing knowledge because the world is changing and growing. We have the possibility of creating weapons—terrible tools, not only good tools. We have to go beyond the concept of truth as sacrifice because it can't work for a contemporary person to believe only in sacrifice. We have this

concept of sacrifice which is the crucifixion of Christ and that's not so different from the concept of the Kamikaze. Christ was a Kamikaze. For truth that is imposed on you, you have to sacrifice yourself.

This world is totally inhuman. Humanity means that you have to study new possibilities of developing life without sacrifice and war. This is what intellectual people should be doing. It should be a mental issue before it becomes a practical one, and then a process between the two.

-llld-   The Houston rap scel

A Reconsideration of the Newspaper Industry in 5 Easy Illusions (2)

Which is the bigger monster—the one out in front or the one coming up from behind?

COUNTV

CD: This is an extraordinary proposition. The education in the most open sense of the word that you provide at the Cittadellarte is about that, about developing a consciousness.

MP: But it's not something that can be done by one person or in one place. It's something that can become a culture, a practical culture. What I see is that there are more and more people who are looking for something like that. This is the enormous change that has taken place since we met five years ago.

CD: Even Biella has changed and the inhabitants of Biella too. There

is a different population. The artist residents here at the Cittadellarte are looking at the Chinese population in Biella, for example, and all the new, different local populations.

MP: Yes, yes, there are many new institutions too; cultural institutions.

CD: But five years ago this diversity was hardly spoken about.

MP: No. It makes me feel bad, everything is going so fast and becoming so dangerous. I'm not a pessimist, or someone who lives in fear, but you can't put your hand in the fire without knowing it burns. You need to have a practical fear in order to raise the value of life. Do you still remember the Cittadellarte when there was the idea of emptiness and no decision, no definition … ?

CD: Yes, and no studio. Do you remember when the exhibition was the studio and the residents were always searching for their own place?

MP: I still think that this empty space is very basic and very important. If you have something that's already been decided on you don't find anything different. What we did was to organize empty spaces in other empty spaces and from there leading to further empty spaces. Organization is not about filling things, but about emptying things. When you speak about offices, I remember about how, in the beginning, we had one cell. This cell was divided into two parts because that's the only way to have a body. You have to divide a cell, not to accumulate but to put less inside and to have more void. Otherwise everything is full. We need to find space between things.

I recognized this within my work with the division and multiplication of the mirror. This work starts from zero and that zero is the mirror. Zero representation means at the same time total representation. When I divide zero I have 1 + 1. From zero I pass immediately to 2. You don't have 1. The only time it is alone is zero. From zero you have 1 + 1 and this is the base. The two mirrors reflect each other and then you have 3, and the more you close the angle the more you have a super division, a super participation of multiplication. But multiplication is the consequence of an act of division. You don't start with multiplication you start with the division of zero. You cannot have zero + zero + zero, instead you have to multiply. This is the idea of the emptiness of the mirror as the reflection of everything which creates a third and fourth mirror, just like a cell dividing. The multiplication of physicality occurs through the division of cells.

CD: This allows us to question scale. The mirror that reflects the mirror that reflects the mirror does not enable us to recognize the scale of what we are looking at. We look at the infinity of the mirrors reflecting, like the cells, they reflect the same morphology. There is no hierarchy of scale.

MP: No. But what's important is that the multiplication of the cell occurs through division. Cittadellarte is the same. It is an empty cell that has to be divided and redivided and redivided. The logo also points to the explosion of cells. But we don't really know anything with certainty. What we know will grow with new information that is brought to us. The world outside at the Cittadellarte is pushed away but reflected within. When we create an empty space it has exactly the same power as the full space, but it can grow too. The full space was empty first and then became full. You cannot push things, you have to create other empty spaces that expand into the fullness of what is already there. Fullness is also a mentality,

a way to think through the work. If you don't have a new way of working you always spend your time making work in a way that is traditional. If you have a new space you have a choice! An artist today has choice, but only one choice, which is to put their work in a collection, a gallery, or in a museum. There's no other choice. But if you make an empty space, perhaps an economy will grow that can enable art to become a job in a different way?

This is why when I speak of Cittadellarte I speak of an empty bubble that creates other empty bubbles and more empty bubbles and so on. Today's situation has become very evident and the need for this void is essential.

CD: With division what you're talking about is a new way of thinking through the institution, and that word institution is not necessarily bad. Institution means an association of people ...

MP: Institution is a fantastic word ... I always explained that in the 1960s we went into the street and made theatre and in doing so we went outside of institutions. But now I'm interested in making institutions. I don't complain about institutions! I complain about institutions that I don't like.

CD: The younger generation that we're dealing with today are interested too in economics, legal issues, in skills and techne, because they are also curious to know what institutions they need and can build. They're not waiting for legacies to be handed down from the empires.

MP: If they were they'd have no reason to call themselves creative. To be creative does not mean to recreate situations that already exist.

www.cittadellarte.it
www.metronomepress.com
www.futureacademy.info

TORSLANDA TO UDDEVALLA VIA KALMAR

A journey in production practice in Volvo
by Jan Åke Granath, Department of
Architectural Design, Chalmers University
of Technology, Göteborg

With footnotes by Liam Gillick

Introduction

The development of production systems through the last four decades in Sweden might be confusing to uninitiated readers. Many international and Swedish students of production systems as well as architects, social scientists and general debaters have taken an interest in the subject. The publicity has been extensive and has been further intensified through the close down (1993) and reopening (1995) of the Volvo Uddevalla plant under the name Auto Nova, a co-operation between Tom Wilkinshaw Racing and Volvo.[1] In some respects the Uddevalla plant is the symbol of the striving to develop humanistic production systems alternative to the assembly line. The fact that Volvo as well as Saab, the other major car manufacturer in Sweden, have developed both short-cycle repetitive production and long-cycle parallel production through the last decades does not contribute to the understanding of the direction of the Swedish practice. These two lines of development are often referred to as Lean production and Socio-technical or Reflective production. The latter are two of the most used terms for a Humanistic approach to production systems design. I will try to discuss this dualism in the Swedish automotive industry at the end of this paper.[2]

The history of development of alternatives to the traditional assembly line is long within Volvo. I will make some reflections on this as an architect participating in the development of such alternative production systems. My point of departure is as an architect professionally responsible for linking the managers' design assumptions into a participatory process where users with different roles in the coming production system take part.[3] Of course this is a long and tedious process where production and quality goals should be integrated with quality of work issues and spatial design.

Primarily I will focus on two extremes, on one hand the Arendal and Uddevalla plants, on the other hand on the Torslanda plant. These are good examples of the Humanistic and the Lean production approach.[4] I will also briefly mention some additional plants that have properties from both these extremes. To make this kind of distinction is somehow a simplification, but is justified for pedagogical reasons in this paper.

Some examples of Assembly Systems Design within Volvo: an early experience from Arendal (1974)

One of the first indications that long-cycle assembly could be an efficient alternative to traditional short-cycle line assembly arose more or less by accident. The production capacity of The Lundby truck plant had by 1974 reached its capacity limit and an extra 400 trucks/year had to be produced. A new temporary plant was set up at Arendal in Göteborg. To reduce investments in equipment in the temporary plant an experiment with an alternative production system was made. A group of 12 people were to assemble two trucks/day, which was regarded as tough. The group was responsible for assembly, materials handling, quality control and correcting defects.[5] The assembly was organized in a two-stage dock with a possibility to buffer one chassis between the two docks. Air-cushion carriers were used for the first time in Volvo to carry and move the chassis during assembly. Already after a couple of weeks the group performed to production goals and after four months they had dramatically decreased assembly time. They often finished their two trucks two or

---

1. As the snow started to fall. Three people were seen. They walked one behind the other. It has been colder. Today there was the sense that a thaw was coming, in the distance was a large building. Light could be seen from gaps in the structure. You couldn't describe the gaps as windows.

2. The prior clarity of the structure had been disturbed, by new openings cut at irregular intervals across each face of the building. The true scale of the structure was hard to read. Until you came close the building was hard to define. The surrounding landscape held no markers. Nothing existed in order to judge size or scale.

3. The three people kept walking. There was nothing to talk about during this long trek. We follow them as they walk. And over time they provide a sense of scale. The true mass of the building soon revealed itself.

4. The size of the cuts in its facade now troubling and excessive. Great tears and raw holes breaking through. Yet the structure remained. Perforated in haste. Revealing now people moving slowly inside. No one reacting to the approach of the three.

Everyone used to the idea of some new arrivals. Walking slowly through the snow.

5. Now inside the building. There are traces of a production line. The people moving around the space are hard at work. Yet rather than using the place as a site of production, they are methodically dismantling everything. Neat piles of machine parts. Stacks of piping and conduit. Barrels of coolant, lubricant and machine oil.

6. In the centre now there was a clear space. Seating had been improvised. Along with large tables.

three hours before the end of the day. The extra time was used for discussing experiences from that day's production and planning the next day's production. As the Volvo organization was dedicated to traditionally-paced short-cycle assembly line production and very sceptical to alternatives, they immediately suspected the trucks produced in Arendal lacked in quality. A quality audit was made and showed that the quality was higher in the Arendal plant than in the traditional Lundby plant.[6] This despite the fact that the most complicated trucks, with the largest needed assembly time, were assembled in Arendal. Volvo could not find any theoretical explanation for this but the scepticism against long-cycle parallel group assembly did not disappear. The Arendal plant was closed down in the summer 1977.[7]

The Kalmar plant is probably be the only Volvo plant that is widely known, and that has contributed substantially to Volvo's image as a Humanistic and responsible car manufacturer. The managing director of Volvo, Per G. Gyllenhammar, was a strong forerunner of Humanistic production systems, and wanted a plant that would communicate this to the market. The final building design and layout was, however, quite conventional and did not communicate the kind of image that was sought for.[8] Evidence from those who took part in the design process tells that Gyllenhammar personally intervened late in the project and urged the architect to design a building that looked more like a radically new assembly plant. Interestingly enough, the Kalmar plant is quite conventional when it comes to production technology and work organization.

The well-known star-shaped building plan contained 27 workstations in sequence with intermediate buffers. Originally the concept contained some parallel workstations. This concept was, however, abandoned, and the Kalmar plant came to be a quite traditional line where every workstation had a view through the window.[9] Originally the buffers were not meant for assembly work but in practice the workers met their cars in the preceding buffer and went on working into the following buffer. The assembly line in Kalmar was equipped with very expensive AGVs. These had ergonomic advantages, as the workers could ride on them and do the assembly work stationary, relative to the car, even if the line was moving at a constant pace monitored by a computer. The AGVs also made it possible to tilt the bodies 90 degrees so the workers did not have to do under-up work on the car and also could have comfortable working situations on interior details like the roof.[10]

In 1987 the Volvo 760 model production started in Kalmar. The new model needed substantially more assembly time than the earlier models. The plant had to be extended with a new wing that made the famous star shape asymmetric.[11] Still, the limited number of AGVs available and shortage of space made it necessary to decrease the number of buffers. The computerized product specification system, however, made it possible to identify every individual car on the line, which made it possible to allow revision of the flow due to variation on the products. In 1989 parallelization was introduced on some subassemblies, and at the marriage point between the engine-axis and body. These changes were made to improve the ergonomic situation but also gave a substantial increase in productivity.[12]

In early 1985 Volvo management authorized a prospective study concerning the establishment of a car plant in Uddevalla, on the west coast of Sweden. Originally, the plan envisaged a complete car plant with body manufacturing, assembly and painting/finishing. A project group was formed to include union representatives in the planning process from its earliest phases. In order to facilitate the new establishment in Uddevalla, Volvo had received permission from the Swedish government to use funds from the company's investment reserves.[13] Early on in the preliminary study both Volvo management and the unions itemized their respective goals in the project. Ellegård has documented this phase of the project in extenso.

The 'vision' of the respective parties is encapsulated in the following phrases: 'a holistic approach to an efficient workplace with human qualities for the manufacture of quality products' and 'technology, process information and environmental aspects shall be well integrated in the complete plant.' Ellegård itemizes the ambitions for the Uddevalla plant in the

And low slung lighting. Surrounding this area, large screens had been erected. On these screens, a mass of text and notation and plans. A complete explanation of what might be done. An improvised analysis of the potential of future production. Attempts to resolve all material relationships. Such an effort. Such precise calculation. An inventory of previous production. Many hours had been spent regretting the early bonfire that had been fueled by notes and comments from earlier times. They used to work in teams. Now they work in a large group. At times they work alone.

Trying to create an archive of all previous working methods.

7. At times this work is punctuated by the sounds of improvised tools tearing at the wall. Everyone stops what they are doing. Assuming that they were doing something in the first place. And many are lying on the ground. For at any given moment, many appear to be resting in the shadows. Those that were resting now spring into action.

8. Grabbing sticks and rods and pieces of old machinery. Everyone goes to the already punctured walls. And begin to hack new gaps into the exterior of the former factory. Some are better than others. So some people help by bending and folding the torn aluminium in an attempt to pull it free. The factory closed a long time ago. Or maybe it was a couple of months ago. There were no aims at the outset. Merely a desire to return and reoccupy.

9. As we know everyone had been well looked after. But the potential of the space remained appealing. In order to prevent it from being reused, people had begun to use the place again. At first merely hanging around and talking about how things had gone wrong. After a while they started to draw out new openings on the walls.

following terms: Finest quality, highest reliability of delivery, maximal cost-efficiency, excellence in personnel development, streamlined administration with few hierarchical levels, and a personal 'manufacturer' for each unit produced.[14]

The Final Assembly Plant
After some deliberation and discussions relating to the concession to operate, Volvo chose in January of 1986 to confine their plans for Uddevalla to a final assembly and finishing plant. The preliminary proposal for the layout of the new plant had many characteristics in common with the Kalmar plant, but not as advanced.[15] Assembly was, for example, to be performed at 150 different stations, located along the walls of the plant. It was to be organized according to the same principle as a line, but would involve assembly in docks. That is to say, bodies would be assembled standing still. Furthermore, the team at each dock was expected to deliver a perfect unit to the next team along the line. Here differences within the project group with respect to production technique preferences which had been implicit in the earlier discussion of goals, surfaced into the open light. The project group included both individuals imbued with the production ideals of Taylor and Ford, and exponents of the Socio-technical approach to work and view of the role of workers in production.[16] The latter proposed parallelization as a means to diminish the losses that line assembly entailed, and they also introduced longer task sequences and buffers to achieve a greater measure of autonomy for both individuals and groups of workers. Thus proponents of the Socio-technical approach were dissatisfied with the proposal currently under consideration. Two features were particularly criticized: the very brief work cycles envisaged, and the fact that line workers were to be held responsible for quality although the conditions under which they would be working afforded no real opportunity to ensure quality.[17]

The project continued as two parallel projects, one by the existing in-house production design group and one led by a production engineer with a socio-technical approach in cooperation with a research group from Chalmers University (in which I participated). The two groups had to prove the efficiency of their designs continuously through the project.[18] A more detailed description of this process can be inferred. After a long design process, the Socio-technical or Reflective approach came to realization.[19] The design process was not straightforward as neither the theory nor the practice were available to design a production system that should meet both high Humanistic and efficiency performance goals.

The finalized Uddevalla plant was divided into six parallel assembly shops, so called 'product workshops'. The product workshops are grouped in two buildings, with a test workshop at the centre of three product workshops.[20] The layouts were different in the two buildings. In the first building the automobile was assembled in two stages and the body was moved between the two stations.[21] The group size was seven workers and normal cycle time 100 minutes. In the latter building the body was not moved during assembly work. At the closedown a group of nine workers circulated between the two stations and the normal cycle time was 80 minutes.[22] The subassemblies were integrated into the workstation system. In the early workshops the workers did both body and subassembly while specific workers did subassembly in the latter workshops. The individual differences were, however, large.[23] Two female workers chose to assemble the entire car by themselves.

Summary of the cases
It might be interesting to look at the development of production systems in Volvo from the point of view of quality of work as well as efficiency of production. The two extremes are Traditional Mass production systems and Reflective production systems. Lean production systems are a modernization of traditional systems with some properties in common with Reflective production systems.[24]

Quality of work
Quality of work contains a number of aspects. I suggest that a system that offers professional, meaningful work is better in this respect than one that only can offer unskilled or semi-skilled work.[25]

10. The dismantling of the machinery only came later once people had stopped going home at night. Anyone passing by would hear people working late into the night. While they believed that things were being made, this was clearly not the case. Merely the sound of action. Often, early in the morning, the place would be quiet. Yet people rarely left these days. Food was being produced in small gardens. Water could be sourced from a pump.

11. A great deal of time and care was put into the gardens. But the primary effort went into calculation. Every available surface had been marked.

12. Every table covered in diagrams. There were lists of materials. And lists of processes. There were shipping routes. And estimates of production times. As the former factory was neatly dismantled. A new virtual production line took its place. But this one was not limited to one location. Instead it included all places on earth. The calculations attempted to explain. All of the relations of production. Now, it sounds as if this might be some kind of devastated near-future. Or a corrupted commune. But these were the normal ex-workers.

13. The people who used to arrive at the factory every day. Many of them had known each other for years. At first they had peopled the production line. After a while they had won the right to organize themselves. At first this had gone extremely well.

14. All predictions of collapse and low production had been unfounded. As soon as this self-organization had taken root it was taken away. Everyone had to go back to the line or leave. There was no explanation and no logic to this.

15. But even a short strike couldn't change the decision. Some decided to leave. Others decided to stay. Within

The aspects that signify professional work are control over methods, time and quality, plus the responsibility to plan ahead and gather the knowledge needed to reflect on work done. It also contains a professional language including theories, concepts and rules. Quality of work also means good ergonomics, appropriate working tools and a good physical working environment. If we look at these aspects, it is clear that Reflective production systems are superior in this respect.

Something like professional assembly work first occurred in the temporary Arendal plant. Compared with the traditional line assembly at Lundby the assembly work in Arendal turned into something quite different. The group of 12 was responsible for the whole product and could, when assembly time went down, also plan their next day's work. There were people in the group assigned to materials handling, control and correcting defects but the group's total work content was basically the entire truck.[26] The actual cycle time was 240 minutes. As a whole, the assembly work in Arendal had very little in common with the repetitive short-cycle work their fellow workers did in Lundby. It took almost 20 years before the Tuve (1991) truck assembly plant came close to what had been achieved in Arendal.

The so-hailed Kalmar plant could not present a work situation much different from the traditional assembly line. The cycle time in Kalmar was substantially larger than in a conventional line assembly, 2–20 minutes, but basically it was a paced assembly line with limitations in work content, high dependencies of the technical system, and very few possibilities to influence quality.

The big improvement was on the physical environment. All workstations were located at the perimeter with large windows. The assembly workers had nicely designed rooms for pauses at the facade. The ergonomic situation was dramatically improved compared to a traditional line assembly.[27]

The Uddevalla is, however, the most radical example of Reflective production in Volvo. This plant was, in all aspects, a humanistic production system.[28] The cycle time was, in general, 480 minutes but one team of two female assembly workers assembled the entire car by themselves. Planning, quality control, corrections and development of methods were all the team's responsibilities. The spatial consequences and preconditions for different production concepts are interesting.

In Kalmar the managing director realized the importance of spatial design and urged the architect to give the plant a visual image different from traditional plants.[29] However, group work with intellectual property demands different physical conditions than detail-controlled, short-cycle, repetitive work. One needs an overview, space for planning and intellectual work, plus a noise level, lighting quality, cleanliness, and workshop proximity similar to those of an office environment. The smallest possible scale of a serial assembly line is enormous compared to a 42-parallel-product workshop assembly like in Uddevalla. The long work cycles also eliminate the need for buffers to make more of the space eligible for assembly work. The number of parts displayed to the assembly workers are also less in parallel assembly than in serial assembly. Altogether this makes a Reflective production system more space-efficient and provides the further benefits of a more human spatial scale and design.

The Uddevalla plant is the most obvious example of a professional assembly system—accompanied by work-appropriate building design—that also communicates something beyond that of a traditional assembly plant.[30] The described development projects at Torslanda show, however, that even extremely large-scale plants can be converted into Reflective production units if some efforts are made to redesign of the space.

Production efficiency

The most important quality of a production system is, however, its efficiency in terms of productivity and quality. In this case I will compare mainly the Uddevalla plant with assembly line production. Engström et al. have, in several papers, questioned the simplified measures of efficiency that are dominant in writings on Lean production. In lieu of a detailed discussion of this here, I will present some empirical figures from Engström et al. on the

weeks the factory fell silent and closed. At first people were drawn to the factory out of boredom. And a degree of frustration that an incomplete project has been abandoned so soon. Initially people would function in parallel to each other.

16. Many merely choosing this place as a location to pass the time. Calculation became the common language.

17. Sharing notes and speculative models. The decision had been made, to avoid anecdotal play. Instead to move focus away from people and onto objects.

18. A desire to account for everything. A need to create a series of equations that could provide a new balance. A desire to quantify relationships. Great lists of materials were created. Routes and modes of transportation discussed.

19. Everything was tied to everything else in a desperate search for balance. People found a way to amuse and occupy each other with this global accounting. It drew them all together and transcended all difference. Some mornings, new people would arrive and marvel at the incredible quantity of work that had taken place. An inverse productivity.

efficiency of the Uddevalla plant. It is important to note that the plant was probably not fully trimmed at the time of the closedown. The work pace in Uddevalla was measured as 115–130% higher than the standard time for the assembly line. The average cycle time was 80–100 minutes. The two aforementioned female workers with the 350 minute cycle time worked at a pace of 105–115%. A subassembly for doors was measured and the empirical data showed that the assembly time in Uddevalla was lower in all but one case. Part of the explanation for this might be found in another empirical study done by Engström et al. of assembly in Volvo and Saab. This study shows significantly lower losses related to materials handling, balancing and system in parallel systems than in serial flow systems. The measured figures are 40% losses compared to 135% losses, relative to an ideal system without losses. As mentioned above, there was an early demonstration of this efficiency of parallel systems in Arendal, where the stipulated work was done faster than estimated. Another example is the Volvo bus plant in Borås with three parallel assembly stations, where the productivity suddenly went 26% higher than on assembly line, and with superior quality.

Reflective production systems seem to relate to variations in different ways than Mass Production systems and Lean production systems. Variations both in systems behaviour and man performance built into the serial systems tend to add up and result in extended losses. Product variation is preferably avoided in serial systems, as they also tend to add up and cause imbalances and quality problems. The cure for this is a high degree of product design. Though this may cause high design and construction costs, this is an affordable problem because very large-scale production will make the development cost per unit reasonable. A serial system can therefore perform efficiently with high product quality under certain conditions.

Reflective production systems, on the other hand, are designed to accommodate variations. With long cycle times, extended work content and overlapping competence within the group, variations in man performance and products do not influence efficiency in the same way as in serial systems. These systems also take advantage of the workers' intellectual capacity to re-plan production, make corrections on-line, and trouble-shoot whenever needed. Reflective production systems are designed to accommodate variations of all kinds. This makes them especially suitable to low- and medium-volume production with a relatively low degree of product design. The flexibility of Reflective production systems can, however, be exploited even in large volume production and has the potential for higher quality and productivity in addition to the proved superiority in work content, autonomy and ergonomics.

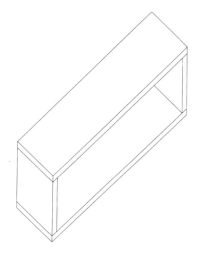

Design assumptions and the actual outcome
We have seen from the above presentation that the company's assumptions or expectations have been quite different from the outcome of the projects. Arendal is the first example of this. The intention was simply to design a temporary production facility that for a short time could meet the extra demand. This had to be done with a reasonable investment in equipment. The outcome was a production system with dramatically improved

20. Over many years the work continued. It initially brought curious outsiders to the former factory. After a while the visitors stopped coming. And left the main group to continue their work. The machinery, by this point, was unrecognizable.

21. All of it had been broken back down into its component parts. One part of the group now specialized in turning these parts back into elements. Not reprocessing for the production of new things but the complete breakdown of former parts. The effort put into this reverse production was as extreme as the early dynamic of capitalism.

22. The core group worked hard on their project at times when they were not involved in refining their calculations. There was an increasing sense that a moment was being reached. A certain level of resolution being achieved.

23. The borders of the building were now completely porous. Gardens extended inside the building. And piles of material were now stacked just outside the factory walls. Some children were born. Some people left.

24. Some people died. A few were maimed in accidents. The old worked alongside the young. There was no obligation to do anything. The texts and calculations formed an enormous archive. A massive log of all potential exchanges. An exhausted but happy group. With a perfect exchange tool. The basis of it derived from experience. A near complete dismantling. Over time the building no longer resembled a factory. It had been absorbed into the landscape. The rigour of the original structure had been lost. Every remaining surface was dented and bent. The roof was missing in places.

25. At night people slept in the former offices. Safely located in the

quality and productivity, providing the first clue that building trucks could become professional work instead of unskilled or semi-skilled assembly line work. In Kalmar and in most of the plants designed during the Gyllenhammar era, a Human Relations-dominated philosophy dictated the projects. A lot of work was done to improve ergonomics, lighting, noise reduction, and the environment, with colours, plants, and more attractive building design. This was intended to result in more rewarding work situations, and involve more worker participation and responsibility. The idea was that these improvements should result in production systems where quality and productivity could be combined into work that would attract the younger generation, and Kalmar was designed to be the ultimate Humanistic car plant. In international TV commercials the plant was presented with happy young people building cars in a handicraft manner, implying the superior quality that must result from such responsible and personal treatment of every car. We know that the reality was somewhat different. The real improvement did not occur in the proposed direction until the late 1980s, when the technical system had improved sufficiently to stand up to the high ambitions. The end result at Kalmar never really stood up to the humanistic ambitions but developed into quite a good production system with some qualities that contributed to worker satisfaction. The design assumptions for Uddevalla were also strongly influenced by a Human Relations philosophy. The first layout sketches of the production system were variations on Kalmar and Torslanda. The vision was basically a traditional production system with strong emphasis on the work environment and some new aspects of work organization and technology. The outcome was a totally new innovation in production technology that proved to be extremely competitive in all respects.

Humanistic values

It is confusing to an outside viewer that Volvo strongly believes in traditional assembly-line production yet continues to attempt radical experiments in alternative systems. It might be interesting to discuss this contradiction. From the 1970s up to the end of the 1980s, Volvo was a company with a much stronger corporate leadership. This made it possible for corporate policies to have a much stronger impact then, relative to today's more atomized company. The managing director of Volvo during this period was Gyllenhammar, a strong believer on one hand in the company as a responsible part of society, but also in the human being as a major resource not only in society but also to the company. In the 1970s this was a quite radical standpoint for a leading industry executive, as mainstream thinking asserted an idealized concept of an automated plant without humans, which were regarded as the weakest part of the production system. The top management of Volvo embraced this more visionary view.[31] This philosophy is well described in a book dedicated to Gyllenhammar, edited by one of his directors in 1985. The title of the book is, in translation, *Work and Dignity*. A small group among the production engineers was well educated in the ongoing development of production systems alternative to paced, short-cycle work. Some of these had ongoing contact with the researchers at Chalmers who had designed some production facilities in other companies.

Investment funds were available

Another influence contributing to the willingness to experiment was that large Swedish companies had, because of the big profits during the 1970s, been legally forced to set aside money in investment funds.[32] This money could only be used under certain conditions. The Kalmar plant was created partly with this kind of money, and so were the Uddevalla plant and the SAAB plant in Malmö. Uddevalla, Kalmar and Malmö were all regions in need of industry, which made it possible to use these funds. The extra money made it possible to design experimental plants that would contribute to more humanized production and make the Swedish car industry more competitive.[33]

Recruiting problems

The unemployment rate was extremely low in Sweden at that time, and it was especially difficult to attract young workers to industry, particularly

---

basement of the structure. In good weather they slept in the main space.

26. Or on platforms suspended above the floor. The few remaining walls were so heavily marked with calculations that they provided a reassuring pattern. Even though some people no longer remembered what this work had been for. Special days had developed over time. Celebrating markers in the history of the place. Moments when ores and fuels had been resolved. Alcohol and food had been accounted for. There was the general feeling that things were working out. A sense that

all relationships in the world had been accounted for. Yet any casual visitor, had they still bothered to pass by, would notice some strange things.

27. What felt like hard work in the former factory would look like almost nothing to someone used to the dynamic of capitalism. The level of work taking place was almost impossible to sense. A group of shy, nearly silent people moving slowly or lying on the ground. But in their minds they were still resolving great relationships.

28. Breaking down structures and accounting for everything. The general health of the factory population was

poor. Their superficial health and appearance even worse. Dentistry had never taken off. Podiatry unknown. Posture was hunched. And mirrors completely absent. New standards had emerged. Connected to the ability to resolve.

29. Yet any attempt to provide an objective reading of this work was now bound to fail. The true effort of the place mainly went into gardening.

30. And even that was barely maintained. Yet there was a sense that this was a better way. Free from the constraints of production and the obligation to improvise. A true parallel

the automotive industry. This fact influenced both quality and productivity in the Swedish automotive industry. Humanization of production seemed to be a way to deal with this problem.

Deeply founded Tayloristic culture
There were, however, some aspects that contradicted these favourable conditions. The majority of management on all levels was both trained in and dedicated to traditional Tayloristic production methods. The fact that the majority of Volvo management saw humanization of production merely as a way of dealing with the current recruiting problems rather than overall production explains certain shortcomings. The humanization was focused on the physical work environment and Human Relations issues, rather than production technology. Participation, group work, learning issues and other soft matters were investigated in some detail, but often the technical systems could not deliver the work content, efficiency and flexibility that was required. Those who should have investigated and developed such systems were not very dedicated because they did not believe in it.[34] This is also why Volvo has never tried to collect, analyze or reflect on the data from the various experiments. Not even when the Volvo Uddevalla plant was closed down—one of the most famous and most elaborate experiments in the world—Volvo intended to keep the documentation of the production system private. This material was saved by Chalmers researchers from being thrown away and is now kept for future research. Such data has been crucial in the design of the Auto Nova plant, located in the same buildings in Uddevalla. Therefore evidence of success related to alternative production has been a surprise. No theoretical explanation has been available, just as no information is available to explain traditional Tayloristic praxis either.

Strategic work is not favoured
The introduction of new production concepts is a very long procedure. It took 20 years after the temporary plant in Arendal was established before a production system with the same qualities was introduced at the truck plant in Tuve.[35] A career at Volvo is not designed for such long-term development. The average 'cycle time' for a career at Volvo is about three years. You will be judged on what you achieve during these three years, not what might be the result of your efforts ten years later. Even if someone were to remember that it was your work, it would not be recognized because somebody else wants to profit from it. Therefore strategic work has low status and no payoff. It pays much better to be tactical and focus on short-term results, even if they might be contradictory to long-term goals.

Humanization as 'band aid' or precondition to competitive production
A large group of managers and engineers saw humanization as a way to get workers to accept the shortcomings of fundamentally traditional production systems. Others focused so hard on the human aspects of alternative production systems that they overlooked the technical aspects of the production systems design. The first group did not really believe in the competitiveness of alternative systems in terms of productivity and quality but saw no other way to deal with the problems of recruiting and absenteeism. The latter group understood alternative production systems mainly as social or democratic experiments. Many projects have therefore suffered either from lack of commitment to the development of alternative systems, or from insufficient technological competence. When Swedish unemployment rates increased in the 1990s, Volvo saw no reason to pursue the search for assembly line alternatives.[36] The book *The Machine that Changed the World* came as evidence that their attitude was right. It is therefore important to stress that the most vital condition for the success of alternative production systems is to base them on technological solutions and theories that are superior to traditional systems in terms of productivity and quality. This has been possible due to technical and organizational solutions that are more flexible, and utilize the human intellectual capacity in a better way than traditional systems.[37] This attitude has been the standpoint of the core group of researchers

had been created. That offered a true illusion of important work. One winter, as the weather grew cold. A small group of people grew restless.

31. The arrival of the three people had recently taken place. They claimed to have come from a similar place. And nobody still lived who could verify their claim. Their story sounded real enough. And their experiences extremely familiar. They too had been part of an improvised community. A long way from here. For a while even the most languid attempts at work were stopped. Many nights were now spent comparing research.

32. The factory space was cleaned up. And layers of writing exposed in order to explain, in reverse, the working of this place.

33. Gardening stopped leading to severe malnourishment. Until one of the newcomers offered to take over, introducing an 'efficient' new technique. Killing animals for cooked meat lifted many from the floor and they too eagerly joined in the process of explanation.

34. Some parts of the former walls were now restored. And a small generator coaxed back into life. It was necessary to show the visitors

everything. Reveal slowly how the resolution of all material relationships had been achieved. Layers of text were carefully cleaned from the walls.

35. Each removal revealing a hidden layer beneath. Papers were stacked and archived. Carefully constructed indexes were produced. Everyone was open and generous. The visitors would sometimes be found searching through the shadows. Initially this was of no concern. But one or two were suspicious. Yet couldn't find any focus for their concerns. After two or three months' work began on reconstructing a computer controlled welding

and Volvo engineers that has been involved in most of the above experiments. Engström et al. have, in several papers, argued that efficiency of a production system cannot be measured by comparing man-hours in assembly, but has to be measured over the whole production process and considered in a specific socio-economical context. They have further shown, in several studies, that even with these restricted measurements, the closed-down Uddevalla plant was as efficient or more efficient than traditional assembly at Volvo was.

Conclusion

The conclusion from Swedish experience is that there are two lines of development: Reflective production and Lean production systems.[38] Under certain conditions, with large volumes, a high degree of design, and effective exploitation of suppliers' competence, the Lean production systems could perform well. Reflective production systems in Sweden have proved to be more efficient than their Lean counterparts, and have potential to be even more so in other contexts. It is clear that Reflective systems are superior in all human aspects. Consequently there is a choice between two efficient systems, depending on the structure of the company, the socio-economic conditions, and values regarding the future quality of work in the automotive industry.

machine. This now joined the paint shop that had been completed a few weeks earlier. One complete wall of the former factory had also been restored. At great effort the facade had been recreated. The effort took its toll. And people died prematurely. Others were weak. But the collective desire to show the work achieved led to renewed efforts. A new, simple, high-fat and high-carbohydrate diet was introduced. Leaving the workers happy for a while. Weight increased. And so did the pace of reconstruction. People were now encouraged to account for their work.

lade a big splash in 2003, "CC

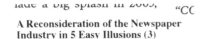

A Reconsideration of the Newspaper Industry in 5 Easy Illusions (3)

Which pile of money is equal in height and width?

36. Complex relationships were forgotten. Everything now had a rational aim. Death was increasingly common. The rate of reconstruction increased. The archive was lost in a fire. The process of explanation abandoned.

37. The work was nearly complete. The three surveyed the work. They were happy with the reinstated plant. Clean and clear. Early on the last evening.

38. The last of the few. Were lined up by the smelter. And no longer knowing what to do ... Slipped into the melt.

'I'M ONLY A DESIGNER': THE DOUBLE LIFE OF ERNST BETTLER

by Christopher Wilson

Let me tell you a little about the Container Corporation of America. Around 1950, under the ownership of Walter Paepcke and the art directorship of Egbert Jacobson, this box manufacturer embarked on an advertising campaign entitled 'Great Ideas of Western Man'. Each ad in the series, which continued for the next 30 years, quoted one Western Man with Great Ideas or another, aligning his words with 'the best in graphic arts'; i.e. the talents of such artist-designers as Herbert Bayer, Max Bill and Paul Rand, among others. The whole exercise was a fantastic early example of meagre content outstripped by style.

Let me tell you a little about Ernst Bettler. In 1954, and possibly unknown to the Container Corporation of America, this 25-year-old was at the beginning of his career as a graphic designer in Burgwald, Switzerland, having completed his three-year apprenticeship as a compositor at the School of Arts and Crafts in Zurich earlier in the year. One of the first clients to walk through his door was an Austrian stationery maker, Androschin AG. As Bettler says now, 'Kurt Androschin showed me the Container Corporation posters. I think he thought he could be the Austrian Paepcke, and that I could be his little Jacobson—one who would cost less money than some Basel hotshot. But I found the CCA adverts vulgar. They were using Magritte to sell cardboard boxes!'

Turning Androschin's brief on its head, Bettler came up with a poster design which tapped into one of the art movements passed over by the CCA designers: Futurism. 'You see, Androschin were one of those clients who, while they are keen to suck the life from the world of art, really know nothing about it. So if a designer tells them that a pioneering Futurist named Depinelli is happy to paint them a canvas for their promotion, they'll be delighted. People have always asked me how I got away with things I did to clients. I always say I am amazed it doesn't happen more.'

Giacomo Depinelli, alias Ernst Bettler, duly forwarded his celebrated 'Dynamic rhythms of postal communication'. The ecstatic client saw in it the dynamic rhythms of postal communication. The incredulous public saw two angular horses (or perhaps cows) furiously copulating in a field of curvy corn. The 'Emperor's new clothes' aspect of Bettler's first piece of subversion was, he admits, slightly undermined by those who congratulated Androschin on their willingness to poke fun at the art world. Nevertheless, the Container Corporation of America has a lot to answer for.

Goodbye to Burgwald

In late 1958 Bettler, now 29, was commissioned by Burgwald-based pharmaceuticals manufacturer Pfäfferli+Huber AG to design a running series of posters celebrating the company's 50th anniversary. He was already aware of reports concerning P+H's involvement in testing carried out on prisoners in concentration camps less than 15 years before, and when the telephone call came, was about to tell this would-be client to '... go to hell. But fortunately the wheels in the brain were faster back then, and I remembered the Androschin job. In that split of a second I had the feeling that I could do some real damage.'

Bettler accepted the commission—a decision which cost him several left-wing friends. 'But I knew I could win them back later. The agony was biding my time. When I said yes to the job, I had no idea how subversion could work with a large client who would check everything over and over. The first set of posters gave P+H exactly what they wanted: a new style of design.'

This 'new style' involved the clean, asymmetric typography and supposedly 'objective' photography which Bettler's big brothers (Gerstner, Müller-Brockmann et al.) were already selling to clients in Switzerland's more significant cities. Scores at the end of the first wave of publicity were as follow: one big, happy client with a dubious but invisible past, and one talented, well-paid designer with a dwindling number of friends and a lot of sleepless nights.

'The only thing I thought might raise suspicion was that the one adult male who appeared in that first series looked very Jewish. But this was the 1950s, and Pfäfferli+Huber were desperate to play down their involvement, even in a meeting with a stupid designer, so nothing was said.'

Early the following year a second set of posters was presented, one by one over a series of meetings, for the client's approval. Only after they had been printed did Bettler's masterplan come to fruition: 'The beauty of it was that, taken alone, each poster was utterly inoffensive. But you must remember that everything has a *Zusammenhang*; a context. These posters would be seen

Ernst Bettler in 2000, and in 1954

together in horizontal rows. And I was very careful with my briefing of the bill stickers.'

On hundreds of sites around Burgwald and neighbouring Sumisdorf, the posters appeared in fours. In the first a clowning child's body made an 'N'; in the second a woman's head was bowed inside the 'A'-shaped triangle of her forearms. An old man's contortions in the third poster ('that took forever to shoot') sketched a 'Z'. No prizes for guessing that the girl in the final *plakat* stood defiantly still, her almost silhouetted profile as stiff as, well, a letter 'I', for example.

The reaction of the usually passive local populace was immediate. The posters were torn down in the streets, the offices of the *Sumisdorfer Nachrichten* were buried beneath an avalanche of complaint letters, and demands were even made for the company's managers to stand trial. In under six weeks Pfäfferli+Huber were ruined forever. Even today, the sooty mark left on the front of the factory building by the long-gone metal logo is less visible than the ancient 'Nazis raus' spray-paint around the rusted gates. If World War II had in part been fought on the battlefield of design, then Bettler's involvement in the downfall of P+H stands as a testament to design's power to change things since then. But how did he get away with it? Wasn't there even a threat of retribution?

'Pfäfferli+Huber took me to court, sure. But as I said, each of the posters was completely innocent. I'm only a designer. As soon as a job leaves the printer it's out of my hands. I can't be held responsible if some buffoon—or a little team of buffoons, say—is insensitive when it comes to sticking the damned things on a few walls in town!'

Even after 41 years, he delivers this gloriously spurious argument with such indignation and hurt that I catch myself almost sympathizing. No wonder the company couldn't nail him.

'Absolutely not. In fact they were ordered to award me damages of 180,000 Swiss Francs—no small amount in 1959.'

Amusing though all this is, one can't help feeling that the possibility of corporate revenge must have played at least some part in his decision to move to England the following year.

Swiss graphic design (or something)

Despite the fact that in the notorious example recited above, the thing which is now known as 'Swiss graphic design' is nothing more than sheep's clothing, it would be wrong to assume—as many of his contemporaries did at the time—that Bettler's interest in visual communication has ever been solely concerned with agitation. Historically, there are those whose work has pushed the boundaries of graphic language but has not set out to change the world, and there are others whose primary motivation has been shock or social change rather than concern with any intricacies of form and function. Bettler's importance stems partly from the fact that he has been able to sit comfortably in both camps at once.

When our conversation turns to more style-orientated matters, I ask his opinion on the current state of all things 'Swiss'. Surely he has seen the work of those who carry on in London some semblance of what his generation began—the 8vos, the Norths. What does he think of them?

'Montaigne said "One must live with the living". These people are not interesting to me. They are no more relevant than a musician who tries to bring back punk rock in the year 2000.'

Playing devil's advocate, I argue that the difference is that punk was a statement on the condition of Britain in 1977. Lohse, Vivarelli and friends, on the other hand,

sought to create a method of working which was objective and therefore good for all time.

'No. Swiss graphic design reflected a period of postwar reconstruction in Europe. It was new at the time. It was about good citizenship. We saw it as a kind of scaffolding on which we could build a new society amidst the rubble of the war. None of us thought we would design in the same way forever, I am sure of it.'

But the eighteen issues of *Neue Grafik* which appeared from 1958 onwards all carried virtually identical cover designs—isn't this a clear indication that the leading Swiss designers thought their work was built to last?

'Now you resort to bad examples. *Neue Grafik* ended in 1965. If it had continued until 1980 then its design would have changed. What is important is that your work deals with the problems of your time. There is nothing more uncomfortable than seeing a working method, a philosophy which you were once part of, being recycled as a hollow fashion statement. And at least with fashion, the clothes change with the seasons. The sort of designer you're talking about uses "modernism" to cloak his lack of imagination, and as a means of parading his slick Pantone colours. Look at the British RAC vehicles.'

I've seen them, thanks.

Would the next Ernst Bettler please stand up?

Despite the fact that his political views have obviously not changed, the work which Bettler has produced in London over the last three decades shows none of his former thirst for subversion. In place of company-toppling posters and booby-trapped corporate identities there is a neat stack of books for small publishers in Britain, Switzerland and the Netherlands. Many of them are related to charities of one form or another.

One of the few existing posters designed for Pfäfferli+Huber Pharmaceuticals (1959)

There are a fair number of art catalogues ('I'm allowed one vice!'). All are assembled with great consideration for the material they contain and for the people who will read them. They exemplify many of the things which Jost Hochuli and Robin Kinross would say are virtues in book design. They are 'Nice Things'. They aren't doing anyone any harm. But all the same, I can't help feeling a pang of disappointment. Though I appreciate their beauty, the books represent to me a fall from grace. Wistfully imagining this Swiss expatriate nipping a soon-to-overinflate concern such as Virgin in its bud at some appropriate point in the late 1970s, I ask if he doesn't ever think of a return to his bad old ways?

'Do you like the Rolling Stones?'

Pardon?

'How old is Mick Jagger? 55? 56? And there he is on that stage, still telling us that he can't get his satisfaction. An 18-year-old should be able to relate to that sentiment. A middle-aged man who can relate to it has a problem.'

So that's it? Game over?

'The struggle is never over, but my own share of the fighting is complete. And one eventually discovers that what you quietly refuse to do can be as important as what you do very publicly. As a designer, as a human, you are defined by what you do not lend a hand to.'

So is he hopeful for the future? If Ernst Bettler has passed on the mantle of subversion by design, who has taken it up? (I have by now noticed a copy of Naomi Klein's recent *No Logo* on the shelf.)

'Corporations are the real governments now, and the public realizes this—even if a little late. What the public has not yet noticed is that corporations can be just as stupid as governments. You would not believe the rubbish I have turned down, even in recent years. One [firm] even came to me because they liked the Pfäfferli+Huber work. That is how stupid these people are. The key is to remember that for all the apparent muscle of the multinational companies, none of them have the stealth of a single man or woman. In a small way, I proved this thirty years ago. So yes, I am hopeful. Perhaps there is no-one protesting in the Bettler way any more, but don't forget that there are other channels besides graphic design.'

He laughs when I suggest that during the years he spent scrambling the sentiments of clients, perhaps he also sometimes wondered who he was as a designer.

'I never suffered from identity problems—I was too busy giving those to other people.'

ST·SEBASTIANI

Sieben

ARMBRUSTSCHÜTZEN·

hundert

GESELLSCHAFT

fünfzig

ANNO 1250

Jahre

HERZOGENRATH

Cover and spread from a book for I.O. Ferdinand Verlag (1999)

AND SO TO BED

by Christopher Wilson

Teachers of Literature are apt to think up such problems as 'What is the author's purpose?' or still worse 'What is the guy trying to say?' Now, I happen to be the kind of author who in starting to work on a book has no other purpose than to get rid of that book and who, when asked to explain its origin and growth, has to rely on such ancient terms as Interreaction of Inspiration and Combination —which, I admit, sounds like a conjurer explaining one trick by performing another.
(Vladimir Nabokov, 'On a book entitled *Lolita*', in *The Anchor Review* #2, Doubleday, 1957)

The second issue of *Dot Dot Dot*, dated winter 2000 and published in February 2001, included my article '"I'm only a designer": the double life of Ernst Bettler'. An editorial statement mentioned two 'aspects' that the issue was 'uncomfortably weighted towards'; the second of these being 'resorting to fiction to make certain points'. 2500 copies of the issue were printed.

Knives and lint

On 15 May 2001 I was contacted by 'culture-jamming' magazine *Adbusters*, whose picture editor Jeff Harris wrote 'Your article piqued our interest in Ernst Bettler. We would like to get copies of his work to run in the upcoming "design" issue of *Adbusters*. I've done some web searches but haven't been able to find any good resources. Do you know who I could contact to get copies of his work?' I replied that the only Bettler-related images I could easily 'lay my hands on' were those which had accompanied my text.

Three days later John D. Berry's review of *Dot Dot Dot* 2 appeared on creativepro.com, the Bettler article apparently exemplifying one of the issue's 'weakest points': 'a certain reflexive desire to smash icons for the sake of smashing icons. [...] Christopher Wilson writes about the brilliantly subversive work of Ernst Bettler in his early career, but then characterizes thirty years of later, less contentious work as a "disappointment," just because it's not a young man's rebellion.' This ignored Bettler's own ample explanation of his latterday stance on the article's last page.

This was soon followed by the appearance of *Adbusters'* 'design anarchy' 'special double issue', which devoted a page to rehashing Bettler's story, here termed 'one of the greatest design interventions on record'. Contrary to agreement, no acknowledgement was made to the source of their information. The nameless rewriter fleshed-out Pfäfferli+Huber as an 'arrogant, brutish corporation', before fumbling an explanation of Bettler's posters: 'Posted in a row, however, they appear to be a series of letters (the "A" is shown here). You can guess what four-letter word Bettler made sure to spell out for the world.' Unsurprisingly, the readership could not guess. 'Call us stupid', wrote one reader in the next issue's letters page, 'but we can't guess what word Ernst Bettler's four posters [...] spelled out. It's driving us crazy.'

On 15 August Andy Crewdson, writer of typography blog Lines and Splines, emailed *Dot Dot Dot*'s editors: 'It has come to my attention that Ernst Bettler might not exist. Would you mind if I post something about this to my web site? (Or, if you have some evidence to contradict this, I'd be glad to see

it).' Soon after this Crewdson posted his suspicions, noting that neither Bettler nor his client seemed to have existed, and highlighting the editors' 'resorting to fiction' remark. (The blog remained online until mid-2002.) The next month, Brian Carnell added a brief text on leftwatch. com: '[...] it appears that *Adbusters* fell for a hoax, which would be deliciously ironic given their holier-than-thou attitude toward the deficiencies of mainstream media outlets. [...] A couple of things stand out immediately that should have given *Adbusters* a few moments pause. An entire major corporation ruined in six weeks by a few posters spelling "Nazi"? Sounds pretty far fetched.' Carnell also noted that *Adbusters* had directly 'ripped-off' their text from *Dot Dot Dot*.

Next came an email from Mike Simons of *Adbusters*: 'It has come to my attention that the story itself was a hoax. Is this true? If so we should perhaps run a correction in our next issue ... although it may be better if the fable continues, I'm not sure.' I told Simons that he now seemed to be 'suggesting that your next issue is going to call me a liar. If I had known that *Adbusters* had intended to treat myself and *Dot Dot Dot* in this way, I would never have agreed to help in the first place.' He replied 'I am only trying to be responsible to our readers and let them know the veracity of the piece. Nothing more than that. [...] Unfortunately we get hundreds of e-mails for each issue of *Adbusters* and many have questioned this work. Just routine follow up work, nothing more.' Such work should perhaps come before rather than after publication. Email contact ended in late October, and accordingly *Adbusters* subsequently declared the story 'too good to be true'. Neither apology nor explanation was offered to their readers, for whom the story's source remained a mystery.

46% brand awareness in three years

'When I joined the [*Daily Mirror*'s] features department, it was administered by Freddie Wills, a former RAF ace [...]. He had a gloriously insane rule that in a newspaper office you did not read newspapers. The reasoning behind this was that you were supposed to have read all the papers before you arrived in the office. Those caught infringing this rule would find themselves stalked by Freddie, who, creeping on hands and knees, would whip out a match and set fire to the pages.'
(John Pilger, 'Forward with the people', in *Hidden Agendas*, Vintage, 1998)

By the year's end, my text had been termed a 'hoax' in at least three different public places, as any online search for Ernst Bettler would have shown. I assumed the saga to be dead. So I read the first email from Michael Johnson, direc-tor of Johnson Banks, with some surprise on 25 January 2002: 'I'm currently trying to write a sort of "ways of seeing" of graphic design + advertising for Phaidon Press[.] I was very intrigued by your Ernst Bettler case study and I wondered if you had any idea if its possible to access all four of the Pfäfferli + Huber (N A Z I) post-ers from anywhere, or is the "A" the only one that exists? I'd like to feature it in a chapter about protest/education'. I explained that the 'A' graphic was the only one known to exist. I had no objection to the story being reiterated in his book, but said I would appreciate due credit for myself and *Dot Dot Dot*, although even at this stage I questioned the concept of a *Ways of Seeing* applied to graphics and advertising—partly because John Berger's book had already covered these issues, and partly because it was difficult to conceive of some-one like Johnson carrying on, from the inside of the design industry, an argument such as Berger's: 'Capitalism survives by forcing the majority, whom it exploits, to define their own interests as

narrowly as possible. This was once achieved by extensive deprivation. Today in the developed worlds it is being achieved by imposing a false standard of what is and what is not desirable.' I voiced this (minus the quote), and Johnson replied that 'You are abosolutely [sic] right, Berger's does examine advertising too—albeit from a very specific period. "Ways of seeing" is my role model in the sense that every foundation student has to read it—the aim with mine (called Problem Solved) is to try to write the definitive text on problem solving as regards design and advertising. There's very little in this area as yet—as you know design books are mostly caught in the thrall of self-promotion and puffery at present. And I always loved the way Berger's text simply described the adjacent picture and read like a lecture, rather than a tedious "standard text". [...] I will of course name check you in the book.' This answered my question. The link between Berger's book and Johnson's would be a purely formal one: images integrated into the text, as per Richard Hollis's layout for *Ways of Seeing*. In February I rode my bike across London and handed in at Johnson Banks a Zip disc containing the requested pictures. Johnson returned this in April, using three 1p stamps. I paid the postman his due, and forgot Johnson existed.

On 10 October 2002 Phaidon published *Problem Solved—a Pri-mer in Design and Communications*. I was surprised by how soon after our contact the book had appeared, and assumed that Johnson must have included Bettler at the elev-enth hour. The 'Kopfschmerzen?' poster was again reproduced and the story retold, Bettler now dubbed 'one of the founding fathers of the "culture-jamming" form of protest'. 'It was only when the posters were put up randomly around town that his client real-ized that their embarrassing roots had been revealed.' Bettler's poster series had of course relied on

the reverse of being 'put up randomly'.

Toward the end of the year, having apparently emailed my former Royal College of Art addre[ss] in vain, Johnson contacted *Dot Dot Dot*'s editors. It had been sug-gested to him by Pentagram part-ner Michael Bierut that the Bettler story was a hoax. At this stage Johnson seemed unconvinced that Christopher Wilson existed, and referred to my RCA address itself as a 'brilliant hoax'—bizarre[ly] forgetting that we'd previously communicated via that very address. I responded by saying that my article was not a hoax, although 'I'm flattered that Mr Bierut is talking about it.' If there is any hoax anywhere in Bettler's saga, then that clause is it, but Johnson replied 'INDEED.' As for the non-hoax, 'GOOD NEWS ALL ROUND', but could I supply him with some concrete evidence, as 'PHAIDON GETTING RATTY'? I repeated: no hoax.

On 4 December, under the name 'ch1cken-ga', Johnson posted the following question at answers.google.com (at the time of writing, it's still there: http://answers.google.com/answers/threadview?id=119027): 'I need to check if a swiss company called Pffferli [sic] + Huber AG actually existed in post war Switzerland. Already know about the reports in the magazines *Adbusters* + *Dot Dot Dot* but http://www.leftwatch.com/discussion/fullthread$msgnum=1199 has alleged this to be a hoax—need to ascertain if there ever was this company or a drug called Contrazipan. Cheers. Michael. Happy hunting'. When researching a company it helps if their name is spelled correctly. This aside, an appropriate response might have been: 'Why don't you do your own research, instead of asking unknown and potentially unreli-able sources to do it on an uncred-ited, unpaid basis?' Nevertheless, a kindly soul named 'Scriptor' responded on the same day:

GUINNESS®

23

Slowest land mammal

The Ai or Three-toed Sloth of tropical America usually moves at 6 to 8 feet a minute but and moments a hurry to reach her infant actually covered 14 feet in a minute

Some choose to educate by more subtle means. Although he is now becoming recognized as one of the founding fathers of the 'culture-jamming'[1] form of protest, Ernst Bettler's way of revealing to 1950s Switzerland that Pfäfferli + Huber AG (a pharmaceuticals company) had Nazi roots was astonishingly subtle.

When commissioned to design a set of fiftieth anniversary publicity posters he suggested four in total. And into each one he echoed the shape of the letters

ABOVE AND ABOVE LEFT
Pfäfferli + Huber Pharmaceuticals
poster campaign
ERNST BETTLER SWITZERLAND 1959

GUINNESS®

282

Quick as a wink

The speed record for giving 24 tiddly-winks is held by Stephen Williams who in 1988 took only 21.8 seconds. He was flipping winks from the standard 18-inch 45 cm distance.

Some choose to educate with tactics that only serve to confuse. In 2000 an amazing example of early 'culture-jamming'[1] appeared to have been unearthed by a graphics journal. The story suggested that in 1950s Switzerland, 'Ernst Bettler' had found a way to reveal the Nazi roots of a Swiss pharmaceuticals company.

It appeared that he had designed a set of posters, into which he 'planted' the letters 'N', 'A', 'Z' and 'I'. When displayed in order, the client's politics were

ABOVE AND ABOVE LEFT
Pfäfferli + Huber Pharmaceuticals
poster
CHRISTOPHER WILSON/DOT DOT DOT
MAGAZINE, 2000

'N', 'A', 'Z' and 'I' through the image photographed (the only surviving 'A' poster is shown opposite). It was only when the posters were put up randomly around town that his client realized that their embarrassing roots had been revealed. There was public outrage. Only six weeks later Pfäfferli + Huber were out of business, thanks to the underground information campaign of Bettler.[2]

When the target market won't come to you, sometimes the trick is to go to them. In the mid-1990s, the British Design Council experimented with a set of posters and accompanying ____ ____ aimed at raising awareness of design within schools by u____ ____ in order to prompt responses. Learning from ____ ____ and targeted specifically at the ____

The idea of the set, ____ ____ with the BBC, was to encourage ____ ____ important ideas of their own and ____ ____ med with the posters, blocks of Pos____ ____ and youth groups around the ____ country set about ____ attacking the tasks ____ by the piece, hop____ inspiring in the ____ the next genera____ Dysons and Br____

ABOVE
Design Decisions poster images
JOHNSON BANKS UK 1996

BELOW LEFT, RIGHT
The Big Zipper poster campaign
and worksheet

revealed. There was outrage and the demise of the company followed. Bizarrely, the entire story has proved to be a fabrication, apparently created to mislead modern designers and their love of the post-war Swiss style.[2] Unfortunately, the story's creators chose to poke fun using perhaps the least funny of twentieth century topics, the holocaust.

Luckily, miseducation is not on the agenda of most public organizations. In the mid-1990s the British Design Council experimented with a set of posters to raise awareness of design ____ ____ ____ ____ ges to prompt responses. Learning from ____ ____ veloped and targeted specifically at the ____ ____ r-olds.

The idea of the set, ____ ____ duced with the BBC, was to encourage ____ ____ eel that they had important ideas of the ____ ____ becoming the next set of entrepreneurs. A ____ ____ -its and work-sheets, thousands of schools ____ ____ set about attacking the tasks set by the ____ piece, hopefully inspiring in the proc____ the next generation ____ Richard Bransons a____ James Dysons.

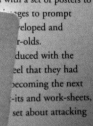

'Dear ch1cken, No final proof so far, but certain evidence:
- The family name 'Pffferli' does not exist anywhere in a German-peaking country. I checked address and phone directories as well as genealocial [sic] data-pases. It is a fake name, made up to sound typically Swiss' (the suffix '-li' is considered a clich [sic] ending of Swiss names). The family name 'Pfefferli'—pronounced much the same—does exist, but since the poster shows the word clearly with an a-umlaut, it has absolutely nothing to do with it.
- 'Contrazipan' does not show up anywhere, neither in tables listing pharmaceutical substances, nor in trademark databases. A quick call at a pharmacist revealed that the name would not even make sense or fit anywhere in the nomenclature of medical substances names.
- The poster allegedly promoting Contrazipan has nothing in common with late 50s' advertisement style. Since I have quite a good knowledge of European 50s' design, I can say for sure that the picture would be an anachronist contaminant.'

Again on the same day, Johnson posted in return: 'mmmmm Well The only extra information I have is that a poster was alledgedly [sic] designed for Pffferli + Huber AG by a designer named Ernst Bettler in 1959. The story goes that there were four posters, one of which is the "a" of the word Nazi. The story was written by a UK based design writer called Christopher Wilson, who until recently swapped e-mails with me at the Royal College of Art under the email address of christopher.wilson@rca.ac.uk. He assures me it is legit but has thus far offered no substantiation. There was apparently something on Lines and Splines about this but it seems ot [sic] be down. Actually, the poster style is quite a good approximation of the infamous "swiss style" of design of the time, so not sure I agree with you there. The creidt [sic] of the "poster" says

Pffferli + Huber AG, Burgwald CH, incidentally. As it happens, I've never heard of a swiss designer called Ernst Bettler either.'

Johnson then emailed me with a 'pretty damming' [sic] list—Scriptor's list, in fact—of reasons why the Bettler article must be a fabrication. He received no reply. On 12 December he again prodded the online forum: 'any more news on this guys? The author of the article is refusing to supply any "proof" of the designer or the client, so I'm keen to nail this as soon as possible / Thanks'. Silence.

Fo[u]rty winks

In February 2003 eyemagazine.com posted a critique by Rick Poynor on 'The "Ernst Bettler" problem'. After relating the public side of events thus far, Poynor asked "What, then, is the point of the hoax? If the aim was to fool credulous browsers into perpetuating the story, then [the reiteration of Bettler's tale in *Problem Solved*] is a triumph. It's now a permanent feature in thousands of copies of an internationally distributed book produced by a major publisher, Phaidon, and it's likely to be taken at face value for years to come. It reveals how skimpy standards of research, validation and basic knowledge can be in design book publishing. Johnson will presumably delete it from future editions, or at least add some explanatory note.' He continued, 'It's certainly odd that Wilson [...] put his own name on the piece. One might have expected a determined hoaxer to cover his tracks.'

Next, Matt Soar gave *Problem Solved* due demolition in *Eye* 47, Spring 2003. Having pointed out the fundamental flaw in the book's concept ('Would any self-respecting creative really take the trouble to thumb through the contents page of *Problem Solved* looking for the "generic problem" that matches their particular needs at that moment?'), Soar examined the terrain into which the Bettler story

had been shoehorned: 'if Johnson had read Naomi Klein's *No Logo* he might be much less self-assured in trotting out his unwavering faith in the bloodless logic of branding, and rather less glib in his dismissal of other people who take this stuff seriously. Since those he does identify are college students, it seems just a little too easy to treat them as youthful idealists who'll grow up to know better. Of one student's anti-McDonald's project, Johnson says: 'will she stay true to her beliefs when, and if, she sees the colour of their money?' Finally, the review deftly summarized the ideological chasm between *Ways of Seeing* and Johnson's writing: 'for all his apparent enthusiasm, the author of *Problem Solved* can't possibly have taken Berger seriously. To do so would have been to confront a sustained critique of advertising and our relationship to images that directly threatens the underlying premise of his own book.'

To these and the review's other criticisms, Johnson was able to muster two words ('depressingly predictable') in his defence. 'On the one hand *Eye* eagerly seeks to encourage "graphic authorship", and on the other, its writers seem affronted when a designer dares to become an author.' Since many of *Eye*'s contributors are themselves designers as well as writers, 'affront' would hardly be taken when Johnson heroically 'dares' to 'become an author'. There is nothing daring about authorship as such; but those who take it up without doing their homework properly should be taken to task. Of his Bettler problem, Johnson flailed, 'I may remove it on the next print run. I may even move it into the "fear and loathing" chapter, since it seems to have been inspired by [Wilson's] desire to de-bunk *Eye*'s original "core" constituency of North and 8vo.' (Poynor had already termed Bettler 'on one level' a 'subtle goad' to one-size-fits-all pseudomodernists.) Design company North did not exist at the time of *Eye*'s inception in 1990, so couldn't have been part of any fictional 'original "core" constituency'.

The memory hole

'Books, also, were recalled and re-written again and again, and were invariably re-issued without any admission that any alteration had been made. Even the written instructions which Winston received, and which he invariably got rid of as soon as he had dealt with them, never stated or implied that an act of forgery was to be committed: always the reference was to slips, errors, misprints or misquotations which it was necessary to put right in the interests of accuracy.
    But actually, he thought as he re-adjusted the Ministry of Plenty's figures, it was not even forgery. It was merely the substitution of one piece of nonsense for another.'
(George Orwell, *Nineteen Eighty-Four*, Martin Secker & Warburg Ltd, 1949)

At the end of March 2004 Johnson popped back up with this breezy email: 'Hi Christopher, Just amending text for the softback edition of Problem Solved—do you want me to put you down as designer of the "Bettler" stuff or shall I credit it to Dot Dot Dot? I'm amending the text accordingly at the moment, would seem best to set the record straight.' I ignored him. Two months later Phaidon published this amended edition. Contrary to his letter to *Eye*, Johnson had not removed the references to Bettler, nor moved them to another chapter. He had merely swapped his original eleven lines for eleven new ones, resulting in my favourite contemporary example of Orwell's memory hole. Where the first edition had begun with 'Some [i.e. Ernst Bettler] choose to educate by more subtle means', the revisionist edition fumbled 'Some [ie. Christopher Wilson] choose to educate with tactics that only serve to confuse'. The Bettler tale 'appeared to have been unearthed' by 'a graphics journal', but 'the entire story has proved to be a fabrication'.

Here Johnson rehashed the 'core constituency' angle he'd already tried for size in his letter to *Eye*: Bettler had 'apparently [been] created to mislead modern designers and their love of the post-war Swiss style.' A note at the back of the book added that the story had been 'since discredited by the Lines and Splines weblog, Leftwatch.com and Eyemagazine.com', though none of these had discredited my text nearly so much as the sources that quoted it. Conveniently, no reader new to Johnson's second edition would guess that the person most famously 'misled' by my article was none other than Michael Johnson himself, in the previous edition of this very book. Not satisfied with this obfuscation of his earlier error, Johnson embellished it by adopting the mantle least appropriate to his position: that of haughty moralist with right on his side. He now dreamed up the sorry concept that I had written the article 'to poke fun using perhaps the least funny of twentieth century topics, the holocaust'. Five years later, the version of *Problem Solved* containing this slander remains in print. Phaidon's website describes it as 'a manual for students and professionals that offers solutions to design problems', whose 'discussions and case studies illustrate the working methods of major advertising and graphic design firms', and whose 'themes include: avoiding repetition, standing out in the market place, reinventing a tired brand, dealing with propaganda, communicating the essential facts'.

18 January 2005: I attended a talk on intellectual property rights, hosted by Own-it at the Design Council in London. One of the speakers turned out to be Michael Johnson, who mentioned to his audience *Problem Solved*, the book he had 'spent a whole summer writing'. A whole summer? If this timespan is accurate, then the Bettler story had already been publicly discredited before Johnson picked up his pen.

The one thing needful

On 8 January 2008 Michael Bierut posted at designobserver.com a text entitled 'Will the real Ernst Bettler please stand up?' After reiterating the story and ensuing saga in yet another variation, Bierut glimpsed something beyond the tedious mantra of 'Why did he hoax us?': 'We need heroes, and we'll make them up if we can't find them any other way. [...] The design world is full of Clark Kents. Are any of us ready to be the next Ernst Bettler?' To return to this question, already implicit in my original text, had taken seven slow-witted years.

At the time of writing, Wikipedia's entry on Bettler states that he is 'a fictional Swiss graphic designer. He was invented by Christopher Wilson in a 2000 hoax article published in the second issue of *Dot Dot Dot*'. And Christopher Wilson? He was 'born August 23, 1979' and is 'a sports humor columnist for Fox Sports' J.T. the Brick and the PostChronicle.com. He is the author of the book Sports Briefs, a collection of his columns.' He 'grew up in Olney, Texas' and is 'married to his wife Piper and lives in Waco.' Though I couldn't have foreseen it at the time of writing my article, the prevalence/popularity of hopelessly unreliable internet sources such as Wikipedia, and the death of proper research, invalidate entirely any finger-pointing exclamations of the how-dare-you-hoax-us variety. Facts are vaguer, and information more useless, than ever before. 'I'm only a designer' is no more or less reliable an article than any other which might now be quoted from online. Insofar as printed books now refer to web sources, or are written by those for whom research is too strenuous a task, they are now also unreliable, and so the disease spreads.

From the outset, I had planned that my article could be received in one of two ways: either as a fiction about a designer who destroyed an objectionable client and got paid for it; or as a true story which might hopefully inspire others to think more like dear Ernst, instead of wasting time creating juvenile 'spoof ads' for their peers to snigger at. For those who took the story at face value, the tale was strewn with sufficient clues (Bettler's name, which literally 'beggar'ed belief and could be found nowhere else in the history of graphic design; nonexistent company with nonexistent name, selling a nonexistent product in two nonexistent locations) to give the game away. A hoaxer does not do this. As for *Adbusters* and Michael Johnson, had they had the nerve to simply play along after realizing their mistake, they both could have saved face. Instead, they took a piece of fiction and hoaxed themselves with it. And, as Poynor pointed out, revealed their 'skimpy standards of research, validation and basic knowledge'.

Finally: if the reactions to 'I'm only a designer'—whether angry, slanderous or simply documentary—prove one thing, it is how utterly uncreative the creative industry truly is. The worlds of advertising and graphic design may abound with professionals 'thinking outside the box', but when, once upon a time, a design writer invented a story, they could not bear it. It must be refuted, labelled a hoax, explained away in amateur conjective fashion. To place a fictional text in the box set aside for design journalism —and thereby perhaps alter the reader's concept of what might be possible via graphic design—was intolerable. It was unacceptable to let the story simply be. It was, in short, impossible to think 'outside the box' of what is permissible in a magazine about design. And for that, the industry really does deserve Bettlering.

Randall McLeod at the McLeod Portable Collator. Photograph by Pamela Harris.

THE UNEDITOR

Randall McLeod in conversation with Mark Owens
July 2008

Randall McLeod is one of North America's leading early modern textual scholars. Over the course of a 30-year career McLeod's work on early printed books and manuscripts has attended to the materiality of texts—from fonts, kerns, ligatures, and bearing type, to the mechanics of printing, folding, and binding—in unorthodox and compelling ways. With the aid of his invention, the McLeod Portable Collator, he has consistently demonstrated the instability of the printed word, arguing for the primacy of material evidence and the value of 'unediting' for both scholarship and literary interpretation. Distinguished by a penchant for pseudonym, neologism, and wit, his widely-published essays offer a continued source of inspiration to those working in bibliography and related fields, such as Renaissance studies and the history of the book. During a break from one of his regular research visits to the Huntington Library in San Marino, CA, I sat down with McLeod and fellow admirer Aaron Kunin, writer and professor of English at Pomona College, to discuss his past work and current activities.

Mark Owens: You work in the domain of textual scholarship, which is to say that you are in the business of looking at books, not necessarily reading them. And yet, the editorial tradition on which literary interpretation depends—in practice, anyway —is founded on the work of textual scholars. By way of introduction can you talk a bit about what drew you to bibliography and what is at stake in textual scholarship?

Randall McLeod: As a kid I wanted to be a physicist. The periodic table and radioactivity fascinated me. My father was an engineer; I think I was trying to get in touch with him, get his approval, that sort of thing. When I was at high school *Sputnik* occurred, and a lot of money was thrown at education. I was in grade twelve then, and the city Board of Education got the local professors at McMaster University a budget for lectures about their respective disciplines to assembled worthy grade-twelve students from across the city. The lecture that spoke to me was not on physics, however, but on etymology. I was then taking German, French, and Latin, and the professor said, 'These tongues are all derived from the same proto-Indo-European language': in words derived from north of the Alps we say a sound one way, [f], for example, and south of the Alps [p]: fish/pisces, father/paternal, fore/pre-, flat/platen, foot/pedal. Etymology gave me a sense of x-raying the various linguistic worlds to reveal a unifying structure behind them. It was a seminal moment for me, and I even teach etymology now, and so thank you, Premier Kruschev.

I think that textual scholarship offers the same kind of revelation for me: behind the appearance of a single book there are structures of variants that are scattered in other copies, and they can somehow be collected by scientific techniques and sorted out. One comes not to trust totally the appearance of an immediate object because there is a reality 'behind' it. At the same time, though, the actual physical object is an end in itself for me, and I don't want to minimize it. Peter Stallybrass once said to me

that 'Things are mystical'—the idea not that you need to get behind or beyond things, into spirit say: rather, physical objects are already there, are intrinsically mystical. I don't know if I've answered your question.

MO: Maybe you could also talk a little bit about the discipline of textual scholarship. For example, particularly in early modern textual criticism, there has been an ongoing discussion over the last twenty years or so about what we include in scholarly editions. Do we need to include two or three texts of *King Lear*, for instance. Especially in the domain of literary interpretation, these have become very real questions.

RM: Well, I don't think it's that we *need* two foundational texts of *King Lear*. We *have* them. The editorial tradition has been one of denying what's there, of synthesizing or eclectically conflating quarto and folio editions in the name of some ultimate *King Lear*, or some ultimate thing that Shakespeare meant. Eventually, I discerned that the tradition is pervaded by learned gentlemanly assumptions I now have little interest in, except as pathology, a worthy subject in its own right. I had to discover, like Joyce's Stephen, my own secular 'Non serviam'. I would not serve. My work came to seem a fart in the Temple of Editing. I'm now an editorial inactivist, an uneditor. I'm into demolition.

Aaron Kunin: But isn't there a way in which you're also interested in that? I mean, in the incorrect collations that get done, which often then become the objects of your analysis and critique?

RM: Yes, I'm interested in it as a textual critic. That intellectual endeavor is closely related to editing, but fundamentally different. When I've got variants, I think I can reconstruct someone's behaviour that accounts for the variants.

*

The Easter Wings Gallery

1. *Speaking Pictures: A Gallery of Pictorial Poetry from the Sixteenth Century to the Present*, Milton Klonsky, ed., New York: Harmony Books, 1975.

1

As this book anthologizes pictorial poems in photo-fac-simile, respect for and intuition about space is surely implied. Isn't it a hopeful sign, for example, that the editor has not cropped one of the two titles? But why are the two headlines, page numbers and catchwords gone? And why has Klonsky turned the image, so that the verses now run parallel to those of "The Altar", opposite? Now it is the *titles* that assert the characteristic internal rotation of the artefacts. As the editor has repeated in modern type just one of the titles, horizontal,

at the top of the page, it is easy (lazily) to overlook the 1633 titles, now redundant – or (industriously) to misconceive them as running heads. Furthermore, as the gutter of the original is no longer apparent, the poems cannot be grasped each on a separate wing of the book: without the diptych-format, the poems no longer allegorize the book, the book no longer allegorizes our hands. The body goes under. The iconic fades. To the unsuspecting viewer Herbert's two poems can scarcely resist editorial transformation into stanzas of a single poem.

Most startling of all: recto and verso poems are inter-changed! The order of the verses is now poetically cowwect. The gutter line could not have simply faded out in the high-contrast repro. No, Klonsky marginalized the centre!

His *Biographical Notes* cite 1633 as the publication date. But look closely. Isn't Klonsky's typeface suspiciously squat and regular for the 17th century? That's because his 1975 *photo-fac-simile* is not of Buck and Daniel's original 1633 edition – *anyone* could have done *that* – but of Grosart's 1876 or 1885 *type-facsimile*.[26]

¶ Eaſter wings. | ¶ Eaſter wings.

Buck and Daniel, 1633 | Grosart, 1876 or 1885

Photography does not lie, of course.[27] You can trust it, because it just *gazes*, like a silly *goose* (the two words are cognate). It does not lie. It does not lie because it does not analyze. It sees surfaces whole, instantaneously. But the underlying type-facsimile is not a *gestalt*; its coming into being was atomistic, sequential, linear – just as the coming into being of the object it copied was atomistic, sequential and linear. It is all these because it is a *reading*, because *reading rationalizes* (these two words are also cognate), because reading is abstract and analytical. In short, reading is too deep – it is not suffi-ciently *superficial* to report the evidence, which lies, after all, on the *surface*. Even if the editor had not cut and pasted his

From 'FIAT *f*LUX' (For full references to all images see bibliography, p. 57)

He might be a typesetter. For exam-ple, Hamlet describes Ophelia as 'pure as snow' in one quarto; the compositor of another sets 'puer as snosh'. The letters 'sh' were printed as a ligature—two letters on a sin-gle type body. In early depictions of the compositors' lower case, the 'sh' ligature is adjacent to the 'w'. If the compositor made a slight muscular error and reached into the wrong compartment, either in composing or distributing, his action was liable to confuse 'sh' or 'w'. So, I wouldn't assume that Shakespeare or Hamlet was *thinking* 'snosh', but that somewhere along the way an acci-dent occurred and it has a physical structure of some sort, and *that* generated 'snosh'. I'm interested in uncovering that structure. I'm interested in *thingking*. I consider that to be *literary* interpretation because it's about *letters*, but it's not a *belles lettres* approach. I'm all

for *laides lettres*, messyges. If we didn't have early representations of the lower case, 'puer as snosh' would help to reconstruct it. I want a form of consciousness of *messages as mediated*. There's usually trouble in that relationship. That's where the action is.

MO: I think what Aaron is also talking about is the editorial or bibliographic tradition, that there is a double-sided interest in that, not only in the wrongness of it, but also an interest in what it still actually can tell us.

RM: I was converted by reading Fredson Bowers. He offers a mag-isterial view of the power of bib-liography, which I initially found seductive. But within half a year of trying to use a bibliographic method to emend Shakespeare's *Sonnets*, 1609, I came to understand

that I needed to use the method to *defend* what I had thought needed correction. The acolyte had become an apostate. But Fredson did spark my passion and I'm loyal to him for that—and grateful.

AK: Mark and I were talking just an hour ago about your essay 'FIAT *f*LUX' and its Gallery of George Herbert's shape poems 'Easter Wings', in which the different editions of the poems you are criticizing take on a demonic energy. They do seem to have a kind of intrinsic interest for you. I guess maybe the question behind this question is: 'What do you want?'

RM: I'm naive. I am continually shocked by error and especially willful error, that editors would not consult original or earliest evi-dence, that they would just follow the previous edition, or fulfill their fantasies. It's fine if an editor or publisher says outright, 'I am now going to fulfill my fantasies.' But if in doing so he says, 'This is Shakespeare; this is Herbert', then that gets under my skin. It's going to be false science. It is ignorant and deceptive. Evidence is paramount.

The struggle to clarify the text is essential. 'The struggle for the text *is* the text.' In a formulation like that I seek to integrate reader and text—or writer and text, for that matter. 'What I want' is to be in that creative, joyful struggle —and not to be distracted from it. The edited world compromises that joy. The reason I like editors —some of my best friends are editors—is that they know that excitement first hand. But some of my worst friends are editors— because they pass on to their readers not the struggle, but the mere result of it, the canned text, the processed meat. The Answer, cooked, not raw. Give me raw, though I will take the cooked with the raw *and* the chef's recipe.

MO: Perhaps you'll allow me to backtrack a bit: your work has shown time and again in various, fascinating ways, that, in the early years of printing and publishing, texts were radically unstable objects. Can you describe what you've come to understand as the conditions of early modern print culture? It seems we are in a moment now where we have various fantasies of seamless transmission from page to screen.

RM: I don't suppose anything has changed. *Transformission*: texts are always transformed when transmitted. And of course, mere reading is a transformation of a text. In my own trajectory there was originally an aspiration to know 'Truth' and 'The Right Answer', but after a while I realized that the fertile part of the enquiry lies in error and metamorphosis. So, now I mostly look at errors and deviations. I don't know whether there is a transcendent goal. I don't seek it, in any case. Just being awake to complexity is enough.

Also Freud has been a big influence. Out front we have these explanations for what we are doing 'We are going into Iraq to spread democracy.' Behind such glib utterances there may be Machiavellian motives, but there certainly are unconscious ones in operation. So, the reason I'm not attracted to editing and the world of stability it often aims at, is because of its

---

—The first catchword in the book (on ¶ 2v) reads "plainely", but the next page begins "plainly".
—On pp. 14 and 15 the difference has to be grasped visually.

,on of loue, together quarels: And in their so- it told them of Orlando, we

we may gather how verie going on emlsassage not lawfull Prince whi

(English printers often acquired their types from more advanced publishing cultures, among whom the Italians and French had little use for the letter w. As a consequence, the w's in English Renaissance books often mix founts. The visual incongruity between the two settings of "we" in this volume is thus a small-scale reminder of the marginality of contemporary English culture—which fact is writ large as the Englished Italian of the whole book.)
—On pp. 22 and 23 we have "growne" and "growen",
—On pp. 134 and 135 "resistance" and "resistaunce"; and so on.

These are homely examples, but they illustrate the theoheretical point well enough: when a Renaissance text talks about itself, it is often not *quite* what it claims to be. Its structural redundancies are, crucially, both *of* its text and *about* it. Any lapse in them opens up contradiction at the heart of the transmission. We therefore do not have to run to fashionable works like *Lear* and *Faustus* for multiple texts; just walk into virtually any Renaissance document, and it is liable to open in its own small ways into multiplicity, into non-identity with itself. By attending to such examples of text's mis-self-representation, we can gauge something of what I call its "transformission"—how it was *transformed* as it was *transmitted*. (And since we don't have texts that aren't transmitted, transformission should cover most everything.)

Oftentimes the contradiction of catchwords may seem to reveal little more than that there were not fixed spellings for English words in the Renaissance. But is this an insignificant message? Isn't it a caution that we don't know why the words in the text take the form they do—even when they happen to be spelled as *we* spell them. In those days each

---

graphic form was more nearly the magic the etymology declares: a *spell*.

Maybe the way to sum up is this: modern re-presentations of Renaissance text have streamlined it toward self-consistency, purging the text of its troubled self-reflections. And it is in this sleek-headed mode that most of us *Lumpenintelligenz* sleep Our Shakespeare. But to his contemporaries Shakespeare's text *as text* presented a complex, ambiguous, contradictory, unhomogeneous—in short, a *hairy* Renaissance face, which his readers just had to—just had to countenance.

*

But sometimes a catchword *agree* with itself! Here is an example from Sonnet 129 in the second edition of *Sonnets*, published by Benson in 1640.

Immoderate Luʃt.

TH'expence of Spirit in a waʃte of ʃhame
Is luʃt in action, and till action, luʃt
Is perjurd, murdrous, blooddy full of blame,
Savage, extreame, rude, cruell, not to truʃt,
Injoyd no ʃooner but deʃpiʃed ʃtraight,
Paʃt reaʃon hunted, and no ʃooner had
Paʃt reaʃon hated as a ʃwallowed bayt,
On purpoʃe layd to make the taker mad.

Made

Poëms.

Made in purʃuit and in poʃʃeʃʃion ʃo,
Had, having, and in queʃt, to have extreame,
A bliʃʃe in proofe and proud and very woe,
Before a joy propoʃd behind a dreame,
All this the world well knowes yet none knowes well,
To ʃhun the heaven that leads men to this hell.

Such textual redundancy gives us more information than could either reading alone. For unlike the other words of the poem, each of which occurs only once in its place in the sequence, the redundancy of "Made" confirms its identity: "Made" is more "Made," for example, than the

---

From 'Information on Information'

'out front' definition of what a text or literary work is. The real action, for me, lies in the turmoil and upheavals, in the volcanic and tectonic shifts in the background, which sometimes map onto the artist's will and desire (Joyce is a good example of an artist who loves accidents, and he runs with them). and sometimes not. I'm ready for the text to ramify in any sphere. It could be an aesthetic sphere or a production sphere—wherever.

MO: I think it's always interesting to hear that we are able to reconstruct, in part, the chaotic way in which early print culture really proceeded. Things were often stopped midstream on the press, and spelling wasn't regularized; so, it was a system that actually worked by breaking down. In a real way, error and variation were part of the way it functioned.

RM: Right. And the lack of regularized spelling is also essential to a Renaissance compositor's way of coping with correction and revision. When he had to insert a word in a line already set, he could alter spellings throughout the line to create space for it. Early printers had a real interest in *not* advancing a system of spelling. But, paradoxically, in the early 17th century, printers' spelling became much more systematic than the spellings in contemporary manuscripts. They cooked their own goose.

MO: There was an investment in not having things regularized, and maybe that leads me to my next question. One of the reasons I find your work really productive is because you spend a lot of time looking closely at things like kerning, ligatures, leading, and the architecture of quires, paper, and binding. These are also the preoccupations of designers, especially book designers, and it seems to me that the story of graphic design's origins in the practices of early Renaissance printing, typography

and reading-and-writing habits is still fairly murky territory that isn't fully understood. Even design history books seem to be fuzzy on the topic. Do you have the sense that there are still questions to be answered and assumptions to be overturned, such as in your current work on the 1501 Aldine italic?

RM: The first Aldine book in italics throughout was the octavo Vergil of 1501. But there is a copy of this text in the British Library which has italic bearer type on the title page (not visible unless one holds the book wrong to the light—with light raking across its surface, that is) which comes from Aldus's octavo Dante, not published until 1502, the next year! Now, there's an explanation for this seeming time warp. The first quire of this copy of the Vergil (and not it alone) was actually reprinted. Other copies may fit what people say about the history of the first italic book, but this one doesn't. This particular copy, however, is the one that is frequently used to illustrate the first use of italic type—because of its association with the Duchess of Mantua, and Vergil was the poet of Mantua. This copy also has a painting of Vergil on the front page and a *trompe l'oeil* shield at the top, in which the title of the first Eclogue appears. Historians of italic assume the image of this first page of poetry in this copy proves their history of early italic. But it is not that early. Aldus had begun using italic before all of the sorts of his new font had been produced. This copy of the Vergil displays more sophisticated ligatures on this page than original copies do. Barker and Burnhill have commented on some aspects of when various sorts come on-stream, but the early history of italic is still 'murky', as you say.
 Modern graphic designers may not be aware that in Renaissance books type was in short supply and had to be recycled promptly. The same conspicuously damaged type might appear on the recto *and* verso of a leaf. Such reoccurrences,

which I read along with the abstract sense of the letters, clarify the production schedule of a book.

MO: There are all these kinds of moments in early print culture: the Aldine italic is an origin point, a place you can point to when something actually starts, and already there are confusions and time shifts from the very beginning. Your work is always urging us to go back and unravel again or look back again at things that we thought we could point to as a beginning, and when you look closely it's already sliding out from under you.

RM: In life there is frequently no precise point of origin, or, say one can always find a point of origin *before* the origin. With the Aldine italic, experts may say that the first use was in the Vergil. But, no, the Aldine letters of St. Catherine came out in 1500, and the woodblock depicting the saint has a few words printed in italic type. Aldus was already trying out italic in the incunabula period. But, he started printing with this font before it was very developed. 'ie*f*us' appears without an initial letter-spaced capital, and without an '*fu*' or '*us*' ligature, but with an oversized long-s (with a spur, as if it were a doctored '*f*'). When the sorts eventually come on stream defines a chronology of italic against which one can test the claims of dating in Aldus's colophons.
 Intricacies of Aldine chronology are also vouched for by colophons. Some books have several of them and several runs of signatures. (One could have started printing such books in three different places. One signing sequence might be with capitals: B, C, D. And then another, with a, b, d, and another one with Roman A then Greek A, Roman B then Greek B.) One colophon in the Philostratus gives the date '1501', but the lines of type in the colophon are crooked. In another copy they are also crooked, but a bit higher;

and in another they are level. Evidently, the colophon was stamped separately from some or all of the rest of the page. Therefore, the two components were not locked simultaneously in the chase. Consequently, the date doesn't stick to the object: '1501' floats free. The roman numerals spelling out the date and how to read them are not in doubt, but what they pertain to is. It's all deliciously complicated. In God's eye there must be a *single* chronology, but on this side of the veil, there appear more.

MO: Such complications are also one of the reasons that textual scholarship has long been one of the most specialized domains within literary studies—the province of a chosen few—but your work, in particular, has also become increasingly important for those working in the broader field known as the 'history of the book' and for others engaged in comparatively recent areas of research such as the history of reading. Have you noticed an opening up of the disciplinary boundaries?

RM: Well, appealing across boundaries may stem from my being playful. I think a lot of people who go into bibliography are 'chosen' by their seriousness, and they see it as science, in a positivistic sense—and the field is surrounded by a high fence with barbed wire. And that is the way I got into it, reading Bowers and thinking that a lot of things could be nailed down. Indeed, they can be nailed down, but, having been nailed, they often disprove more than they prove. Yes, they may become secure points of reference, but they don't tell you what Shakespeare meant, or what the true text is, or what '1501' pertains to. I think I have nailed down that '1501' floats free. Many might see this as a pyrrhic victory for scholarship, but I find it *liberating*—as the etymology of that word implies.

MO: There does also seem to be a renewed interest in the materiality of texts and material culture more generally that your work resonates with.

RM: When I was getting started, David Greetham founded the Society for Textual Scholarship, which brought out the journal *Text*. I think that it was a genuine sign of the times, and it provided a big umbrella under which textual people could come together. At the banquet of the first conference I was seated beside an Egyptologist, and I thought, 'Well, that's the way it should be.' All of these people were concerned with systems of communication and information. Group it under 'information theory', if you wish. It was the right time. People were ready to come out of the woodwork and ignore professional boundaries. For me there was an expansive sense of identity. I can work on English, Latin, Greek, and Hebrew texts without much facility in the foreign languages. I feel I can do cutting-edge research in all of them because I'm looking at the texts as texts. I'm still trying to be a physicist, I guess—succeeding in being one, in a metaphoric sense. In this way, I suppose I'm typical of those who are galvanized by material.

MO: You also mentioned the playfulness of your writing as a way into bibliographic concerns and as something that distinguishes it from other work in the field. And certainly one of the many things that I've continued to find inspiring and productive in your work is your particular discursive style. Your essays have appeared under a number of pseudonyms and tend to include conversational asides and other rhetorical moves that are both seemingly loose and even whimsical, but at the same time are absolutely rigorous and force the reader to pay attention to his or her own reading process and assumptions. Can you talk a bit about how you've come to re-imagine the scholarly essay? For example, you have published 'essays' that are over 100 pages, that have tables and elaborate diagrams, and that break off and have conversational moments in them. There is an absolute rigour in this, but almost as part of the rigour is this porosity built into it as well.

RM: It's absolutely important to me. I would stifle and die if I didn't think that each essay required its own form, and maybe its own author's name and its own voice. Otherwise, I would just be repeating myself.

I like mixed genres. I Like the Clown in Cleopatra's suicide scene: 'Those that do die of it do seldom or never recover.' I don't see a need to differentiate poetry from scholarly writing or to keep wit apart from seriousness. I tend to latch onto projects that force me to learn something, and when I learn that something I'm someone else—and with each a new genre, or a new voice. I think that's essential to my personality—I don't want to do the same thing twice. I mean I *am* always doing the same thing over and over, because the skills you build up you keep on honing and re-applying them, but it's as if you have a symphony orchestra, but not with a piccolo yet, and here comes a piccolo. You add in the piccolo, and you can make new music. And then there is the *electronic* piccolo, and you keep on tweaking your product. So, I think I'm kind of selfish in this way; I'm not part of some institute which has a goal, like, 'We are going to produce all of Raleigh's texts in the next twenty years.' I'm really interested in things that are weird and unexpected, and I will follow them when by chance or hunger they cross my path. I don't have a five-year plan, though maybe I should.

This Montaigne I'm working on now is a case in point. I've always thought, I guess since reading McKerrow—whose introduction to bibliography reigned before

Gaskell's—(and by keeping my nose really deep in Shakespeare) that the letter 'u', which at that time was pointed at the beginning of words (the 'v' shape) and round elsewhere (the 'u' shape—and hence their 'vuula' is our 'uvula'), or the letter 'i', long at the end of words (the 'j' shape) but short elsewhere (the 'i' shape) was the style in English books up until around 1630, and then changed into current usage, although they didn't have the *letters* 'v' and 'j' or the *names* for them even until a century later. Johnson filed 'under' and 'very' under the same initial, but 'very' first—because 'e' precedes 'n'. (They counted 26 shapes and 24 letters; we count 26 of both.) Recently, I wanted to find out exactly when in 1630 this change took place. So I latched on to a particular printer, Donne's printer, Flesher, and I hired someone to go

through all his books of this and adjacent years. For some reason I happened to look at the 1603 Florio translation of Montaigne's *Essays*, and realized that his usage was thirty years ahead of the shift. Then in my bibliography class someone was working on the 1609 Spenser—and I saw again the modern usage: the pointed 'u' for a consonant, the round 'u' for a vowel (except for the first letter of a word, where the 'v' shape was always used), decades ahead of when I thought the shift had occurred. So, now I've devoted a couple of months just to Montaigne, to surveying his text, collating copies of the 1603 edition, looking especially for variants of the sorts v, u, i, j—those two letters. The Huntington copy turns out to be a presentation copy by the translator, and the revisions may very well be in Florio's hand. (My nose is now taking me from type to

handwriting). And this hand also has a habit of taking whole phrases and making them compounds by putting hyphens between successive words. So, now I'm following hyphens. I don't have a plan. I don't need one. If it's weird, I'll follow. I've been taught to know what's normal, and I've decided not to identify with it. Time to tear up a model I've used for 40 years. There is a point of origin before the point of origin. I might find it on the continent, as John Florio the translator is really Giovanni Florio.

MO: You mentioned briefly that each essay might occasion its own voice or even its own author's name. As I mentioned, you've published under a number of creative pseudonyms, including Claudia Nimbus, Random Cloud, Random Clod, Sir Greg Walters,

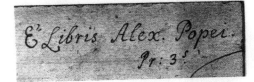

Now, let me show you how a reader four centuries ago coped with your insoluble problem. Youll never guess. There is an *inexpensive*-paper copy at Hartlebury Castle, formerly owned by three-shilling Alex Popei.

—which is painstakingly altered (seemingly by a single hand throughout). I deduce that the corrector followed the "Faults escaped" alone, for two reasons, because (1) no alteration is made in the crux 1 referred to which is not listed in the "Faults escaped", but which is generally altered in the expensive-paper copies, and (2) because several instructions in the "Faults escaped" are carried out in this copy, which are never among the hand alterations in the expensive-paper copies. It seems obvious, then, that the corrector of this copy was not associated with the press (and so did not have access to the *unpublished* faults list used by the pre-publication correctors), but was acting solely on the authority of the "Faults escaped" published at the back of the book in hand. In short, a conscientious private reader. The spelling of the alterations as a whol points to the late 16th- or early 17th-century.

As "tne" never did occur in this copy, the instruction to alter it mu have been as baffling to the Renaissance reader as it was to you. And Hartlebury had to *find* tne crux first, and without being told that "p.8" in the "Faults escaped" meant "p. 80"! And that wasn't easy. The *sequence* of page references in this early part of the "Faults" is not the give-away you might assume: . . . 60, 69, 63, 82, 74, 77, 76, 8, 82, 98, 92, 90, 89, 100. . . . It seems to have been laid down partly at *random*, partly in the

order of the printing or proofing (of formes), but not in narrative sequence (of pages), which is in effect later in the "Faults escaped."

Once past the wrong page number, any reader faces a problem with the phrase "Notes Allegory tne" in separating (a), the location, from (b), the quotation of the error. Is the location "Notes Allegory", and the error "tne"? or is "Notes" the location, and "Allegory tne" the error? If the first, then the four-line Allegorie section near the bottom of p. 80 is the small field in which to hunt for "tne"; if the latter, then the whole bottom half of the page is the field, and all the occurrences of the word "Allegorie" are the potential sites. In fact, there are only two such occurences. One is the marginal heading just mentioned—but there is no exotic "tne" nearby. So, it must be the other one, right?—the fifth-last word in this section. But bafflingly, for this occurrence too there is no accompanying "tne", let alone a prosaic "the".

Our Renaissance reader seems eventually to have concluded that "tne" was yet another error, an error *per se* in the "Faults escaped", rather than an accurate reference to an error in the body of her volume (or, unthinkably, *though correctly*, in the body of some other, uncorrected, copy).

And so, she must have ignored "tne", or regarded it perhaps as a redundant but garbled version of "the", which word stood seductively at the end of the note after the injunction to "r[ead]." And *read* it in she did, linking it with the word "Allegorie", which, she must have resolved, was not the field but the site. The inventive result is shown in the blow-up below, which I have referred to the passage as Hartlebury saw it before she penmistakenly obeyed orders.

From 'Information on Information'

Spellbound: Typography and the Concept of Old-Spelling Editions*

RANDALL McLEOD

This paper consists of extracts from an extended account of Renaissance typesetting problems. It differentiates old spelling from old typesetting, and asserts that editorial uses of the former concept lack philosophical rigour, and that its general application in so-called old-spelling editions has distorted the subtle texture of accidentals which they are designed to convey.

The *prime facie* evidence is limited to ink on paper, from which can be inferred an arrangement of typefaces and types during printing. The relationship of printed image to typeface and to type is concrete, and our inferences about composition are necessarily tied to an actual historic event. Inferences about spelling, however, are highly abstract, and we have no clear evidence a given compositor spelled as he set type. There is something about spelling, this editorial abstraction, both in theory and certainly in practice, that smacks of "spurning the base degrees." Once we have made the abstraction, we pull the ladder up after us, and, though we may lower it in a new old-spelling edition, we have grossly altered material circumstances. We are headed for a fall to the extent we take pride in our conservatism.

Let us look first at the early quartos of Dekker's *Shomakers Holiday*. In signature B3ʳ of Q3 we find

amongſt .

The ſ and t constitute one graphic shape, a ligature, printed by one type, noteworthy in that it back-kerns. A kern is vulnerable typeface that extends off its own typebody. To survive printing it must be set where it can rest on an adjacent type shoulder; but as the g occupies

*An earlier version of this paper was presented at a conference on "The Preparation of Old-Spelling Renaissance Play—Texts in English," Glendon College, York University, April 12-13, 1978.

this very place, *ſt* cannot be set after g without causing the kern to foul, and thus to bend or break:

amongſt

Accordingly, we can deduce the gap between the g and the *ſt* correlates in the original setting with spacing type or types. Now look at the equivalent passage in Q1 and 2.

amongeſt

kerns

Is e part of the spelling? part of the pronunciation? Is it not perfectly plausible that the e is merely a weak vowel whose body is being used by the typesetter, who may care nothing for her intelligence?

* * *

About "amongest." We can look to the *OED* spelling profile (arranged grossly by centuries), and find that "amongest" is a legitimate 16th-century "spelling," but not 17th. But how does the *OED* know what the spelling is if it gathered its information from type, since the whole question of the spelling *per se* of this word in type (though not, perhaps, in ms.) is challenged by the example from Dekker? Unfortunately we frequently cannot separate ms. "spellings" from type "spellings" because the sources of the profiles are not extant. As there is no Dekker concordance, the prevalence of the form in his work cannot easily be determined. But what would any other italic occurrences tell us, for there is no ready way to surmise a ms. value through such type exigencies? It would be interesting to learn if the e were found only in italic settings, where alone the fouling potential exists. (Q1 also offers two settings each of "amongest" and "among" in black letter.) More than a Dekker concordance we need one for Valentine Sims, the printer, and an analysis of his founts and compositors. Some founts, by the way, had a non-kerning allotype of the ligature, and contemporary examples of this rarer type are not hard to find, though there is none in *Shomakers* Q1:

Amongſt .

From 'Spellbound'

Ana Mary Armygram, Orlando F. Booke, R. MacGeddon, and R. McEden and I've also noticed that almost all of your essays are dedicated to someone. It seems to me that these two moves, these prefatory gestures, are a way of immediately opening up the essay form.

RM: I don't want to be alone, and so I imagine a relationship. I would give someone, the dedicatee, a gift, and that other person would (in my imagination) give me the gift of listening to a new me, tolerating me, sparking me, licensing me. I imagine surprising them all. Well, they have their own personalities, which I know, and so, one of them is stiff, say, and one flexible. If I pull the rug out from under a stiff person it would be different from pulling it out from under a flexible person. So, I try to be cheeky with them,

or woo them, or whatever works. These are social projections that keep me from being alone when I research and write. Because writing is lonely. These tricks amount to a displacement of a social scene, I think. They *work* for me. I don't strive to understand them. That's a legitimate project for the reader or the dedicatee, perhaps, but I don't need to know much about it. (I do know it relates a lot to how I spoke to my mother in later years—with a Scots accent or in French, always with grammatical oddity and broken rules of one sort or another. I avoided talking straight.)

MO: It's a very solitary sort of activity. But I also really like—and it's something I always try to bear in mind as a writer—that there isn't just an undifferentiated audience 'out there'. Rather, there is a

performative gesture being made. So, when I talk about you re-imagining the essay form—particularly in literary criticism, where there are certain protocols in place —that's one of the things I find really productive.

RM: Well, Napoleon, I am told, said rules are for those who are too weak to break them. But there is an art to breaking rules. One has to know them well to break them well. They are worth honoring, and breaking them well does that. But also, dedicatees can be people who taught me to see in a particular way—trail blazers.

My first dedication, in 'Spellbound', was to Harry Carter, a historian of type. He helped me understand kerns and ligatures —on the basis of which I challenged old-spelling editions, for type is *set*, not necessarily *spelled*.

In italic 'amongeſt', for example, 'e' keeps the 'ſt' ligature from breaking its kern on the 'g'. Knowing this, one hesitates to say that 'e' is part of the *spelling*. When I sent him my essay, he said that he was dying and was sorry he would not be able to meet me, but that I had written kerns on the blackboard for all to see. Until now I have thought only of my own loss, that I never got to meet this fine thinker. But, being older, I can appreciate that my 11th-hour missive might have mitigated his dying in some small way. Fathers and sons. It's a lonely business. I don't feel lonely tonight with you, however. I'll be Harry, you be Randy.

MO: I think there is something about a dedication that gives you a certain permission as a reader as well. Even though it may not be dedicated to me in particular, it sets up an expectation that, as a reader, nevertheless also gives me permission to laugh. I think so much of a certain kind of criticism is taken up with adversarial finger-pointing and chastising. In your work, for all of its rigour there is still a generous impulse there.

RM: It's nice to hear you say that there is a generous impulse, because I am aware that I might seem savage to people. In the Herbert Gallery, I am tearing stripes off editors. But when I go like that at people I *know*, I'm taking the mickey; everything I say is in quotation marks. There are ways of softening attack as in the wit and the laughter, but I'm not sure other people will know that. They may think that, man, McLeod is a ferocious disciplinarian; don't cross the line!

I don't use aggressive tones in the classroom. I have a very different voice there—I try for many voices during a class. Writing and teaching are *very* different modes for me.

MO: But that's the interesting dialectic for me; there is an absolute rigour on the other side of the playfulness.

RM: I don't think that I could play in public unless there was the rigour. I would be dismissed as frivolous. Perhaps, I court being dismissed—at the reader's peril! And laughter forestalls tears.

MO: That, as much as anything, is the reason that it's also important. The work is also, quite clearly, taking itself very seriously.

RM: It would be stifling, I think, if the rigour I imposed on myself was carried out in the execution of the essay. It would be frightening. The wit is a pressure valve to blow off the steam. Plus, I like to be funny, especially by punning, for it exposes the instability of language. I think that humour is also an attempt to compensate for the obsessive side of my critique. I just spent eight hours today hunched over this little book on the trail of some guy who scratched over the letters and wrote something else—I've got to be sick. But if I can have a cup of wine and talk to you guys afterward and laugh about it, not only can I pick up tomorrow where I left off, but I'm a little balanced.

MO: We also touched on this briefly before we sat down—the other thing that is interesting about your work is that since you are dealing with material texts your essays also have this added task of presenting the physical properties of rare, centuries-old books to the reader and, often, of explaining fairly complex printing and binding processes. So, graphic design also has a role in your work in the form of things like photo-quotations from archival sources, diagrams, and very careful attention to the ways your essays are put together on the page—even moments of typographic play in some of them. Maybe you could talk a bit about that as a part of what you are doing.

RM: Well, I'm married to a photographer. She certainly educated my eye. I learned to look at a text without reading it. I aimed to understand the text, but not by reading.

Also, when I was a kid and I was learning how to use a typewriter, there were carbon papers. When I was an undergraduate we used to type on corrasable paper. I don't think this is sold any more. If you made a mistake, you could easily smear it off. But then, it must have been in my second or third year of college, I discovered xerox. At the same time, Scolar Press was producing photo-facsimilies. Photocopying was a revolution. In my PhD thesis, I was using The Variorum and the Arden editions of Shakespeare, and then in the last chapter, which was on *Sonnets*, I came across a photo-facsimile of the first edition. And I said, 'Well, I don't *need* these editors.' That is it in a nutshell. I was, for once, in the right place at the right time: here was an invention that short-circuited the product of a Renaissance printing house (you can equate that to 'the artist and his times', if you want) and me, a modern reader. The intervening centuries of editorial screwing around with the text were just gone, and I soon knew it. They had gone. Eventually, in a single day, I un-edited all of Shakespeare. It wasn't an act of reading everything and judiciously weighing cruxes one at a time, it was just an act of dismissal. Tremendous power came to me at that point. I predicted that there would be a revolution, when everyone else disowned Malone, disowned Pope—but it didn't happen, of course. Mine was a private apocalypse. That world goes on without me.

MO: We also talked about the fact that you have gone so far as to actually lay out some of your more recent essays before you submit them to a journal, so that you have a certain level of control over how they are put together.

RM: Well, I'm trying to compose like a painter, who wants to know from the start the canvas size and texture, and the colours of the palette. At the beginning of my career, I thought I had to court the journal editors and tailor my articles to them. But quickly I learned that they were actually looking for idiosyncratic pieces, and that I could state my demands. Or, they would come and ask me: 'Have you got anything?' I'd say, well, yeah, but it's got these 32 photographs. I guess I really didn't have to worry about marketing because people sought me out. I feel fortunate that many editors have understood that the oddity of my work was potentially essential to its success.

MO: We often think of such things as, well, very designerly, something you have to do in order to prepare books for print. But it really has put control in your hands, particularly as a scholar who has specific needs, to the degree that you want a page to end on a specific word, or are doing interesting things with pages misnumbered. There are things within the essay form itself that require a certain level of attention.

RM: Well, at first I tried to communicate all of the concrete features of layout to the editors in square brackets—'[This word to come at end of line.]' And I was dragged kicking and screaming to InDesign for more efficiency. I resented that I didn't have an artist's immediate expression in a physical medium, and I don't have great skill in InDesign, though I am committed to it and getting more adept.
I used to write all of my essays with the images merely in my head. Or, the images might be on paper, but not integrated with the words. At the 11th hour, when it came time to assemble word and image in a layout, I always found that I hadn't really understood the image. So, I craved a medium in which my composition of words and image would

be integrated from the beginning, so that the errors I continually made in understanding the image would work themselves out during the whole composition process and would not surprise me near the end. Very reluctantly I've taken time from research to bang my head against InDesign. A designer, Brandon Besharah, has helped me. He is the one who makes all of my diagrams look professional.
I depend upon the relationship with Brandon very much because it is one of the things that keeps me from being lonely. In our inevitable miscommunications during revision I also learn to refine my work. Having a collaborator who misunderstands is essential. It keeps me from being absorbed by my own idiom.

MO: Your work in particular also makes certain demands in terms of how you explain the architecture of a book to someone, how it has been stitched, or misfolded, or when things have printed on top of one another. Graphic design is also one way that you try to communicate that.

RM: When I was in school I did take drafting, in grades 6, 7, and 8. And my father was an electrical engineer and a draftsman, so I bonded with my father through that. Cartesian geometry in grade 12 was really big for me—the expressive power of numbers, spatial relationships, diagrams, and mathematical formulæ.

MO: Perhaps that is related to one of the other things that I quite like about your work—as an interesting analogue to your graphic interventions—which is your penchant for neologism, which is another economical way of conveying a dense combination of concepts.

RM: Like 'theoheretical'.

MO: —or 'obliterature' or 'unediting'. And what was the other one?

AK: 'Transformission'.

MO: Through neologism you tend to bend the discursive demands of the essay to your will. On the level of language you have this interesting ability, if you need to convey something. And it's playful, but it's also a succinct way of getting at complex ideas.

RM: Well, I admire James Joyce —or Beckett: 'In the beginning was the pun.' And as I said before, I studied languages in high school and I enjoy exploiting etymology when I write. For example, the part of the Dante that appears as bearing type on the title page of the 1501 Vergil comes from Canto XXVIII of the *Purgatorio*, when Dante and Vergil have just entered Paradise and meet Matilda standing across a brook, Lethe. Vergil's name, the only word inked on the title page, comes in just here, and the next two lines of verse become reversed. At the collision of 'V E R G I L I V S' and Lethe the poem *forgets* itself! Vergil, Dante, and Aldus intended this joke no more than Shakespeare intended 'snosh.' But there it is.
Anyway, 'Lethe' is cognate with 'latent', so I'm going to call the essay dealing with this example of bearing type 'Latent Image'. I toy with having as a frontispiece for the essay an etymological tree, starting with Indo-European and coming down variously through Old Slavic, Old Norse, Latin, Greek 'lethe' to English, 'latent'. Finding the title for this essay comes from the accident of the Dante appearing in the Vergil, and the particular stanza on Lethe that's rearranged.
You haven't seen the picture of this, so let me show it to you. [Produces raking-light photo.] Here's the title page. It's printed on vellum. If you shine a light, a raking light, as the photographer did, you see it: 'T *al qual di ramo in ramo si raccoglie*'. That is the first line of verse on the page. What's happening here—routinely—is that lines of type are rearranged

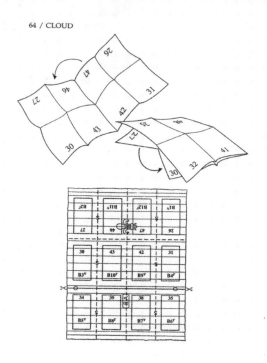

path of sewing

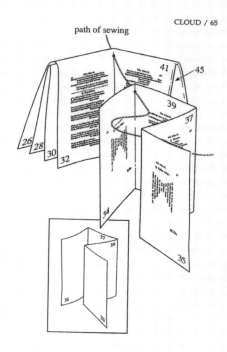

From 'FIAT ƒLUX'

when recycled as bearers. Right here [points] is about the river Lethe, and these are the lines that are interchanged. When I shine the light like that, I can read all of the type, intended or not, I enter a world of strange juxtapositions. Here coherent language is beginning to melt, as when you fall asleep, and the syntax, blurs, garbles, and flows in various directions.

Bearers are liable to be in any early book. Wherever you see a blank space at the top or bottom of a page in these bigger formats, a folio, a quarto, or an octavo, they are usually not blank. Most of the time you can't see the bearers, because you don't think to look, or because there has been flattening of the text block with a hammer or a standing press to hide this evidence—unless you look around from copy to copy—which is always

what I'm doing with my Collator anyway.

Maybe the most important thing to say—and this pertains to my teaching too—I try not to enter the classroom with a single version of a poem. I always prefer more than one, because there will be differences, and they open up a place where you can put in your crowbar and start wiggling. And the temple of something or other will collapse. Now, if you are coming from the top with Aristotlean criticism, or you're coming from the bottom with Freudian criticism, you're still imposing an 'ism' on a text. But bearers reveal a structure that is *in* the book that can't be seen until you have a knack for exposing it. The critical language that follows is one derived from the object. It's not an extrinsic 'ism'. That's the appeal of it for me: the unknown language hiding in

the object, the book's Song of Itself, and then to attempt a reading of the object as originally perceived in the light—or darkness—of the newly revealed text.

MO: To clarify, in instances of bearing type their bulk is what is filling out the space of the page and supporting the platen—so, they are simultaneously leaving behind traces of what they say, as well as evidence of a purely architectural function.

RM: Yes, it is their bulk, but their bulk comes on stream at a certain time, because these are elements in a chase, and you pull them together and put them in a particular syntactical and grammatical formulation, following copy. But then, when waking day is over and sleep comes, these things move around in the night. And, although the shuffled forms we often find the bearers in may no longer convey narrative sense in terms of, say, the *artist's* narrative, it *is* a narrative of what is liberated from his purpose at a particular time. It is like a satyr play reworking the themes of the tragedy. Now they float free into some other arrangement. There is a new purpose for the type bodies—stabilizing a platen.

But the rearranged letters are still literature. Now they are communicating something of Aldus's publishing program and of his schedule of reprinting. Look at this map of the sources of bearers on the title page of the Aldine Philostratus. [see p. 53] These revelations are like Carbon-14 dating. They tell you, in this case, that part of the first quire of the book was printed from the inside to the outside. The first quire, a, has eight leaves—or four bifolia—and printing seems to have started in the middle with leaves 4 and 5, and then moved to 3 and 6, and then 2 and 7, which is where we are here, the source of the bearers on leaf 1. So, leaves 2 and 7 appear in the dream state on 1. I am reading the Philostratus for its own backwards chronology. I said that I like to go into class with at least two versions of a text; well, this text is *already* two versions. It's got the narrative reading 1 to 8, and another reading progressing from 4/5 to 3/6 to 2/7 to 1/8. What you do with this multiple chronology is up to you, but there *is* another story going on. For me the startling thing is that no one else sees this textual complexity. But it is on the surface and merely requires close reading. I don't get it. On the other hand, I enjoy being the first to map it. I don't like the thought of being scooped.

MO: Also, when you are talking about this other narrative that is behind the narrative, it reminds me of your term 'obliterature'. We were talking about neologism, and 'Obliterature', for example, is the title of an essay in which you are examining a censored manuscript copy of Donne's quasi-pornographic elegy, 'To His Mistress Going to Bed' that is almost entirely marked out. This seems like an interesting model for a critically engaged practice, which is to *begin* by looking in the place where there seems to be nothing going on or nothing immediately visible. It's similar to the bearing type. It's this place where there seems to be nothing, or nothing of interest, and beginning there as a point of departure. It's not just simply looking to the margins for no reason.

RM: Well, nothing is marginal, really. You know, the definition of God as 'a centre everywhere and a circumference nowhere'? Text is, as it were, divine—everywhere, in every margin. I think we are fallen when we regard meaning as confined to the centre. You don't have to really be too mystical. Just reading Freud tells you that there are these boxes and concepts or beliefs that you put them in, but as soon as you fall asleep, or as soon as you've had too much to drink, or as soon as you've broken down, you realize that everything is flooding and weaving. The walls of the box are ripe for transgression. Always. And you don't need a reason to look to the margin. When one looks to the margin, reasons there will reveal themselves. Let the margins reason *you*.

MO: There also seems to be something in 'obliterature' as a concept suggesting that just because there seems not to be something there does not mean that it can't also be pregnant with meaning. Particularly in that essay, where in fact you can see a few letters of the text that escaped the censor.

RM: Well, with a technological breakthrough—infrared reflectography.

MO: But also even just the letters that you can make out in normal lighting, if you carefully examine the manuscript.

RM: And if you count up how man lines should be there, you figure, well, it's a 48-line poem in a run of poems by Donne; it's got to be *this* one. That's reading body language

MO: That's another impulse that I'm interested in. I suppose it is part of bibliography, too, which is about looking at things closely, carefully.

RM: Well, wrong to the light, too, transgressively, abnormally. Like, with raking light you've got not to flood light in the way a photographer would normally. To light it, to illustrate it, you've got to hold it strangely. In fact, the funny thing about vellum, it becomes more translucent wher the type bites into it. So, you can actually read the uninked text with *through* light, as well as with *raking* light. On paper, through light doesn't reveal bearers.

MO: You spoke about looking wrong to the light or askance to the light, which makes a perfect transition to the collator. Because the other big part of the actual day to-day work of textual scholarship and analytic bibliography is comparing texts, and you've developed the McLeod Portable Collator as a device that, really, uses 19th-century optical techniques to collate two different copies of the same text. It's interesting to me also because this is a technology that doesn't seem necessarily to be improved upon by computers, for example. You could scan things an superimpose the images, but this is much more immediate, portable easier, visceral, faster.

RM: Yes, it's of the body, it's visceral. In fact, you don't have to use the Collator to this end, thoug it is convenient. Just cross your eyes. Let the left eye look at the right object and the right at the le At first, you see four images. Keep

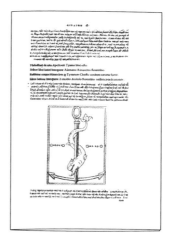

title page as inked   title page as inked plus bearers

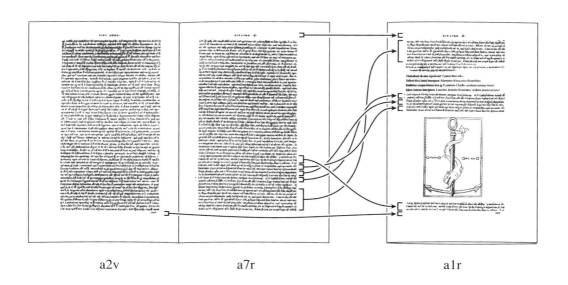

a2v   a7r   a1r

the sources on a2v | 7r of the title-page bearers

on crossing, and there's a point where you see only three, and one instinctively locks one's eyes there. The middle of the three images is the fusion of the two peripheral ones. They are transparent, but the middle one is solid. If there is any horizontal displacement of type in a line of one copy but not the other, the composite line in the fused image in the middle will appear in 3D against the stable 2D background of the invariant rest of the composition. Understand that in normal vision two independent functions of the eye are linked: so that one focuses where the two eye-beams converge. In cross-eyed collation, one focuses on the objects beyond the point of convergence. (There is no object at this point. It is just where the eye-beams cross.)

MO: Maybe you could talk just informationally about how you developed the Collator. Did you see a gap that needed to be filled? Or was it your engineering background coming home to roost? A bit of both?

RM: When I was a kid I played with View-Master and a magic lantern and became fascinated with periscopes and projections and tracing, and with looking cross-eyed. My uncle had a 35mm camera and he gave me his reject slides to play with. My dad said, 'Let's build a projector and we'll project them.' So, he bought a lens and a lamp and things, and I became fascinated with the projection of images —a process I came to articulate in drafting, geometry, and psychology. Now on the Collator I'm projecting a different image for each eye. So, I had that background from childhood.

When I was a young teacher, a colleague who was an editor of Renaissance drama, Dick Van Fossen, gave a talk about the Hinman Collator, which is a sophisticated electro-mechanical device—too sophisticated. And once I realized what its principle

was, I could make my own low-tech version. Unlike any other stereoscopic instrument I know, my Collator halves the optics. Such devices usually have symmetrical optics, two ocular mirrors and two objective mirrors, as in a pair of binoculars. In mine, one object is close and seen through two mirrors and one remote and seen directly, but the optical distance between the two is equal—unless one object is reduced, is a photocopy, say— in which case, I move one object closer or farther away until the two have the same angular height and width. Each eye then focuses at a different depth. If that works for you, you've just saved $3,500.00!

MO: Maybe I should mention one other thing for the benefit of those who don't traffic in textual scholarship. It's maybe unclear that your work doesn't just take place between the covers of books; you are also looking at multiple volumes from Los Angeles to London and every place in between. There is a peripatetic, archival part of your work.

RM: 'Peripathetic!' Well, ideally you have to see them all. There's no such thing as really completing your study until you've seen all the copies—or, in practice, enough copies to show that your original hypothesis was too limited. I like to write essays governed by some original misunderstanding, which I break out of with some new piece of evidence. In my study of a monument of Greek textual criticism, *A Dissertation Upon the Epistles of Phalaris* by Richard Bentley (1699), when I realized that the book was full of remote offsetting I wanted to map it. And I saw about 40 copies in Britain that summer. I was just going to every library I knew that had copies and mapping the offsets—each copy different from the next. You'd think 40 was enough. But I'd read about a copy at the University of Alberta in Edmonton, a place I'd been only

once, to give a lecture. So it's really far off my beat. But I felt that there was something essential about that copy, for it was bound with another text—one that Bentley's text referred to, and was dedicated to Bentley. I wanted to see how my understanding of Bentley's work might be affected by this physical association. Satisfying that curiosity cost about $600, but it revealed something that blew the top off my earlier understanding: the two books were originally intended to be released as merely one, joint-authored.

It's like a myth of the Fall. The good things of Eden are dispersed, and by the sweat of your brow you have to recollect them. The myth of editing is that you can capture the text and make a thousand copies and send it out to people, and they won't have to travel to the evidence. But that's not the way it works for me. We are fallen, and the body of Christ or Osiris, or whomever you wish, is dispersed and has to be remembered, harvested. This one copy hearkened back to the original plan. Its provenance is lost, but it must have been closely associated with one or both of the authors, the printer, or the publisher.

MO: I think that is also a part of your work that is easy to forget about. You don't just go down to the corner and find these things. One can't even just walk into the Huntington Library—you have to write letters to gain entry. It's like diplomacy, like getting into an embassy.

RM: Once one is an advanced doctoral student or has significant publications most libraries are easy of access. But yes, you can't just go to the corner to find these things. I acquire photos from many copies over years. Once I start an essay, a judicious selection among the photos eventually makes all seem straightforward. But, most of my articles take about ten years, because I need a long lead time to see the evidence. When I start a project I know that *something* is there, but I don't know what it is. It may be after two or three years that I will know what the project really is, or learn its name or whom I might dedicate it to, and then many libraries will have to be revisited because I then know not merely what to look for, as I may have on my first visit, but how to *see* it.

MO: That's actually a perfect place for me to move to my last question. I came to your work over ten years ago now, during my time studying early modern textuality in graduate school, tracking essays down in various library journals and different places, and now that we've connected via email, asking you for things that I haven't had access to. In researching for this interview I ran across a short biography of yours from a few years ago that mentions a forthcoming volume of collected essays titled *Material Shakespeare*, and there have been rumblings that there was going to

be a collected group of essays at some point. Is that still something that is going to possibly happen?

RM: Yes, well, I would love that. And various people, realizing that I had a gap there and was not able to do this, like Peter Stallybrass, and Margreta de Grazia at Penn, and Stephen Orgel at Stanford, tried to facilitate it. And I think I alienated a lot of people by seeming to be clueless about the process. So I would like it to happen. My dedication is to what I'm working on at the moment, rather than repackaging old work. But I think the project is important—knowing you would like to see it convinces me of that—and when you showed me Jonathan [Goldberg]'s collection of published essays [*Shakespeare's Hand* (2002)] I thought, Why don't *I* do that?

MO: It seems to me that your work in particular would be very demanding for someone to put together in a volume properly, especially when you have essays

like 'FIAT *f*LUX' that run to 110 pages.

AK: It would just be convenient to have a volume that one could tote around.

RM: I think partly my problem is that I think that each time an idea is expressed it needs a new container. I like the essays. I work on them for so long I'm sure of the material, and I don't tend to be alienated from them when I revisit them years later. But the idea of going back and picking up something that's 15 years old and reentering it—aargh, it sounds like a mountain of work.

MO: I was joking earlier that I just need to take my xeroxes and make a facsimile, or a PDF.

RM: Well, maybe I should do that. Just historical layers: this is what I said in 1984; this is what I say now.

MO: Still, part of me resists that. It would be nice to have it, because

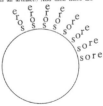

From 'from Tranceformations in the Text of *Orlando Furioso*'

you could just go to the shelf and pick it up, but I can also remember having so much fun searching out each essay. Maybe that goes back to the appeal of your work, in a way. It's like your favourite punk rock record. If it was in every store and easy to find it might not be nearly as exciting. It has a little bit of that quality for me. I had to work to track everything down. Even in graduate school I certainly wasn't looking stuff up on the web, just going to the library and finding it, or inter-library loaning it and xeroxing it so I could have my copy. There's something about that that I think is the proper way to experience your work, to have to go after it.

AK: The pseudonyms also make it difficult.

MO: But I like that. That's perfect.

RM: And I think I make demands on readers—once the essay is in their hands. 'You're not going to get into this essay unless you are willing to struggle with this first sentence.' That kind of difficulty. I experience it in Faulkner.

MO: But I think that's part of it. That also makes it more meaningful. That whole process of coming to the work—at least the way I came to it—made it more meaningful to me. So, part of me would love to see a book of collected things, of Shakespeare pieces or whatever it is, but at the same time I resist it because I like my xeroxes.

RM: I think I'm conflicted in the same way. You're as bad as I am.

AK: Could you talk about that in terms of the concept of change, the theme of change in your work? Like the word we were trying to remember, 'transformission', or the idea of flux—which might be related to the element of surprise, or the spirit of play, that maybe goes back to something you were saying at the very beginning of the

conversation: the idea of a reality beyond the immediate object. I was trying to articulate this before—like the way that editorial work becomes, really, not secondary, but primarily creative, and then the criticism that you do on the editorial work also becomes, not parasitic, but primarily creative, and then ends up producing these other persons, these pseudonymous personalities. I guess what reminded me of that in what you were saying is that each project needs its own container, or has its own form. Putting the essays in a book would mean, I guess, making them something new, transforming them.

MO: Maybe another way of thinking about change is as a certain kind of vitality, a 'livingness'. It's not that these books, or the different editions of a book, have a kind of organicism to them, not exactly. I think anyone who considers a time period 300 years ago, a culture that's pre-cinematic and pre-televisual—it's very easy to forget that this is a completely different dispensation in terms of the way people are interacting with these objects. Maybe that's part of the 'history of the book', it gives the book a life—it's gone through transformations, it's gone through 'transformissions', it's an elastic, unstable thing with secrets to tell.

RM: It's also showing the changing life in me. I think when I began looking at books as a small child I did find them distant and alien. I was not a fast reader, was a very slow reader, in fact, because I looked at letter shapes. And so I think I'm constantly trying to take care of that little boy who was slow at it. Now, I'm even slower because I feel it is worthwhile to delve into the meanings of material things, to which many other people seem not to have access. I have a role to play.

MO: There is a kind of designerly slowness, too. If you were designing

a book, for example, you would pay attention to the spacing around em dashes, or the shape of the capitals, or how this block of text sits next to that illustration, or running heads, or any of those fine details. All of that is incredibly meaningful for designers, especially when you may spend a week trying to settle on the right typeface for a particular book. Those decisions all come hard-won.

RM: Well, designers are under a time constraint that academics may not be, thanks to tenure. I think that I would not flourish in a world without tenure. I'm smart—I *could* perform on schedule, but I would be alienated outside academe, I think.

MO: I think it's valuable to be looking at these founding moments and these earlier texts and realizing that they operate as a kind of information design—I'm thinking of your article 'Information on Information'. Designers understand that close attention, and I feel like you've got potential allies all around you in other disciplines.

RM: I don't really think I have much of a sense of who my allies are. I'm always surprised when people like you contact me. I don't assume that I am read. Maybe that feeling stems from my being Canadian, or a younger brother —or maybe from awareness of the blind spots in our traditions of editing and interpretation. I assume that most things are witnessed shallowly.

MO: The good thing about working on material culture more broadly is that there aren't necessarily the constraints of art history, for example. It's open territory. Also, there is a way in which its natural state is to partner up with other disciplines, partner up with architecture and design, partner up with bibliographic or textual criticism, and find the productive points of contact. It's the porosity of it that is one of the most exciting and enabling things about it.

RM: That, for me, is what textual criticism is, since one can work profoundly in any language without knowing A, B, C.

MO: Your work seems like a natural fit for a group of people that are going to pull different things from your work—they're certainly not going to go out and edit Shakespeare.

RM: We've had enough of that, anyway.

MO: But they can draw inspiration from it for work in completely different disciplines. I've tried to talk about it a little bit in pressing you about pseudonym, or playfulness, or the dialectic of rigour and openness. I think all of these are productive things for anybody who is engaging seriously with something. Do you have anything you want to add?

RM: Well I guess I'm looking for inspiration, and I find it in material, touching material, finding that it has voices that are previously unheard, or haven't been heard for centuries, or that my training in the academy has predisposed me not to hear. There seems to be inexhaustible surprise in things.

Thanks. I've really enjoyed talking with you.

SELECTED BIBLIOGRAPHY

– Randall McLeod, '*Gon*. No more, the text is foolish.", in Erick Kelemen, *Textual Editing and Criticism, An Introduction*, W.W. Norton & Co. (2008).
– Randall McLeod, 'Chronicling Holinshed's Chronicles', in Cyndia Susan Clegg, ed., *The Peaceable and Prosperous Regiment of Blessed Queene Elisabeth: A Facsimile from Holinshed's Chronicles (1587)*, Huntington Library Press (2005).
– Randall McLeod, 'Obliterature: *Reading a Censored Text of Donne's 'To his mistres going to bed*", English Manuscript Studies 12 (2005).
– Randall McLeod, 'Gerard Hopkins and the Shapes of his Sonnets', in Raimonda Modiano, Leroy F. Searle and Peter Shillingsburg, eds., *Voice Text Hypertext: Emerging Practices in Textual Studies*, University of Washington Press (2003).
– Ana Mary Armygram, 'The Triumph of King James and His August Descendants', *Shakespeare Studies* 28 (2000).
– Random Cloud, 'Where Angels Fear to read', in Joe Bray, Miriam Handley, and Anne C. Henry, eds., *Ma(r)king the Text*, Ashgate (2000).
– Randal Mc Leod, 'ALTVM SAPERE: Parole d'homme et Verbe divin. Les chronologies de la Bible hébraïque in-4° de Robert Estienne', in *La Bible imprimée dans l'Europe moderne (XVe-XVIIIe siècle)*, Bertram Schwarzbach, ed., Bibliothèque nationale de France (1999).
– Random Cloud, '*Enter* Reader', in Paul Eggert and Margaret Sankey, eds., *The Editorial Gaze*, Garland (1999).
– Orlando F. Booke, 'IMAGIC / *a long discourse*', Studies in the Literary Imagination 32.1 (1999).
– Randall McLeod, 'Unemending Shakespeare's Sonnet 111' (1981), reprinted in Stephen Orgel, ed., *Shakespeare, The Critical Complex*, Garland (1999).
– Randall McLeod, 'UN *Editing* Shak-speare' (1982), reprinted in Stephen Orgel, ed., *Shakespeare, The Critical Complex*, Garland (1999).
– Random Cloud, 'Shakespeare Babel', in Joanne Gondris, ed., *Reading Readings: Essays on Shakespeare Editing in the Eighteenth Century*, AUP (1997).
– Random Cloud, 'What's The Bastard's Name / Random Cloud', in George Walton Williams, ed., *Shakespeare's Speech-Headings*, AUP (1997).
– Claudia Nimbus, 'An Evening without Mrs. Siddons', *Critical Survey* 7.3 (1995).
– Random Cloud, 'FIAT *f*LUX', in Randall M Leod, ed., *Crisis in Editing: Texts of the English Renaissance*, AMS (1994).
– Randall McLeod, 'Il collazionatore portatile McLeod: una veloce *collatio* dei testi a stampa come figure' in Marco Santoro, ed., *La Stampa in Italia nel Cinquecento*, Bulzoni (1992).
– Random Cloud, "The very names of the Persons': Editing and the Invention of Dramatick Character', in David Kastan and Peter Stallybrass, eds., *Staging the Renaissance*, Routledge (1991).
– Random Clod, 'Information on Information', *Text* 5 (1991).
– Random Cloud, 'from Tranceformations in the Text of *Orlando Furioso*', *The Library Chronicle of the University of Texas at Austin* (1990); also issued in *New Directions in Textual Studies*, Dave Oliphant and Robin Bradford, eds. (1990).
– Randall McLeod, 'McLeod Portable Collator', *Newsletter*, Humanities Association of Canada (1988).
– Random Cloud, 'The Psychopathology of Everyday Art', in George R. Hibbard, ed., *The Elizabethan Theatre IX: Papers given at the Ninth International Conference on Elizabethan Theatre held at the University of Waterloo, in July 1981* (1986).
– Randall McLeod, 'Spellbound', in G.B. Shand and Raymond C. Shady, eds., *Play-Texts in Old Spelling*, AMS (1984).
– Randall McLeod, '*Gon*. No more, the text is foolish', in Gary Taylor and Michael Warren, eds., *The Division of the Kingdoms*, OUP (1983; reprinted 1986).
– 'McLeod's Portable Collator', *Bibliography Newsletter* (1983).
– Random Cloud, 'The Marriage of Good and Bad Quartos', *Shakespeare Quarterly* (1982).
– Randall McLeod, 'UN *Editing* Shak-speare', *Sub-stance* 33/34 (1982).
– Randall McLeod, 'Unemending Shakespeare's Sonnet 111', *Studies in English Literature* 21 (1981).
– Randall McLeod, 'Spellbound: Typography and the Concept of Old-Spelling Editions', *Renaissance and Reformation* n.s. 3.1 (1979).
– Randall McLeod, 'A Technique of Headline Analysis, with Application to *Shake-speares Sonnets*, 1609', Studies in Bibliography 32 (1979).

THE SKY IS NOT THE LIMIT

by Angie Keefer

529.10 It is one of the strange facts of experience that when we try to think into the future, our thoughts jump backward. It may well be that nature has some fundamental metaphysical law by which opening up what we call the future also opens up the past in equal degree. The metaphysical law corresponds to the physical law of engineering that 'every action has an equal and opposite reaction.'

(Buckminster R. Fuller, *Synergetics*, 1975)

The Space Shuttle *Challenger* exploded in the sky above Florida approximately 90 seconds after launch on January 28, 1986, killing all seven crew members, including Christa McAuliffe, a teacher. I was eight years old then, and, like many students around the country, I was watching the event live on television at a school assembly. I recall from my faint memory of the broadcast that Christa McAuliffe's mother was in the audience on the ground at Cape Canaveral. She was looking up at the sky, using her hand as a visor to block the sun from her eyes, presumably so that she could take in a view of what would likely have been for her —as it was for my third grade class—an incomprehensible sight.

What was a rocket headed towards outer space one second, disintegrated into a cloud of smoke the next. My mother, who had been working for several years on programming of the controller for the Space Shuttle Main Engine, picked me up from school early that day. I recall that she spent the rest of the afternoon, and several days that followed, crying intermittently, covering her face with her hands while our television replayed the tragic event *ad infinitum*.

The Rogers Commission report on the causes of the disaster, which was released in the summer following the explosion, assigned blame to faulty design of an O-ring in the solid rocket booster, and, moreover, to the managerial culture of NASA, which had stifled safety concerns voiced by shuttle engineers. As part of a general campaign to secure funding and support, NASA leadership greatly deflated the probability of loss of life on a shuttle mission to 1 in 100,000, against engineers' estimates of 1 in 100. Physicist Richard Feynman was blunt in the appendix he wrote to accompany the official investigation report, wherein he asked, 'What is the cause of management's fantastic faith in the machinery?' Feynman concluded pointedly, 'For a successful technology, reality must take precedence over public relations, for nature cannot be fooled.'[1]

Yet, to attempt to fool nature, or at least one's audience, by employing strategies of obfuscation and hyperbole is a service for which businesses and government organizations in the U.S. currently pay over $6 billion dollars per year to a booming public relations industry. As everyone who works in public relations, marketing, or the psychiatric professions realizes, our conceptions of reality are malleable, subject to our desires. Feynman discovered that even within the parameters of aviation engineering, with its highly specific criteria for safety certification, a 'slow shift towards a decreasing safety factor' occurs as myriad, ostensibly sustainable compromises to standards, and facts accrue —compromises that serve the immediate interests of some aspect of a system, without consideration for the larger interests of the whole.[2] Over time, previously held distinctions between licence and deviance in representing reality are obscured and redrawn. Only when deviance results in a spectacle of destruction does the culminating effect of the slow shift register, however briefly.

I grew up awash with images and souvenirs of space travel, but I remember clearly the autographed photo of Ms McAuliffe in her official NASA-issue blue flight suit. NASA had distributed promotional materials to schools in anticipation of the launch, which was to have been the first of a series of shuttle missions to carry non-professional astronaut teachers into space. Jones Valley Elementary School, where I was a student, had been following the *Challenger* mission closely. Though I was aware during the time of the *Challenger* catastrophe that my mother worked on the space shuttle project, I would not infer until years later that her reaction was related to a sense of personal responsibility. Following the tragedy, the shuttle program was suspended for 32 months. During the initial months of the suspension, previously undetected cancers rapidly metastasized throughout my mother's body. She died within three months of diagnosis. She was 45.

The call for systemic reform issued by Feynman in the Rogers Commission report was not heeded. In February 2003, the Space

Illustrations by Chris Evans

59

Shuttle *Columbia* and its crew of seven astronauts were destroyed during re-entry into Earth's atmosphere as a consequence of damage sustained to the vehicle's external fuel tank during launch. Again, the official investigation into the underlying causes of the catastrophe revealed that NASA's management had long suppressed engineers' safety concerns. Again, significant risks were foreseen. Again, those risks were not addressed. Feynman, who died in 1988, was not around to restate his case against the triumph of public relations over reality.

The *Challenger* and *Columbia* episodes mark a confrontation between two modes of thought. On the one hand, is the scientific approach, a mode of rational inquiry characterized by a suspended state of doubt, during which evidentiary facts are collected, from which conclusions may be drawn and further objects of inquiry identified. On the other, is the mode of belief rooted in the fluctuating phenomena of opinion and bias, including the speculative formulation of ideas to rationalize desires. A range of personal and political possibilities for any given lifetime or culture is inscribed through the ongoing process of negotiation between these two modes. Both are powerful cultural forces, not entirely separable, as each contributes, like NASA management and engineers, to delimiting the other's scope of influence.

502.22 Among the irreversible succession of self-regenerative human events are experiences, intuitions, speculations, experiments, discoveries, and productions. Because experience always alters previous experience, the process is both irreversible and nonidentically repetitive.

Last Fall, as news of the global economic meltdown emerged, an announcement was made that the space shuttle program would be terminated in 2010. U.S. astronauts would hence travel to space on the Russian *Soyuz* between 2010 and 2015, at which point NASA is set to reinitiate manned flights with a new program called *Constellation*. Some weeks before the announcement, I visited the Dymaxion Study Center, a reading room installed as part of an exhibition on the life and work of engineer, inventor and thinker Buckminster Fuller. The shelves were stacked with books Fuller had owned or written. Notes, photographs and sketches reproduced from Fuller's archive lined the walls, providing a thumbnail timeline of the evolution of his salient concepts. I spent some afternoons there, reading *Synergetics—Explorations in the Geometry of Thinking*.[3] Referred to as the *Synergetics Dictionary*, the book is a compendium of Fuller's ideas, arranged axiomatically, in numbered sequence. Matters under Fuller's consideration included time, space, thought—the phenomena of experience. The clarity of the book's structure paired with the breadth of its contents give the impression that one might find inside such an ordered tome concise answers to complex questions. In fact, I was more affected by the poetic obliquity of Fuller's language than by its precision. I transcribed selections from the book onto index cards, which I carried with me during the following weeks. My intention had been to assimilate Fuller's ideas about time—the relationship between past and future as he conceived it is mutable, navigable via thought, not linear as per Newton, but relative as per Einstein. The cards instead became an inverse field guide to subjectivity, either making relevant again basic perceptions that had grown so familiar as to disappear from consciousness; or providing novel vantages upon familiar ideas, such as the individualized process of observation, association and formulation, which is thought, itself.

When Buckminster Fuller asked how can we 'make the world work for 100% of humanity in the shortest possible time through spontaneous cooperation without ecological damage or disadvantage to anyone?',[4] he brought ethical matters of purpose and process to bear on the goals of technological innovation. Fuller's vision of a sustainable future society made possible by technological innovation was not only utopian but democratic, with a small 'd', based as it was on a bottom-up idea of cooperation among individuals. Like Feynman, who insisted that NASA owed it to citizens to be 'frank, honest, and informative, so that these citizens can make the wisest decisions for the use of their limited resources',[5] Fuller was committed to the idea of political progress hewn through public discourse.

The idea of *cooperation* expressed in Fuller's statement differs categorically from that of Edward Bernays, the founding father of public relations. Bernays, the nephew of Sigmund Freud, pioneered with remarkable success the systematic application of psychological principles governing human behaviour for the explicit purpose of manipulating mass opinion on behalf of the business and government leaders who were his clients. Fuller's ethical position was and remains anathema to the militaristic command and control perspective modeled by the efficacious practice of public relations formally developed by Bernays during the early 20th century, then brought to bear upon scientific research, economic theory and government policy in the post-World War II era. In 1928, when Buckminster Fuller was 33, Bernays' book *Propaganda* was published. Bernays writes,

The conscious and intelligent manipulation of the organized habits and opinions of the masses is an important element in democratic society. Those who manipulate the unseen mechanism of society constitute an invisible government which is the true ruling power. We are governed, our minds moulded, our tastes formed, our ideas suggested largely by men we have never heard of. This is a logical result of the way in which our democratic society is organized. Vast numbers of human beings must cooperate if they are to live together as a smoothly functioning society. In almost every act of our lives, whether in the sphere of politics or business, in our social conduct or our ethical thinking, we are dominated by the relatively small number of persons who understand the mental processes and social patterns of the masses. It is they who pull the wires that control the public mind.[6]

Fuller viewed prevailing systems of social organization as inhibitive of the expression of innate acuity and creativity—as well as uneconomical and ecologically destructive—and he therefore worked to replace those systems by encouraging scientific attitudes towards problem-solving. Bernays accepted these systems as inevitable. His concept of the cooperation necessary for the 'smooth functioning of society' would more accurately be called obedience or conformity, a top-down approach. His constituency was not humanity *per se*, as was Fuller's, but a particular clientele of those 'men we have never heard of' who 'control the public mind'. Bernays' purpose—the purpose of public relations—was to maximize economic and political power for his clientele by creating, distorting and controlling information available to the general public, from whose actions power would be derived. This purposeful manipulation of mass opinion is a fundamental aspect not of democracy but of autocracy, though the methods of public relations are a culturally permissible commonplace in democratic societies.

509.30 You cannot program the unknowns you are looking for because they are the relationship connections and not the things.

I first heard about Fuller from my parents, who must have mentioned him when explaining geodesic domes during the family vacation we took to Walt Disney's Epcot in the time between the *Challenger* explosion and my mother's death. Epcot, *Experimental Prototype Community of Tomorrow*, part of the Disney World theme park in Florida, is a wholesale usurpation of Buckminster Fuller's ideas, translated into an immersive brand environment for the park's diverse corporate sponsors, including in turns Exxon, Nestlé, GE, GM, MetLife, Hewlett Packard, AT&T, Siemens and others. The Epcot concept was significantly influenced by the World's Fair of 1939, for which Bernays had been publicity director. Albert Einstein and six other scientists associated with the World's Fair were averse to the Fair's deliberate channeling of scientific wonderment into the presentation of consumer goods, but they were unsuccessful in their attempts to steer the exhibition. Epcot, like the World's Fair, tells the story of how science and enterprise partner to bring good things to life all over the world. The park's iconic centrepiece is an enormous geodesic structure called *Spaceship Earth*, apparently a reference to Fuller's well-known 1969 book *Operating Manual for Spaceship Earth*, though Fuller is not credited, and perhaps rightly—Fuller's notion that systematic decentralization of power is necessary to foster ingenuity would be at odds with the public relations-driven branding of ingenuity at Epcot.

Inside the geodesic sphere at Epcot is an amusement ride based on the history of communications technology, from the inception of language, through the current day, into the unknown future. The *Spaceship Earth* ride opened in 1982, the year before Fuller's death. The ride has since been rebuilt several times, to keep pace with changing historical interpretations, but the basic conceit persists—that of traveling through time to observe civilization progressing in tandem with developments in communication technology. I remember some scenes from *Spaceship Earth*, though my recollections are conflated with memories of the movie *Tron*, a Disney feature released the same year that *Spaceship Earth* opened. *Tron*, one of the first movies to combine live action with extensive use of computer-generated special effects, is the story of a computer programmer who becomes trapped inside of a video game, from which he must battle his way back to freedom against a malevolent AI. Both *Spaceship Earth* and *Tron* are spectacular narratives propelled, respectively, by enthusiasms and fears about new technology.

529.11 The future is not linear. Time is wavilinear. Experience is expansive, omnidirectionally including and refining the future. ... It is both a subjective 'now' and an objective 'now'; a forward-looking now and a backward-looking now which combine synergetically as one complete 'now.' Because every action has both a reaction and a resultant, every now must have both a fading past and a dawning future.

Fuller's *Synergetics* was published in 1975, when my mother was 34. She had already been living for some time in the town where I would be born, two years later. At first glance, many of that town's significant architectural elements resemble those on view at the Epcot theme park, as they were constructed in the image of fantasies of the future defined by the prospect of space travel. The civic centre, inaugurated in 1975 with the premier of a locally commissioned symphony, *Galileo Galilei*, features a white arena structure reminiscent of the disc-shaped portion of the Star Trek *Enterprise*. Rockets, positioned upright in the landscape as monuments alongside the elevated I-565 connector, mark the city limits. However, despite a superficial similarity to the internationalist, technophilic gist of Epcot, the future vision underpinning the cultural narrative of my mother's adopted town was not informed by a utopian outlook. Epcot's—and Buckminster Fuller's—vision of the future had been predicated on technological solutions that would benefit humanity. The local economy of my hometown was driven by the aerospace defense industry, populated by engineers tasked with weapons development, oriented towards ominous probabilities. This world was more like *Tron* than *Spaceship Earth*.

An image of a church steeple and mosaic from my hometown conveys the ethos of that place in time. During my mother's youth the novel political and extraterrestrial concerns of the post-War era displaced a fervent religious culture in the south,[8] where church had been the primary institution of authority permeating rural family and social life. This transitional design of mosaic and steeple from the 1960s melds the modern embrace of technology and enterprise with the spectre of violence and religious tradition. Nowhere has fantastic faith in machinery been rendered more explicitly. Even still, I failed to notice, when I was

a child, the correspondence between the steeple's silhouette and that of the *Saturn V* rocket, which had been developed in my town. I did not recognize the obvious allusions to galactic bodies in the mosaic of Christ or the suggestion of Jesus as astronaut. Nor did the implications of these analogies occur to me. An affinity between a transcendent God and government sponsored space exploration—not to mention its shadowy sustaining partner, the aerospace defense industry— was apparently so mundane, so uncontested, as to have been invisible, except in retrospect.

The town in the foothills of the Appalachian Mountains where the church sits was before the 1960s known primarily for its downtown neighbourhood of intact antebellum houses. The place had been fixed on nostalgia for its fantasized past until pre-eminent Nazi rocket scientist Wernher von Braun, whom the American government had imported along with his colleagues at the end of the war, descended upon it, switching focus to the fantasized future. Here, Dr von Braun led NASA at the Marshall Space Flight Center during the development of the Saturn and Apollo programs, in the initial boom period of the burgeoning aerospace industry. During his 20-year tenure, the local Chamber of Commerce saw fit to supply this quiet, suburban town with the moniker 'The Rocket City' and adopt as its slogan *The sky is not the limit*. At the height of his fame, von Braun was satirized in a popular song by Tom Lehrer, 'Once the rockets are up, who cares where they come down? / "That's not my department", says Wernher von Braun.'[7] The aforementioned civic centre bears his name.

512.01 Mechanically and chemically, a steerable rocket embraces a complex of internal

and external energy-event transactions and omni-interacting, resultant 'motions' in Universe transcendental to earth motions, where the observer-articulator is extraterrestially positioned.

Since the earth is moving as a dependent motion-complex in respect to the Sun's and other planets' motions, and since the Sun is engaged in a plurality of internal and external motions in respect to the galactic system, and since the galactic system is a complex of motions in respect to other galaxies and supergalaxies, and so on, and since the whole set of motion events are nonsimultaneous and of uniquely variant durations, and since the intereffects of the events vary vastly in respect to eons of time, it is obvious that any thinkably meaningful conceptual coordination of event interrelationships in the meager lifetime limits of humans is inherently limited to a relatively local set within universe and within a time sense, and the relationships may be measured only in respect to the angle and

frequency magnitude characteristics of any one subsystem of the totality.

My early awareness of the space program was gleaned as much from pop culture as from direct exposure to the aerospace defense industry, which was the lifeblood of my hometown. By contrast, my mother came of age at the onset of the Space Race, before the first satellite missile had been sent into outer space. *Sputnik* was launched in October of 1957, the fall semester of my mother's last year of high school. The nation was seized by fear and shock over the unexpected technical prowess of their Soviet nemesis. Competition with the Soviets over space exploration, and in particular the goal of sending a man to the moon, soon became a national obsession. Students all over the country joined model rocket clubs. However, President Eisenhower, who was simultaneously overseeing the desegregation of Little Rock High School, and was in a position to know the true status of the U.S. missile defense program, expressed more concern over public concern than over the threat of Soviet attack. David Callahan and Fred Greenstein write in *Spaceflight* and the *Myth of Presidential Leadership*, 'What startled Eisenhower far more than the advance in Soviet rocketry was the intensity of public concern. *Sputnik* was not true proof of a Soviet advantage in ICBM development, but it *appeared* to be—and this idea was terrifying to many in the United States.'[8] Though the first satellite did little more than beep, *Sputnik* proved highly effective as propaganda.

Six and a half years after *Sputnik*, in spring of 1964, my mother finished graduate studies in mathematics and went to work as a rocket scientist. She was 22. She, and later my father, worked in the Simulations Lab of Computer Sciences Corp, creating digital and hybrid simulations of components of the *Apollo* Program, including the *Saturn V* booster, which launched the *Apollo* Spacecraft; the Lunar Lander, or Lunar Module, which carried the three-man *Apollo* crew and ultimately landed on the surface of the moon; and the Lunar Excursion Module, or Moon Buggy. Later, when my mother worked for Rocketdyne, which was then a division of Rockwell, she was involved in reprogramming the Motorola 68000 processor to replace the Honeywell computer originally used as the Space Shuttle Main Engine (SSME) controller. This same 68000 processor family, which subsequently powered Macintosh computers and UNIX based workstations until the introduction of the IBM Power PC processors in the late 1990s, is still in use today, thirty years after its introduction. The SSME controller project occupied the last years of my mother's life, until her death in 1987.

My mother was born four days after the attack on Pearl Harbor, in 1941, in rural St. Clair County, Alabama, like her mother and her mother before her. Two years before, James Agee and Walker Evans published *Let Us Now Praise Famous Men*, documenting the lives of tenant farmers living in nearby Hale County. During a childhood that I imagine against the backdrop of Evans' photographs, a childhood typical of the pre-industrial, agrarian south, my mother spent her early years labouring on the family's small farm, harvesting turnip greens. She was born in a house without plumbing, and at age nine, around 1950, helped to build the bathroom. That she would be employed in the fledgling space program only a few years later is testament to the radical cultural transformations that occurred between the 1940s and the 1960s. The possibility emerged then for people whose parents were barely literate to migrate from subsistence farms to astrionics labs. In my mother's case, this trajectory would likely have been fueled as much by native intelligence and determination to escape the oppression endemic to hardscrabble farm life, as by the cultural ambience of nationalistic zeal and fear. The shadow of World War II, the looming Soviet Threat and the national ambition to dominate the Space Race would have provided precocious Alabama schoolgirls with fodder for both.

My mother's father, Luther Crow, was a farmer and a logger. During the war, he had been a welder of the hulls of ships. I remember him as a sober man whose facial features I could hardly discern, so camouflaged were they in the creased and mottled texture of skin thickened and scarred by decades of physical labour, sun exposure, and abstinence from expressions of joy or tenderness. Luther had come from the hills. In the shorthand of his culture, this meant that he came from a poor and barren place, compared to the lush farmlands of the valley. His father, Mr Crow, whose first name I never heard spoken, had been a tenant farmer. Luther belligerently opposed my mother's ambitions, adamant as he was that college was no place for modest women, though his descriptors were hardly so polite—suffice it to say he found the prospect of his daughter studying mathematics and engineering personally humiliating. My mother's family was dominated on her mother's side by another patriarch, one of a more conspicuously religious persuasion than Luther Crow, though no more supportive of scientific education than Luther had been. My great-grandfather Alvin G. Tucker was better known as Papa Tucker. He notoriously displayed a fistful of his wife's hair on the mantel to remind his family and anyone else, of the violent consequence to befall those who would test his authority. He was the seventh son of a seventh son, reputed by nature of this fact to possess otherwise inexplicable powers of insight, influence and healing, including the ability to divine underground sources of water; to subdue menacing animals through mere presence of mind; and to cure babies of the thrush by miraculous means. Papa Tucker started a Baptist church and a dairy farm. *Sputnik* was not his concern.

502.23 Since experience is finite, it can be stored, studied, directed and turned with conscious effort to human advantage. This means that evolution pivots on the conscious, selective use of cumulative human experience and not on Darwin's hypothesis of chance adaptation to survival nor on his assumption of evolution independent of individual will and design.

I recall my mother as disinclined to extremes of emotional expression—unless reserve and psychosomatic illness qualify as emotional expression, in which case she was exceedingly demonstrative. Her stoicism I attribute to mettle developed through years lived in steadfast, albeit tacit defiance of the normative pressures of culture, class and gender. She had chosen, as a young person, to leave behind the rural mores of her upbringing to pursue an education that had been beyond the reach or interest of her family or her ancestors. She had chosen, as a young woman, to enter a field of study and, soon after, a profession that was and remains significantly male. She made these unorthodox choices in the late-1950s, in the deep south, in a cultural milieu in which codes of propriety had historically discouraged and devalued intellectual curiosity, particularly in women. That these options existed for my mother was a function of a national cultural embrace of public education and technological innovation wed to a clear political ambition to spread democracy and capitalism while suppressing the opposition force of Soviet socialism. Concurrently, the mass media achieved a sufficient degree of public saturation such that the prior dependence for ideological foundation on institutions of home and community was effectively supplanted by communications technology, even in the agrarian south.

Particular historical circumstances give rise to particular conceptions of self, and vice versa. Over the course of four and a half decades between 1941, and 1987, my mother's life was adapted directly to the major political transformations of the post-War period. As her moves from farm to school to lab, from relative poverty to relative affluence, from a culture defined by family to one defined by professionalism, and from the providence of religion to that of science attest, the fields of sociopolitical possibility and personal choice are mutually determined. John Dewey described the relationship in his 1939 essay, *Science and Free Culture*: 'The assumption that desires are rigidly fixed is not one on its face consistent with the history of man's progress from savagery through barbarism to even the present defective state of civilization. If knowledge, even of the most authenticated kind, cannot influence desires and aims, if it cannot determine what is of value and what is not, the future outlook as to formation of desires is depressing.'[9] That is, desire is culturally determined and therefore historically contingent.

530.03 The parents tell the child he cannot have both the sun and the moon in the picture at the same time. The child says that you can. The child has the ability to coordinate nonsimultanaeity. The parents have lost the ability to coordinate nonsimultanaeity. One of our great limitations is our tendency to look only at the static picture, the one confrontation.

When I was perhaps eight or nine years old, around the time of the *Challenger* explosion, I read about the principle of Mutual Assured Destruction (MAD), the strategy of nuclear containment in which aggression between adversaries is deterred by each side's fear of retaliation. I was shocked then to learn that the nuclear armory of the United States, alone, could destroy the world, many times over. This seemed unreasonable. I raised the issue with my mother, whose rationale I must have found unconvincing, as I recall being inconsolable. I had not grasped yet, at that earlier age, that my own parents' employment was directly related to this worrisome matter. I would later learn that the accepted strategy for maintaining peaceful equilibrium among heavily armed nation-states is in fact based upon a mathematical model of human behaviour that excludes the probability of irrational moves or of cooperation among subjects.

Nash equilibrium—the concept underlying MAD—posits players acting in hyper-rational self-interest against entirely hostile opponents. Equilibrium in this system, derived from game theory, is achieved when, given knowledge of the other players' strategies, no participant stands to gain by changing his or her own strategy. The possibility of trust among adversaries is precluded. Rational choice theory, the result of the research conducted at the RAND Corporation by John Nash and others, is underpinned by models of predictable, fundamentally invariable norms of human behaviour unmediated by historical contingencies. That Nash was suffering at the time from paranoid schizophrenia may be relevant.[10]

In 1949, experimental testing among secretaries at RAND determined that 'The main lesson from this limited experiment is that the social relationship between the subjects can have a controlling influence on their choices.'[11] The secretaries did not act rationally, according to the theory. Instead, they chose to assume each other's cooperation in sharing a sum of money, which resulted in each participant attaining half of the given sum, whereas Nash's theory predicted results of a 2:1 split. Further testing of a 'non-cooperative pair' showed a similar empirical incongruence with the outcome predicted by Nash's theory.

In a press conference conducted in the wake of *Sputnik*, Eisenhower had responded perspicaciously to the military pressure to dramatically increase defense development, which was amplified by widespread public fears of Soviet attack. He explained, 'I am always a little bit amazed about this business of catching up. What you want is enough, a thing that is adequate. A deterrent has no added power, once it has become completely adequate, for compelling the respect of any potential opponent for your deterrent and, therefore, to make him act prudently.'[12] Nevertheless, it was the idea of Nash equilibrium that prevailed as the Cold War strategy of ensuring political sovereignty and deterring nuclear war via maximal increase in nuclear armament, on the assumption that opponents would likewise be bent on political domination by amassment of destructive means. Prudence was flagging.

Though the U.S. and Russia have signed several arms reduction treaties in recent decades, following the end of the Cold War, and neither country has tested a nuclear weapon since 1990 (Russia) or 1992 (U.S.), the arms race now shows signs of resurgence. In the wake of Russia's invasion of Georgia this summer, Poland agreed to host an American missile defense base. It is either ironic or seemly, depending on how one spins the issue, that the site on the Baltic Sea where Russian President Dmitry Medvedev plans to install short-range nuclear-capable missiles to counteract the planned expansion of the U.S. missile-defense program in Poland is Kaliningrad. Now part of Russia, Kaliningrad—formerly known as Königsberg, East Prussia —is the birthplace of Kant and the categorical imperative, 'Act only according to that maxim whereby you can at the same time will that it should become a universal law.'[13] Kant presumed a markedly different conception of human being than did Nash. But, then, Kant lived in a time before technologies of mass destruction changed the stakes for conflict irresolution. Upon signing the agreement with Poland, U.S. Secretary of State, Condoleezza Rice, offered the assurance that 'Missile defense, of course, is aimed at no one.'[14] Ms. Rice, coincidentally, is also a native of Alabama, and was a member of the Center for International Security and Arms Control at Stanford, from 1981–1986, now renamed the Center for International Security and *Cooperation*. Edward Bernays would no doubt appreciate the wordsmithing.

509.10 The thinking process results in varying degrees of lucidity of the arrayed residue of focal-event patterns uniquely consequent to

the disciplined deferment of irrelevancies. Thinking is a putting-aside, rather than a putting-in, discipline. Thinking is FM-frequency modulation—for it results in the tuning out of irrelevancies (static) as a result of definitive resolution of the exclusively tuned-in or accepted feedback messages' pattern differentiability. And as the exploring navigator picks his channel between the look-out-detected rocks, the intellect picks its way between irrelevancies of feedback messages. Static and irrelevancies are the same.

Recently, I was defrosting my antiquated refrigerator as news of the global economic meltdown emerged, and an announcement was made that the space shuttle program might not be terminated in 2010, after all—rather, old shuttles would be re-tinkered for continued use, given the resurgent conflict with Russia and the corollary unlikelihood that U.S. astronauts would be permitted to travel on the Russian *Soyuz*. As chunks of ice dropped from the roof of my freezer to the kitchen floor, I was reminded that the world's glaciers are today melting into the sea at a rate roughly two times faster than in 1975, when *Synergetics* was published.

Four years after publication of Fuller's book, President Jimmy Carter delivered his infamous *Crisis of Confidence* speech. He suggested that the root causes of the nation's disillusionment would not be ameliorated by the empty promise of material consumption. Concurrently, Fuller determined that humanity had reached a point of technological sophistication such that selfishness no longer made sense. I was taking my first steps around that time, now 30 years ago, as Carter recommended that Americans 'face the truth', 'reduce consumption', and 'increase conservation' or suffer the consequences, including 'chaos', 'immobility', and 'failure.'[15] Carter was pilloried. Fuller was temporarily forgotten, his more palatable ideas co-opted and re-branded by Disney. Reagan was elected on a platform of supply-side economic reform, winning by a landslide majority. The mainstream sense of foreboding was reversed. Confidence was restored, with the result that 30 years after Carter's speech, sometime proximate to the defrosting of my refrigerator, the future has arrived, according to an ersatz plan of short-term gain over long-term viability based upon diametrically opposed models of human behaviour—as either hyper-rational or wholly irratio-nal—which have been championed by media savants operating on a principle of cynicism towards the public sphere.

We have underestimated ourselves.

I will never know with certainty how my mother perceived the arc of social and technological progress in her lifetime. Nor will I know whether she was conflicted by the complex political contingen-cies inherent in her work, the work for which she had taken a great leap of faith as a young person. I do know that, while our family was ostensibly irreligious, my mother had in the years preceding her death attended a Methodist church. The Pastor of that church visited our house in my mother's final weeks, leaving behind two books on Agnosticism. I am inclined to believe, therefore,

that she retained doubts about the delineation of faith from reason.

101.01 Synergy means behavior of whole systems unpredicted by the behavior of their parts taken separately.

NOTES
1. Feynman, R.P., *Report of the Presidential Commission on the Space Shuttle Challenger Accident, Vol. 2: Appendix F—Personal Observations on Reliability of Shuttle*, NASA, June 6, 1986.
2. ibid.
3. Fuller, R. Buckminster (in collaboration with E.J. Applewhite), *Synergetics —Explorations in the Geometry of Thinking* (New York: MacMillan, 1975).
4. Fuller's question was the instruction for his World Game proposed in 1961, later renamed World Peace Game, a simulation game 'intended to be a tool that would facilitate a comprehensive, anticipatory, design science approach to the problems of the world.' From the Buckminster Fuller Institute: www.bfi.org.
5. Feynman, op. cit.
6. Bernays, Edward L., *Propaganda* (New York: Horace Liveright, 1928).
7. For a live performance of Tom Lehrer's 'Wehrner von Braun' see: www.youtube.com/watch?v=QEJ9HrZq7Ro.
8. Callahan, David and Greenstein, Fred, 'Eisenhower and U.S. Space Policy', in Roger D. Launius & Howard E. McCurdy, eds., *Spaceflight and the Myth of Presidential Leadership* (University of Illinois, 1997)
9. Dewey, John, 'Science and Free Culture', *Freedom and Culture* (New York: G.E. Putnam's Sons, 1939).
10. See John Nash interviewed by Adam Curtis in Curtis's documentary series *The Trap: What Happened to Our Dream of Freedom*, originally aired by the BBC in 2007.
11. Flood, Merrill M., 'Some Experimental Games', U.S. Air Force Project Rand Research Memorandum, RM-789-1. The report was published in 1952, but refers to an experiment conducted in 1949.
12. Callahan and Greenstein, op. cit.
13. Kant, Immanuel and James Ellington, *Grounding for the Metaphysics of Morals; with, A Supposed Right to Lie Because of Philanthropic Concerns* (Indianapolis: Hackett Publishing Co., 1993).
14. Kulish, N. and Rachman, T., 'Rice Signs Missile Deal With Poland', *The New York Times*, August 20, 2008.
15. Jimmy Carter's televised *Crisis of Confidence* speech, also known as the 'Malaise speech', was delivered July 15, 1979, and can be seen at www.youtube.com/watch?v=1IlRVy7oZ58

THE ADAPTER

Jay Baldwin in conversation with Raimundas Malasauškas
San Francisco, Summer 2008

Among thousands of kilograms of paper, scores of unpublished techno-scientific inventions, and an inspiring series of love-letters from Mrs Anne Hewlett Fuller, Buckminster Fuller's archive at Stanford University contains the *Dymaxion Chronofile*, a large scrapbook that Bucky supposedly updated every 15 minutes. Contrary to Andy Warhol's time capsules, the *Chronofile* is organized rather like a calendar: it contains both past and future as active, simultaneous domains that one could affect from any point of time. Following this logic, Bucky would add new records both to the past and future as if they were elastically changeable. Occasionally he would also slip speeding tickets in there.

The following conversation unfolds like an another endless story. Without any central subject or destination, it stems from one of the 1951 entries of the *Chronofile*: 'Met with Jay Baldwin.' They had dinner, and you can find out what happened after that meeting from Wikipedia, even if Jay himself is not sure who actually maintains his page there—this most common tool of 'self-academization' proves to be rather enigmatic. Yet it is clear that this meeting led to his becoming one of the main characters in Fuller's 'comprehensive design science revolution'. It also made Fuller fuller: Jay Baldwin was one of the few people who was actually able to adapt Fuller's concepts to material conditions and make them work. How he identified the cause of the chronic leaks in geodesic domes (and how he solved it) is explained here—between myriad other topics connected to the 'know-how of designing your life', like: What are the origins of colourblind policies

in employment? What did the 102-year-old man at the old ice cream parlour know? What do you do when being chased by someone bigger than you? Why is there a special place in hell for gym teachers? Where do you find a drive-through funeral parlour? and Who was Jay Baldwin playing poker with while waiting for the Russians to attack Tbilisi in 1989?

So who is Jay Baldwin? An artist? A life-design inventor? A genuine California visionary? A man who couldn't float? Talking to him one morning in San Francisco, I felt a little like Andy Kaufman hounding Fred Blassie at breakfast in LA. His wide-ranging thoughts on the technologies of living were convincing and eloquent, in quite another category of symbolic weight to my half of the conversation. Talking to him felt like decompressing an eternally incomplete archive.

After reading this uncut stream-of-consciousness transcript, Jay paused for a moment, then commented: 'My rants are all part of an attitude towards life that is not linear, but rather circular, or even random. On the other hand, I am, after all, a designer, and as such take advantage of events and coincidence as they appear. My life has been guided by some self-inflicted rules I generally follow, e.g. not to hurt anyone, not to act in a way that will require an apology, not to mess up nature, and not to speak with forked tongue. I consider myself to be what Buckminster Fuller called a 'comprehensivist', attending the connections between phenomena as I search for synergetic arrangements. In short, I am interested in everything. You would be closer to clarity if that was noted as underlying the scattered subjects I touch upon.'

Jay Baldwin: There's a woman who's going to interview me later today and maybe she changed it—or did you change it?

Raimundas Malasauškas: No, I didn't. Did she make you younger or older?

JB: Older. I don't know who put my stuff in Wikipedia. I have no idea, but whoever did knows me pretty well. I am not much of a schmooze. I don't know that many people that well. When I go home at the end of the day, I go home and shut the door. My wife and I have been married for 28 years and in that time we've had four couples over for dinner and we haven't gone over to anyone else's house, not once!

RM: That's amazing.

JB: It's just that when we're home, we're home. When we're on the job that's different. I have a portable machine shop which is open to anybody. If you want to build something, just call me up as long as you know how to use the tools. I'm not insured and I don't have any money worth mentioning other than tools —and nobody can sue you to sell your tools. That's illegal.

RM: To go back to this Wikipedia page: you didn't establish it yourself?

JB: No, I don't know who did.

RM: Is its content sampled and compiled from something already existing or is it new?

JB: Some of it is, but a lot of it's not. Like I have a nickname—that is only used by lovers—and that name appears in Wikipedia. There somebody who knows that and I don't know who it is.

RM: So it's probably one of your lovers.

JB: It took me three tries to get a wife to keep—that would stay with me. As far as designing, one of the reasons I agreed to talk to you is the fact that you said that you design your life, and I consider the way I ended up living is my best design. I think a lot of artists think that. I never had any urge to have a house or station wagon for a lot of reasons, but one of which is that, if I had a mortgage to pay every month, as Bucky Fuller said, 'You can either pay rent, or pay rent to rent money.' You're still paying for it, since money is 100% interest. So that means you have to make twice as much money in order to live the same way, and then you end up owning the house, and then die. It's not called a mortgage for nothing. So I never thought about giving a bank half my money, and then if they sell the house again they make the same amount of money again and again and again while not having lifted a finger or taken any risk whatsoever.

RM: And your kids are supposed to keep paying your mortgage when you die, no?

JB: Not usually. Right now I don't owe anybody anything and I only buy cars for cash. I have only ever worked project to project—which is what artists do. When you're done with this painting you take off the canvas and put up a new one and paint some more. I've lived 15 years where we're living now—it's the longest I've lived anywhere in one place. It's a very handy place, but we're renting. We live in a chicken coop.

RM: What's a chicken coop?

JB: A chicken house—where they keep chickens. Except there aren't any chickens in the house, but there used to be. We joke about things that go cluck in the night. Some of our neighbours have chickens. I like living on the edge of town in the country. The air is cleaner. It's quieter.

RM: Have you always lived in the San Francisco bay area?

JB: No, I came here in 1962. Before that I lived eight years in Ann Arbor, Michigan. And I was born in New Jersey—in the same hospital as Springsteen, except I'm older. I spent my summers in a tiny town in Iowa until I was 12. It's the town that you see in Grant Wood's *American Gothic* with the guy standing with the pitchfork. That's the town, and that town is still 350 people. I actually mowed the lawn of that house. Grant Wood changed the house a little bit—it didn't have that peak, it was just a plain house and a little old lady lived in it. She gave me a dime to mow the lawn. That's what a picture show cost. The town didn't have a theatre but they had a screen.

RM: A drive-in?

JB: No, it was in a warehouse. It was OK. I came back to that town when I was 38 with a girlfriend and I went to the ice cream parlour and it was still there. The man who would serve me ice cream when I was a kid ...

RM: He was still there?

JB: And he thought that the woman I was with was my sister. When I came in and sat down he looked at me and didn't even say hello. He immediately put a malt on the machine, a vanilla malt, and he served it to me. And the girl I was with said to him, 'How did you know what he wanted?' He said, 'That's what he always orders.' So he was 102. In those days if you lived past 50 you were going to live a long time unless you had bad luck. My great grandmother on my mother's side, who came from that same town, lived to be 103. She died when I was nine while doing chores on her farm.

RM: How long are you planning to live?

JB: I don't know. I've had repairs and some of them not so good. My maternal grandfather had a bad valve in his heart, my father did also, and so did I. In me, the valve broke when I was 58. So I have a mechanical heart valve. I haven't had any trouble. It's been in there since I was 58. It's noisy and it gives me a random heartbeat. I don't have a steady heartbeat —it's completely random.

RM: A random rhythm?

JB: It has no rhythm. At all. None. It's all over the place.

RM: What's it like?

JB: It's noisy. I can hear every heartbeat.

RM: Like a drum set?

JB: It's a click. You could hear it if there wasn't all this noise in here. On the other hand I feel fine. Everything is working fine.

RM: The interesting thing that's happening now—due to advancements in medicine—is the increasing average duration of life ...

JB: Yeah, when I was born my life expectancy was 52.

RM: ... and at the same time the retirement age stays the same, which means people have more and more time to be retired and experience what it means to be 'old'. I wonder how you see this social shift.

JB: Fewer and fewer people are retiring at 65. I never had any intention to retire because I saw what happened to people when they retired: they died. Especially people who worked very hard. They feel like they don't have to work anymore and my theory is that their body says OK, clunk. Like my father. He was born in poverty and worked his way up to a big office in the Manhattan

Telephone Company—a big executive. In 1946 he established a colourblind hiring practice at Bell. At the time there was only one telephone company worth mentioning in this country and it was Bell. Way before Martin Luther King and those people were making any noise about it, my father put this into practice.

RM: What kind of practice?

JB: Colourblind—meaning they didn't care what colour you were.

RM: That's good. And that was Bell?

JB: Yeah. They were probably the first big company to be colourblind. At least in New York Bell, but in the south they were far from colourblind. So my father lived to be the age I am now, but he was pooping out at the end. He was the kind of man who would get out of the car and then lean on the car a minute to get his breath before moving away. My cardiologist said, 'Do you want to be one of those?' I said, 'No.' He said, 'OK, you have a big surgery ahead of you.'

RM: You never had to retire because you were never in a full-time job …

JB: No, I never intended to.

RM: … but you were working as a freelancer hopping from project to project.

JB: Not exactly. There's a subculture in this country—and there has been for a long time—based on what would now be called 'sustainability' … people paying attention to nature, inspired by Aldo Leopold and Buckminster Fuller among others, and a number of philosophers. Among my favourites would be Gregory Bateson, Wendell Berry. I don't think much of Bill McKibben. I think he's younger than I am. He's too much of a grump. He sees the bad side of things and puts too much energy

into it. You can make almost anything look bad if you want to. A lot of divorces happen that way. Nobody has done anything really bad but you know the woman could say, 'I couldn't stand my husband, I had to get a divorce because he would never sit up straight at the table!'—or something like that. And the man could say, 'She would always grind her teeth while she was combing her hair!'—something equally stupid. What it really is, actually, is the outside sign of simply getting sick of somebody, like cabin fever. You can't stand somebody getting too close to you. I don't really know what happens.

Jus heads are better than one

RM: In this respect, do you see looking on the positive side as a strategy?

JB: When I was a kid I was raised up to be a good Christian and I saw right away that you had good luck and bad luck. The thing is, I learned to read early and well. I learned to read when I was three, and by the time I got to kindergarten, when I was five, I was reading *Treasure Island* by Robert Louis Stevenson—the original version, the adult version. I was reading a lot of stuff I really didn't understand. My grandfather had given

me one of those huge dictionaries —it was about this thick—a giant *Webster Dictionary* under the table and I could look all that stuff up. So I really liked the dictionary and I spent a lot of time reading. There wasn't a lot of television.

I also learned early that my father didn't know everything. He was a nice guy, but he had to work at it, work hard. So in grade school I would work hard to get good grades. One of the reasons he built his house in the town I came from, in New Jersey, was that it had a great high school. Everybody in that high school would eventually go to college. It was a very high level high school. All white—there was one black guy in high school and no black girls as I recall. Anyway he said, 'You go to a good college and get good grades. Then you choose a good company with a good retirement plan and work there for 45 years. Then you can do what you want to do after that.'

I saw he took the same electric train and the same ferryboat to Manhattan to the same telephone building for 43 years. He had three Masters degrees. He was a nice man, a powerful man. He was way bigger than me, just about as big as men get. Big guy, size 16 feet. In fact, wearing the shoes I have on now—I have big feet for my size—I could stand in his shoes with my own shoes on. When he died we were getting rid of his stuff and I tried on a pair of his shoes with my shoes, and looked really funny. They looked like clown shoes then. It got a little macabre laughter out of people. Do you care about what I'm talking about?

RM: Yeah, totally.

JB: I didn't float when I was a kid and I still don't.

RM: Float?

JB: Float.

RM: You mean swimming?

JB: Yes, but not swimming. If I jump into a swimming pool I hit the bottom as hard as ...

RM: Cement.

JB: Exactly. So my father and everybody else said the reason I didn't swim was because I was a sissy. I know the reason I couldn't float is because I couldn't float. So I was afraid of water, and especially afraid of uncles who'd say, 'Just throw him in the deep end and he'll swim! Har har har!' Everybody says that. We had friends with swimming pools and sailboats and all kinds of stuff. I didn't even dare walk on a dock. The final straw was the gym teacher in grade school who said I didn't float probably because I was a fairy.

RM: A fairy? A homosexual?

JB: Yeah, a queer. And that cooked my reputation. Even in fourth grade the girls didn't want anything to do with me. So I didn't go to parties. I didn't have parties. We had a small family anyway and at Thanksgiving there were six people at the table, sometimes eight, whereas with my wife, who's Hawaiian, we had a terrific dinner one Thanksgiving with 70 people all from the same family. Hawaiians have these huge families. They're like Italians, it turns out. The mother runs the show but quietly and the uncles are the enforcers. Somebody screws up in the family and the uncles go over to pay a little visit and straighten it out. They don't always succeed. So anyway, I spent a lot of time by myself.

RM: Who said you're queer because you didn't float?

JB: The gym teacher, and in public.

RM: Gym teachers are the worst people. I had a problem with a gym teacher as well.

JB: There's a special place in hell for gym teachers.

RM: Exactly.

JB: And also I was small for my age—I'm still only five foot seven—but I had big hands and big feet and a big head. When I was much smaller I looked stupid. I looked like an ape. Even now I can stop a volleyball. I can just put my hand out and stop it and keep it or wipe it, and the referee says, 'I didn't hear it. I didn't hear that.' I didn't like sports. I never liked sports because of the reading I did. I was raised up while there was a depression going on, then in 1941 we were listening to the radio while Pearl Harbour was being bombed. So we were raised up then and it began to be obvious what was going on with the Jews in Europe. Our town had a big Jewish population. When the war ended, I was in junior high school, and the Jews were asking questions—If there is a God, he's not taking very good care of us ... and I thought that too. I asked my parents about it and they said we don't talk about those kinds of things in this family. I could never find out anything from them.

RM: Why?

JB: I don't know. They said the floating was a question of courage, or that I didn't try. They used the word 'gumption'.

RM: Gumption?

JB: Gumption is a driving force. I know that I didn't float. I said, 'Look I don't float', and my father said, 'That's ridiculous.' My mother said, 'That's ridiculous' too. 'Do you know anyone else who doesn't float?' And I said, 'No.'

RM: So now you can swim?

JB: Yeah. What happened was, at the time polio was a big fear. There was no penicillin, no antibiotics. So I actually know somebody who died of diphtheria, a kid my age. In my high school there were

a lot of kids with polio. Just in my senior class of 100 there were four of us that died from polio. One guy died in a single day. He came down with polio overnight and he didn't live through the next day. That sent us thinking. I noticed from what I was reading that there's all this business of wars, people killing each other, and slapping heads off dragons. It was sort of thrilling, but it also sort of wasn't to me. I read a figure somewhere that approximately 30,000 people a day die of starvation. Right now, and back then too. You have to understand that at the time I was in high school the population of the United States was half what it is now, and that the population of automobiles was 90% less. So if you go outside now, for every ten cars you see take away nine. That's how many cars there were back then. That would mean out there would be 20 cars instead of 200. There are a lot of cars out here. I was more interested in playing the game. I regarded life as one big game. I was more interested in continuing the game and getting good at it than I was at winning, because when you win that means somebody else is dogshit. And I didn't know anyone who wanted to be dogshit. I was afraid of bullies. Being small I got bullied a lot, but I had good luck. I could run like a deer. No bully could catch me. And I was even faster on a bicycle. I could make one of those fat tire shards really go. Once I got it up to speed you weren't going to catch me. So I was not so much afraid of bullies because I could outrun them. I got a book about bullies.

RM: What was it called?

JB: *Defending Yourself*. I learned some nasty tricks.

RM: Like putting your fingers in somebody's eye?

JB: There's a trick if you're being chased by somebody bigger than you. You slow down just a little

71

bit, acting like you're running as fast as you can and at the last minute you drop to your knees with your face under your arms and stick your ass in the air —they hit your ass, fly over you and land head down in front of you. So you go jump on their stomach or their head as you go by. Then you start running again. It works really well. Especially at the top of a stairwell.

RM: You did that?

JB: Yes, and I didn't go back and see what I'd done either. I could tell by the crunch that I'd done something bad.

RM: Yeah. Maybe they're still there.

JB: I don't know. A few dirty tricks, just if you got desperate. I think I've only been in two fist-fights in my whole life. One I initiated very stupidly when a man threw a fire-cracker to a squirrel. It thought it was a peanut and picked it up. It blew the squirrel to bits. And that just pissed me off.

RM: He took a firecracker, threw it at a squirrel and blew it up?

JB: Right, because the squirrel thought it was a peanut. He was in law school at the University of Michigan. I don't even remember. There was nothing to do but attack the bastard. So I did, and we had to be suppressed—and I was not winning. He mounted a big attack. Another time I had a guy lie in wait for me one night—I played a lot of poker in the military ...

RM: Because you won at poker?

JB: Yes, and one of the things I know how to do is—you never hear it anymore—Boogie-Woogie.

RM: What's that?

JB: It is a piano style. At the time I was in high school the men who had invented traditional—what

would now be called Trad Jazz— Dixieland, Boogie-Woogie and the Blues, were all still alive. They're all gone now. They were in New York. Their music was not popular anymore—it was all Big Band Swing at the time, Benny Goodman. But the old guys were still alive and we would go to nightclubs in New York. If you could see over the counter to give money to the guy, they would let you into any club in New York where the old Jazz guys played. That's what you went for, not to get drunk. It's great music.

RM: Which clubs did you go to?

JB: We were going to a boxing club called Werderman's Hall. It was a big empty room like a gymnasium with a boxing podium in the middle for prize fighting. This was not big time boxing. You know people would bet on the fighters and they were all local people, boys, golden gloves, pugilists. On Saturday nights if there wasn't any boxing, they'd put a band on there. Word would go out and then we would all go on the bus. I think I went in starting at 14 or 15. They would let us in. They weren't supposed to let us in. I never saw a cop. This was in Greenwich Village.

RM: The boxing place?

JB: Right, Werderman's Hall, and there was another one called the Stuyvesant Casino. It was similar. It was upstairs. You'd go up a big freight elevator that brings trucks to the top floor. You open the door and this big blast of music would come out. It was terrific. Then, at two in the morning, it all had to close down. Sometimes somebody would say, 'We can all go to my house, I live just up the street', and we would all troop into some old building some guy owned and keep going. My parents thought it was cool as long as I was with my friends. We got beat up once by Puerto Ricans. I assure you that *West Side Story* notwithstanding, Puerto Ricans do not break

into song and dance in the street. And it's wise to run fast—they all smoked so if you could outrun them for a block you could get away. Some of them were good runners, but not with tap shoes on and smoking. The smokers are not slower for the first block but they sure are for the second block.

RM: You never smoked?

JB: No.

RM: I remember once in New York I was on Broadway in the Upper West Side and there was some kind of emergency. Four or five cops got a radio signal and started to run after something. They were running, running, running, but one cop was very big, and at some point he started to slow down, suddenly grabbed the wall and collapsed. He wasn't able to run anymore and it was sad to see.

JB: When I was a kid you did not want to piss off a cop. They had a nightstick about this long and they were going to brain you with it. They did not kid around. There was no way you were going to sue a cop. If a cop knocked your block off it was because you had it coming. Know what they did that was really evil? They would hit your feet with it. The top of your foot. It hurts so much. You did *not* mess with them. They didn't have radios then, because a radio was a huge thing. It took up the whole back of a car. So they had radio cars but not many of them. That meant that the hot rods—I had a hot rod in school—

RM: What's that?

JB: A hot rod. You'd get an old car, mainly Fords because Fords had the V8 engine and it was the preferred car of gangsters. Bonnie and Clyde—they even wrote Henry Ford how good his cars were, they could beat anything. Well, it just so happened that you could mess with a Ford engine and make it about double power—and that was called a hot rod. The hot rod culture started in LA. In New Jersey it wasn't all too common. My senior class in high school was the first class to have cars. During the depression no kid could afford a car. When the war was on all car companies stopped making cars. Ford made airplanes, General Motors made tanks—and by the way, Ford and General Motors made all the trucks of Hitler's Nazi Panzer *and* got the profits from it. That's another story.

RM: Going back to the idea of games, you say you prefer to be good in a game and play the game well rather than win ...

JB: Yes, I wasn't much into games. I never played chess. I don't have time to play chess and really think it through. In the military we spent a lot of time just sitting around waiting because our duty was to wait for the Russians to attack. Well, they didn't attack and that's tiring after a while, so we played poker. I learned to play poker pretty well. I haven't played a single hand of poker since. It's a different kind of poker than you see on television.

RM: What other games did you play?

JB: One of the few games I really liked playing was racquetball. You play it in a small room. You have to be really quick. It's like handball only with a racket and the ball going 120 miles an hour. You really have to pay attention. I understand all the geometry. I know if a guy hits it over here it's going to end up over there. If it's bouncing on the wall twice or the ceiling, I know where it is going to go. I'm awkward physically. I am somewhat dyslexic. I can't back out a car without looking. I can't look in a mirror. Absolutely hopeless. I can't do mathematics. My mind will just not do it. I squeaked through college by hiring a tutor

to get me through calculus and algebra. That's where I stopped. For making domes I know the geometry. That doesn't bother me. It's the strength—how big a tube I should use. When I need to know how to get maybe 200 coins in a small bill like fives, to make a nice roll, I go over to Berkeley Civil Engineering Department and ask the postgrad students, 'Who wants to make 200 bucks quickly? Who knows how to do a finite vector analysis?' And I get, 'Me, me, me!'

RM: They do the technical engineering while you provide the concept?

JB: Yes. I always make my own prototypes whenever possible, because in my view if you don't make your own prototypes something gets lost in the translation. Even Fuller had trouble having someone else make his prototypes. He had his students make his prototypes. A lot of his artifacts had troubles that they wouldn't have had if he'd got his hands dirty. It's not that he didn't get his hands dirty. He was a machinist. He had a machinist union card, but he didn't actually build his cars, he had them built.

RM: He didn't have time, I guess.

JB: His cars were an interesting design, but they had features that

ended up being critical that he didn't research far enough. He thought he was researching far enough. This always happened. His cars were built by aircraft engineers and boat builders. They wanted the car to be aerodynamic but they didn't realize the more streamlined a car is the less stable it is. Fuller's car was very unstable in a side wind, and what it needed was a big tail, a router-type, vertical stabilizer. People didn't put them on cars yet in this country, but in France there was a guy named Andreau who did put big tails on cars in the mid-1930s. They were a little weird looking but they would have helped Bucky's car a lot. A big tail. And his domes leak. Geodesic domes are notorious for leaking.

RM: Why did they leak?

JB: Well, I decided I'd find out —and I found out by doing experiments that should have been done by someone else but weren't. The geodesic domes leak geodesically. And other domes don't leak because they're not geodesic. Do you know the difference between stress and strain? Stress is force and strain is how much something moves. When the dome is stressed the strain is distributed equally through the whole structure. So on a hot day the sun is shining on one side of the dome, and parts of it expand.

RM: Because of the temperature?

JB: Yes. On the cold side of the dome the parts are not expanding, but because the strain is evenly distributed the seams have to open to make the dome bigger, and they pull it apart so the rain gets in. This also happens if the dome has a different temperature inside than it is outside. There are a lot of ways this can happen. I have found photographs of domes that are bulged on one side. On a hot day you can see that bulge. So I said, 'I'll make a dome that doesn't have any seams.' They said, 'Well are you going to pour it out of concrete and get monolithic?' And I said. 'No, that's too heavy.' 'So what are you going to do?' What I decided to do is to make an inflated skin, and Fuller had already figured this out. His very first dome stood up by itself. It wasn't commercial, he had it made with students. It had an inflated skin but the plastic to make an inflated skin was practically unavailable. Then in 1972 DuPont came out with a plastic that's not eaten by sunlight. That stuff is strong. I would make a dome out of this. So I found someone who could make triangular pillows. It turned out to be a company that makes inflated women for adult use. Their main use is actually in the diamond lane.

RM: Diamond lane of what?

JB: For commuting. If you have two people in the car you can go in the fast lane. So you have a fake person, an inflated person, with clothes on and so forth. You paint their face and put a wig on.

RM: When was that?

JB: I see them every morning commuting. They're not so common now because they've cut down on the number of cops, but I would say half the number of people in the diamond lane are there illegally. It's a big fine. They're going to raise the fine—make it huge so that people aren't going to ride in the diamond lane anymore. When they raise the fine to 500 dollars people are going to say … well, you're going to have to be in a big hurry. Bucky kept his speeding tickets in his *Chronofile*. The cops didn't have any radar then and all they could do was use a stopwatch. They had a telephone when they saw him burn pass they'd say, Fuller just left Ipswich, Connecticut and he's heading towards Norwalk. So the cops in Norwalk would be waiting with their stopwatch … synchronized watches, yes …

and then they would wait and see. So he was going 120 miles an hour and they'd catch him, so he'd get the ticket and place it in the *Chronofile*. He was proud of it.

RM: What year was that?

JB: I hesitate to say. 1934 or 1935, something like that.

A Reconsideration of the Newspaper Industry in 5 Easy Illusions (4)

Sitting Duck or a March Hare?

RM: What was the normal top speed of a car by then? 80?

JB: A Ford V8 would do about 70. Sometimes fast cars are not what you think—like my favourite car of all the cars I owned was a big Citroën DS.

RM: I remember you saying that.

JB: Yes, lovely. I have a picture of it. It was a safari station wagon. It was a three-quarter-ton vehicle. It could hold a big weight and it behaved itself. The top speed of that car screaming was 100, but it would cruise at 85 like a swan. That was the speed it was made to go. It liked going 85. Everything in that car was adjusted to be perfect at 85. It didn't have any reverberation from the four cylinders, the wheels didn't patter on the street, it didn't move around, the wind didn't shove it. It was rock steady. You could have two fingers on the stirring wheel at 85. Even today very few cars are comfortable at 85. They'll *go* 85, but if you have to swerve around something then you'll see. Like a Toyota Camry

will cruise at 100 if you dare, but like most Japanese cars—not all of them—it'll cruise at a fast speed but if an abnormality occurs and you have to make a maneuver, something goes wrong, or the tires blow out, and then you'll find that your Camry or Lexus is not as good as you hoped. Whereas when a Mercedes or Volvo goes wrong at a very high speed they'll just say, 'Uh, what was that?' The car just keeps doing what it wants to do and won't go crazy.

RM: Have you ever had some kind of archival structure like the *Chronofile*?

JB: No, I have a good memory.

RM: Yes, I can see.

JB: And pretty accurate. The only person who I've met who has the kind of memory I have is Lynn Margulis, a scientist, science writer and biologist. She goes right to the heart of things. There's all this crap flying around and she says. 'What's really happening is *that*.' And *that* is what turns out to be important. So maybe I see some things as important which other people don't notice. It boils down to that. That's what designers need to do. A lot of people have trouble understanding Fuller's writing. I don't have any trouble. I have trouble with certain sentences and there are a couple of chapters in his *Synergetics* that I look at and think I'll let someone else figure out. I understood most of what Bucky was talking about and what the important parts are the first time I heard him talking, which was 1951. At the time he hadn't yet built a sellable dome. He was just about to make one for Ford.

RM: Your students are really noisy behind the wall …

JB: I gave them an interesting exercise. What happens if you're skiing and you sprain your ankle or something and it gets dark and you didn't make it back? Are you going to be a statistic the next day— a Monday morning frozen corpse —or are you going to get away with it? So they're designing something you have with you in snow sports that would enable you to spend a night in the high Sierra. Maybe even two nights if there's a storm or something. You don't have to be comfortable, you just have to be alive. You're not allowed to design anything new, only using existing products. They have to design the package and how it's attached to you. They have to design what goes in it and why and how you're going to carry it.

RM: That's a good task.

JB: In three weeks. If they had a little extra time I'd have them spend a night in a meat locker at 20 below zero, then we'd see whether they come out or not.

RM: Tell me what it's like living in geodesic houses.

JB: It was fine. It's really very nice. If I have the money, and if I live long enough, what I'd like to do is to make a big geodesic house, maybe 15–20 metres diameter, and put it right over the trees and bushes and everything—living out-doors indoors, using the building as a climate control. Fuller didn't consider his domes to be buildings, he considered them to be weather shields.

RM: What are weather shields?

JB: You control the weather. He called them valves. A valve either opens to let something out or it lets something in. So it's con-trollable. He used the term a lot, actually, with respect to buildings. So I think I could make a building that would raise most of its food, make all of its electricity, collect its fresh water and purify its waste, all by biological means, indoors, and control the climate regardless of what is going on outdoors. You'd

be able to control your privacies if you wanted to. The thing would essentially be a greenhouse. In our democracy it is illegal to live in a greenhouse in every state—unfit for human habitation. I've worked in communist countries and they say, 'Oh my god, I can't believe that!' We can't do that here.

RM: What countries?

JB: I had a job in Moscow, and in Tbilisi. Tbilisi is the most interest-ing place I've ever been. What a city ...

RM: When were you there?

JB: 1989.

RM: Right when the USSR was collapsing.

JB: In fact, while we where there the Russian army was returning, beaten, from Afghanistan. They came through Tbilisi. And at the same time Gorbachev had the president of Georgia saying, 'We're going to resign from the Soviet Union.' So Gorbachev had the army there in the city. We were in our hotel not far from the Government Palace and we heard this big noise outside. We looked out, and there were so many people that you couldn't see the streets. It was all people, solid people. One of the concierges in the hotel was actu-ally KGB and we knew that, and he knew we knew. So we asked him, 'What's happening out there?' He said, 'You don't want to go out there—all hell has broken loose and there's at least a million and a half people on the street.' And being Georgian they're all armed. Like how all the Swiss have guns at home, all the Georgians do too. So it was just bristling with guns. Everyone had rifles and pistols and then here's the whole army. And the tanks had their guns depressed, moving them back and forth look-ing at the crowd. We looked out the window with binoculars, which upset the KGB guy who didn't

know we had binoculars. We could see the signs in Russian on the shell boxes on the outside of the tank were white ferrous. Those are the shells used to burn people. So the President of Georgia came out of the palace, he had a micro-phone and big speakers, and said, 'Soldiers ...'—and of course we had our interpreter tell us this— 'The crowd you see before you are Russians just like you. Are you really going to kill us? If you are, start with me.' Brave words. So they put their guns away and shut off the tanks. It was not a very fun party, but we were out there and we had our little American flags—here are the Americans. There were 14 of us, very small out of a million and a half people, and we had a very interesting day. I thought we weren't going to see the sunset, all because if one person had fired a gun, just one, even a backfire would have done it. All hell would have broken loose —a total massacre—but it didn't happen. And then Gorbachev won. He won that round in Russia.

RM: What was your mission there?

JB: We went there to teach the 16-year-old boys and girls. The juniors in technical high school had to do solar energy calculations because the Tbilisi climate is just like San Francisco. They have a river running right through the town. It's a really old, old city, and it has very odd aspects to it. For instance, there's nobody in Tbilisi my age. They were all killed. There are no men or women between 65 and 80. There's a whole group of people not there. So you see a lot of young people and a lot of old people, but nobody in between. The Nazis never got there. They got to the top of the Caucasus and were going to sweep down on Tbilisi and take it. The men were all fighting the battle of Leningrad, which was a nasty battle—a million or more Russians got killed, you'll never know.

The women and children in Tbilisi, all the boys who could walk, and the older, injured people went to the top of the pass where they knew the Panzers were coming. There was a big snowstorm and they laid down and let the snow cover them rolled up in blankets. The Germans came and set up camp to prepare for the attack. At three in the morning the Tbilisi people came up out of the snow and all they had was knifes. They knifed the whole Panzer division but in the fight they were all killed too. So it was a terrible fight, apparently, and our guide said there weren't enough people left to bury the dead, so they just left them there. He said if you go up there now, there're bones lying all over the place. Nobody ever took care of it. Tbilisi has been sacked 32 times.

The city has some interesting features—typical are the bakeries. They have a big thing in Tbilisi about fresh bread. So if you're going to have dinner they usually send the boys out to go and get some bread. We noticed kids running down the street with a smoking sack in front of them. These bread ovens are underground—glowing fires underground—and they lower these baskets of dough into the fire and then pull them up. So we asked the interpreter how old the building was. He said that the ovens haven't cooled down in over a thousand years—they've never turned them off. And the bread is terrific. If they sold that bread here that's all anybody would eat. Best bread I've ever eaten in my life.

RM: By the way, on Geary and 19th Avenue in San Francisco there's a place called the Russian Bakery which is owned by a Georgian man. He sells *Khachapuri*, this cheese bread ...

JB: That's right near the Jewish bagel place ... ?

RM: Yes, 19th and Geary.

JB: In Tbilisi I liked getting up in the morning, watching, just sitting there. I got up—avoiding the KGB—and went out early to watch people going out to work. There were some kids—eight, nine, ten years old playing soccer. One of them had fallen, hitting his head, and was lying unconscious ... and people just went around him. Nobody picked him up and wiped him off. I thought the teacher would run over there or something. Finally he got up and there was blood on the side of his face and the teacher said, 'Wipe your face off and get back in the game.' I thought, well, in this country they'd have an ambulance or something. Here when a little kid gets injured, some-one's going to sue. There, it's 'Stand up and go back to work. You got knocked up the head and it's not a big deal. Don't make a big deal out of it.' That's how they were. And we got some surprises there too.

RM: Like what?

JB: We went back again. The first year we were there we got nothing done. The second time we brought 50 American 16-year-olds carefully chosen from technical school, and we invited—this wasn't done by either government, this was privately done—the whole class of Georgians to Aspen, Colorado, to visit us. That was a scene. We didn't know how the American kids would take Tbilisi, but they were fascinated and the Tbilisi kids were fascinated. For them, if a boy and a girl go together, they have to have an aunt with them. They weren't allowed to hold hands or anything. The American kids were all lovey-dovey, so the Tbilisians were taken aback by that. The kids got along really well. Then when they came to this country they were amazed. They got off the plane in Denver and there was a short wait for the plane to go over to Aspen—a couple hours—so we took them to the nearest Wal-Mart and the kids were angry. They were pissed. 'We came all this way

and you show us a government showplace. What kind of shit is this?' This is the kind of thing they do in Moscow. We said, 'OK, get back on the bus', and we took them to another Wal-Mart. At the third Wal-Mart they began to see what was going on—and all the cars! They said, 'All these cars were brought here to show off to us!' 'Nope, sorry. This isn't even rush hour ... ' So we made sure to get tangled up in rush hour. We just sat there between millions of cars. Denver is a big city. They began to get the picture. So we gave each kid 300 bucks and said you can buy anything you want. They all went running into the store and spent all their money on Nikes.

RM: Nikes?

JB: Running shoes. They wanted to buy tape decks—because they didn't have CDs yet—but the tape decks didn't work with European tapes ... so it took them a while. Then we got to Aspen. We landed at the airport and they saw this red Cessna which was just like the one that landed on Red Square. They all wanted to have a photo taken with it. They had a KGB in their group of students disguised as a student. He was just a young-faced guy. All the kids knew who it was but we weren't supposed to know. They had been threatened not to tell us. One of the boys who was having his picture taken said, 'Can I get a driver's license here?' He was 16 years old, and one of the Colorado people said, 'Sure just go down town and get it.' The KGB guy said, '*Nyet*.' So then he was revealed.

The kid who wanted to get a driver's license saw a Ferrari on the streets of Aspen, which is pretty common—a 12 cylinder, the kind with the lines on the side where the radiators are. So he was looking at the car. God, he had never seen one before and the guy who owns it comes out and says, 'Where are you from, kid?' The kid says, 'Tbilisi.' The guy said, 'Where's that?' The kid said, 'Georgia.' 'Is that near Atlanta?' 'No, no, no ...' So finally the guy says, 'So you are a Commie?' 'Yeah, yeah.' 'Have you ever met a filthy capitalist pig? I'm a filthy capitalist pig and I invite you to lunch at my house.' He had a six million dollar log cabin on the hill above Aspen. You could literally play basketball in his living room, it was that big, a huge place made from logs. So he said, 'The rest of you will have to walk or take a taxi but you, kid, can ride with me.' The kid had his eyes stuck out. So everybody had to take his picture. He was a filthy capitalist pig. He was a dealer of art. He sold paintings to people in Aspen. A high-class art dealer. Multi-multi-millionaire. His house had an original Degas on the wall.

RM: Did you ever consider making art?

JB: I worked as a potter. I'm pretty good at throwing on the wheel. I made a lot of ceramics, big stuff. I learned to throw great big things. I was a late bloomer in school. I didn't get what the authorities wanted me to do, what the school was asking for. What I didn't realize at the time was the school asking me to learn stuff that wasn't good design. I'd already figured that out, but the school wasn't teaching it. So I had bad respect for the school—and rightly so, it turns out. Then I joined an architecture fraternity and that's where I learned a lot, by living in the fraternity with 54 architects, designers, and artists. It was supposed to be only architects but it wasn't.

Then they invited Bucky for dinner, and I was sitting right next to him. I didn't know who he was. He was going to speak that night and we got into a conversation about cars. He noticed the picture in my room and he said, 'I have a car too.' So I insulted him about his car. I said, 'If that back wheel that does the steering blows a tyre, you're not going to be able to steer and you're going to be in real

trouble.' And I said, 'Furthermore, I bet you don't even have a brake on the back wheel.' And he said, 'No, I don't.' I said, 'I know why, but I told him if the back end is steering and the back tyre slows down and you're in the middle of a turn, it's going to have a abnormal gyroscopic effect on steering—it's going to be really bad.' It turned out that the car was very evil at high speeds. His later design had steering at the front but in a turn all three wheels steered. So it could move sideways into a parking space and come out sideways as well. You could do a u-turn in a two-car garage and come out the other way by having the car rotate around itself. This was in 1951.

Then once we were eating breakfast in Japan in 1982 —we were just eating and he said, 'By the way old man, you were right about that tyre', and we laughed. He had remembered it all that time. All his subsequent cars had dual tyres side by side in case one of them blew. The last car he designed had all dual tyres, and the wheels themselves were motors. He had invented electric wheels, with a small generator—not carrying batteries, but a constant speed energy-efficient engine. You can make a piston engine that's pretty efficient if it doesn't change speed. You can make it exactly right. That's why I made a sports car that used an outboard motor as its engine, because it was made to push a boat into high speed. I put a radiator on it, so you have this cooling water. The motor is standing up in the back, straight down. It was fast and loud. Boy, a two-stroke engine is like a big mega-phone.

RM: Have you considered writing an autobiography?

JB: I have considered it. I'm writing a book right now, which isn't an autobiography but it does have me in it—as a fly on the wall watching what's going on. I'm involved in it.

RM: I like that idea of watching from a fly's perspective.

JB: The book is about managing a designer's mandate. It addresses the dark side inherent in any technology. Every technology has a dark side. Even an ambulance can run over people—and they do. It's difficult for most people to see the dark side. Henry Ford, for instance, could foresee accidents happening, but he would have never been able to predict a drive-thru funeral parlour where you have the open casket and can drive through and look at it without stopping, which they have in Elk Grove up near Sacramento.

RM: How does it work?

JB: Well, it had been a fast food restaurant, and they just opened up the wall where you got your food and put the casket there. So you drive through.

RM: Really?

JB: Yeah, I don't know what it's called but I went there once just to watch. It's in the town of Elk Grove, south of Sacramento on the 99, I think. It's a pretty bizarre idea.

RM: So your book is about aspects of technology?

JB: I'm writing it as a novel, and the reason is that I want the proletariat to read it. I don't care whether academics read it or not. It's done like a famous book from the 1970s called *Ecotopia*, in which California secedes—separates from the rest of the United States—and California, Oregon and Washington become a separate country. Even with all this talk of recession, California's economy is the sixth largest in the world. So if we were a country we'd be the sixth richest in the world— and we have enough people to be a country. Actually, more people live in Los Angeles than all of Canada, so in that sense LA is much bigger than Canada—not to mention the economy. All this talk of recession … what happened was that the economy didn't grow quite as much as they thought it was going to. But it still grows. That's a recession? I don't think so. Not if you've got any smarts. People are gullible and greedy. That's the way it's always been. You read the Bible —same thing. That's one thing you learn from the Bible: things have not changed.

RM: When will your book be finished?

JB: Well, I'm about halfway through. I've been working on it for nine years, on and off. I have it figured out. I've decided on the people in the book. It's almost true, but I can't make it a documentary because some of the people involved are still alive, and that would cause a lot of trouble. Also, the very basis of it has got trouble written all over it, so I have to be discreet about it, and I have to be honest. It didn't happen exactly the way I'm showing it because I couldn't do that—naming names and all that. Much in the same way that my Bucky book isn't a biography of Bucky at all. I selected certain things he designed and concentrated on going at the basic principle involved, and how he thought about it. I'm mainly interested in how he thinks about things, and that's why what he said is the most important. The way he thought about, the way he came up with, and the way he approached design problems.

RM: It's not necessary to answer the question but to reformulate the question.

JB: Well, he starts with what human beings are for. The basic work of all human beings is to make human beings a success on Earth as a species, and everything else is less important than that. Therefore if you're able to contribute, it should be some sort of move towards making life better for everybody. As long as there are people starving— and 15,000 babies die of diarrhea every day—that would be really easy to fix if somebody wanted to. As long as I have food and the one sitting next to me is one of those starving people … that's the basis of terrorism, despite all the talk otherwise … it's not purely greed. As long as people don't have the basics of life, there are always going to be people interested in killing other people to live better.

It's one of the things Bucky preached right from the beginning—that there are plenty of resources and know-how, and that everybody could have a fantastic standard of living, without messing up nature either. We just have to think about it and do it right —and it *is* possible to do it right. He called it 'a comprehensive design science revolution'. And that's what I've been doing with my life, that's what I continue to do, and that's what I teach. I am defiantly subversive. I don't make a big noise about it here. It's an expensive school.

I'm showing people like Dean Kamen, who designed the Segway PT. The government gave him an interesting assignment recently. They said, 'All these veterans are coming back with their arms shot off, there's a big outbreak of missing arms compared to other wars.' That's because they're sitting up with a gun on top of their Humvee and something hits them. So they said, 'After all this talk about prostheses, why don't you come up with an arm so that a person can tell the difference between a grape and a peanut and can pick it up between two fingers and eat it.' They had a guy on television with a completely missing arm and shoulder who had this arm strapped on, and he picked up a grape and a peanut, he shaved, he put his hat on and off and shook hands with people. He could eat and swivel his arm around—it's all electric— because Kamen put his mind to it and he used things he had already learned from the gyroscopes and sensors from the Segway. All you have to do is put your mind to these things.

I have students saying, 'Why doesn't someone do something about people starving, someone should be able to do something about that.' Fuller figured out what to do about it but nobody's done it yet. Now it's possible to figure out how to do it because at last we have international communication. That's what it takes, because somewhere there's a pile of rice, and here are the people starving, and somewhere there's an empty freighter that doesn't have anything to do and it's returning to its home port with nothing in it. All you have to do is get them together—it can be done if you keep track. Well now you can. There are people whose business it is. They know where everyone is. So if you know that, you certainly know where the rice is. There's big stuff coming up on this kind of thing very soon, and I'm considering getting in on one of those deals. I've never looked for a job as an adult, but I have, I will admit, hung out where the action is in case somebody needs something. I've kind of ended up being the person who builds things. So if you need something like this, I will make it. And I think Kamen and I get along just fine.

(…)

CHAPTER 9

CONCERNING LOVE

"Not so flat, was it?" he laughed to himself.
Opening the door, he walked in, and – to
continue on the day's course – I followed,
in the idea of a moment to sit somewhere
quietly and chew over everything that I'd
seen, heard and talked about since leaving
home. "'ll go look for him," he said, going
indoors and yoo-hooing ahead.

My sight was drawn along the unbroken
– except for the eight vertical steel frames,
of about three centimetres wide and joined
below at a wide sill that ran the full breadth
of this sun-room, where it turned a corner
back at the door – line of the horizon. Inside,
the first steps I took were directed towards
an especially long, worn, plywood, trestle-
ish table with narrow but adequate iron legs,
with a high-backed bench the length of one
side, and the sill – doubling for bench with
its back to the window – on the other. I sat,
and stared out at the sea and what must've
been the same four boats that had kept up
with us, with their rust-brown red sails.

Concerning Love

    The frames were unevenly spaced, and
despite my good eyesight, I hadn't noticed
this difference between the glass that was
slid back, and the open space it left behind.
As all else fell away, I don't think it was the
the increasing volume of the waves breaking on the shingle down below, more than
their growing presence in this quiet room,
that told me to get a better look. I stood up
and walked round to the other side of the
table, closer to the window, and sat on the
oiled oak sill, still looking out over the sea.
From up here there was a fuller view of the
garden: stepping down to the beach were
four terraces of varying widths, with a worn
brick path zigzagged. On the first terrace,
directly below me, the path we had come
off to get up into the house continued to
the left, giving access through the beds of
veg and flowers that continued on from-
and into those of the neighbours. After the
huge fig, and at foot of the oak, the porous
red path ran right, down and between flat
lawns and slopes of kale, all the way to the
beach. The bottom terrace, banked by the

small stones thrown up by the high tides,
continued left and right, unbroken by any
structures as far as the eye could see. Like
earlier on in the park, people sat in groups
with abundant picnics spread out on blankets between them, or on the beach grilling
fish and veg on small pits in the shingle.
From the jerking downward movement
of various elbows, it was clear that they
were sharing fresh oysters.

Turning back into the sun-room, I saw
that the wood of the bench I was sitting on
was pocked with a chaotic pattern of dark
rings left by years of flower pots. I could only
assume that in Winter and Spring this room
served as a nursery for the plants and flowers below, though a lot of the smaller rings
and stains closer to where I was sitting were
more likely to be left by glasses and cups.
I pictured the groups on the beach heading
up the path and stopping here as the cool
evening set in.

Looking back in, the table was framed
by a wide opening into a higher, cooler space
beyond it. The light dimmed gradually, the

closer it came to a white plastered wall eight
or nine metres further in. The objects in it
only highlighted the darkness behind them,
but also brought them forward: a modest
yet large kitchen, to one side of the space,
clearly able to feed friends after a day's walk
along the seashore and terraces; in the middle of the other side was a table – with six
wooden chairs – whose top looked like a
long chopping board, with a black-topped
silver flask, a pair of slightly conical glasses,
a jar of flowers and a white-handled nail-
file; there was also a rocking chair nearby
with a red cushion with an open book lying
face down on the woven seagrass floor next
to it. Besides a few small framed drawings
on them, the long white walls were only broken on one side, the right, by a large fire-
place whose grate was framed by two black
arches receding back into the chimney. This
whole was surrounded by grey marble, with
a wide grey mantlepiece containing a few
small objects that were hard to distinguish
from here, except one: a small book bound
with three metal rings, open at a page

containing the lines AZURE & SON/
ISLANDS LTD/ OCEANS INC.

In the two far corners were even darker
openings, without doors, leading from this
space into others in the house. From the
darker of the two Dick emerged, talking to
the man who was following him, who saw
me and turned his words in my direction:

"So now... Will, you brought news from
overseas? How long you been away? Dick
says we've all got some catching-up to do.
Says you find everything altered, 'n I might
answer some of the questions he can't. So
now... bin round a bit longer than the old
Common Knowledge, see?"

"I see." I offered, shaking his hand. He
watched, expecting me to begin, but after
a few moments' silence, he continued, "Oh
sorry, me again: ask a question and get talk
for hours. Tell you all you need in the course.
Do me a great service if you've come to get
my old tongue wagging. My love of talk
grows on me, though I don't think the others preciate me, they can get all they need.
Oh, there I go. So now... ask me questions,

Concerning Love

ask me questions about anything; since
I *must* talk, make my talk profitable to you"
　　This "you" was joined, punctuated by,
and rhymed with a hoo, and we all turned
to see her coming up, through the garden
towards the house in a red everyday dress.
It was Dick in particular whose "Hallo!",
followed by '?But she said she didn'eed
any errands" made me look: "She" was
the "She" we'd met this morning, just after
"She"'d cut open the pages of a booklet.
The blood ran to my face at the memory
of how – on hearing my attempt at how
I thought I should say something, like,
"Kay." – of how the blood ran to my face.
　　She took the wooden stairs, and the
door opened to frame "Hallo" in a red dress
sliced in white pleats. The old man walked
towards her saying, "eve Blossom, no! You,
yours, you to you, I to you, you to me,—we?
That (by the way) is beside the point!
So now… here's Anna, if you please, two
sandwiches short of a packed lunch!"
　　"White or brown?"
　　They hugged, and kissed once on the lips.

"Writin'gain?" he asked her knowingly.

"Why didnyou say?" Dick asked, pulling away from her. "We could've taken it all the way. You mus've been just behind us the whole way down."

"U-uh. Came down on The GLEANER."

"Ah. No wonder we did'know till we heard you… oh, where's my manners? Will, meet Anna. Just in on what is the *only* way to go."

"Hello again," she said, smiling. "Did you have a nice walk?" Pronouncing each word as though I may not follow her otherwise.

"Yes, lovely, thanks. It's been…quite a lot to take in, and I haven't had time to get my head around it. Yet." I admitted, losing the sense of covering up for what must've made me look pretty stupid up till now. Nevertheless, she stared blankly, as though I'd said something in a language she didn't understand. After a split second her expression changed and she raised her eyebrows.

"D'you come over on The WELCOME?"

"No, but I feel it. Very.…I mean, you've all been perfect strangers to me. But you have to excuse my ignorance. I've been away for a long time." (Off I went again: white lies for perfect strangers. This was going to take some time, but I knew that it was easier to learn by pretending to understand through having the sense to say yes or no at the right time. Nine times out of ten, you'd give the right response, and the other would carry on informing you. On the odd occasion, you simply corrected yourself by saying, "No, sorry, I mean no", and they'd continue, until you knew enough to ask a pertinent question).

"So what brings you here, Anna?"

She looked at Dick questioningly, as she also had done this morning, but before she found the chance to answer me, the old man broke in: "She's come to drop off something she's written. That's why most people come to me...Well, not entirely true. Normally it would be handed down to me and eventually one of my neighbours'll drop over every now and then. Usually it's a sheet, folded twice, in an envelope, slit open to just before the spine. That's more than enough space

120

for most to copy, you see? But when people pick up a pen and make a dedication, most 've never written a single word in their lives. It's Common Knowledge that it's best to just start writing out what it is you want to say, though some still only work on their abcs. Through this practise we manage to distill things into a few meaningful lines. I think this's what you'd call 'a labour of love'?"

"Sounds like it. But are you saying no-one writes any more?" I asked.

"This'd be a sad place if no-one did. Nah, we only have the need to write a few times in our life. Only once or twice for some. It's just not necessary when we all know the same things. We have so little to tell each other. Haha.

"So now… when we do want to write something out, we quietly ask a neighbour for a pen, then shut our doors and start to put things to paper and – of course – as soon as the pen moves, and the words find themselves on the page they become Common Knowledge. Pen moves, and the whole world knows what's up. Haha."

"But how?"

"How?... Oh, see what you mean. So now... there's every kind of a history of every one who ever can or is or was or will be living. So now... there's a history of every one from their beginning to their ending. So now... a history of all of them, of every kind of them, of every one, of every bit of living they ever have in them, of them when there is never more than a beginning to them, of every kind of them, of every one when there is very little beginning and then there is an ending, a history of every one so now... a history of everything that ever was or is or will be them, of everything that was or is or will be all of any one or all of all of them. So now... there's a history of every one, of everything or anything that is all them or any part of them and so now... there's a history of how anything or everything comes out from every one, comes out from every one or any one from the beginning to the ending of the being in them. So now... there's a history of every one who ever was or is or will be living. As one sees every one in their living, in their loving, sitting, eating, drinking, sleeping, walking, working, thinking, laughing, as any one sees all of

122

them from their beginning to their ending, sees
them when they are little babies or children or
young grown men and women or growing older
men and women or old men and women then
one knows it in them that there's a history of all
of them, that all of them will have the last touch
of being, a history of us can give to them. (Haha,
been a while, speaking lines like that.)"

"Know! Next time you walk through a garden,
tell someone *all* the names of *all* the flowers."

"So now... That's why all this writing ends up
here. Writing's this thing, so the person they're
writing to knows exactly what's being put on
the page, as they do it. So now...why would
they do it? you might ask. Besides the fact that
I can usually tell them a little something only
I can know of what it is they've copied out."

"Copied?" asked Anna.

"Well, yes, essentially. Well, 'written', would
be the word we would use, so now...you'd call
it 'copying', wouldn't you Will?"

"Would I? Yes."

"So now...a copy would presume that there's
an original somewhere..."

"AN original?"

"Well, yes… in a sense that what Anna copied out existed somewhere else first."

"As Common Knowledge."

"Well, not exactly. But in another place."

"But how can it be a copy? Anna wrote it, didn't she?"

"Of course she did, but someone else did before her."

"Really! Who?"

"Well, I could be wrong. What was it that you wrote Anna? Frost– was it?"

"M-hm… 'Design'."

"I found a dimpled spider," said Dick, as the old man looked off, into the corner at the door, and said "Mhm, thought so! Hang on!" With the speed of someone half his age, he ran off through the door in the far corner. All the while Dick continued "fat and white, On a white heal-all, holding up a moth."

"Where's he off to?"

"To The Library," Anna answered

"Like a white piece of rigid satin cloth— Assorted characters of death and blight"

"Oh, is there one that close by?"

"Mixed ready to begin the morning right,"

"Garden Flat IS The Library."

"Really? So what's the Mote House if it's not the library?"

"Like the ingredients of a witches' broth —A snow-drop spider, a flower like a froth, And dead wings carried like a paper kite."

We heard the sound of running up- and downstairs, then the old man came back in, smiling (before my question could be answered): "Here. Anna, wheresyours?"

Anna pulled out the thin book she had cut open, and gave it to him.

"Q."

He sat down at the long table and opened it out. Next to that he put a sheet of paper, which had either faded to a very light green, or was of the sort commonly used in offices. Or both.

"*Green*!"

"Oh, we got all sorts here," he told her.

Anna caught her breath, as he smoothed out the sheet next to her pages.

"So now…"

125

'Design'

I found a dimpled spider, fat and white,
On a white heal-all, holding up a moth
Like a white piece of rigid satin cloth —
Assorted characters of death and blight
Mixed ready to begin the morning right,
Like the ingredients of a witches' broth —
A snow-drop spider, a flower like froth,
And dead wings carried like a paper kite.

What had that flower to do with being white
The wayside blue and innocent heal-all?'
What brought the kindred spider to that height
Then steered the white moth thither in the night?
What but design of darkness to appall? —
If design govern in a thing so small.

— Robert Frost —

I found a dimpled spider, fat and white,
On a white heal-all, holding up a moth
Like a white piece of rigid satin cloth —
  Assorted characters of death and blight
Mixed ready to begin the morning right,
  Like the ingredients of a witches' broth —
A snow-drop spider, a flower like a froth,
And dead wings carried like a paper kite!

What had that flower to do with being white,
The wayside blue and innocent heal-all?
What brought the kindred spider to that height,
Then steered the white moth thither in the night?
  What but design of darkness to appall? —
  If design govern in a thing so small.

        Robert Frost

Concerning Love

So now... there's so few words in the world... think I get most of them here. Sometimes there's writing that is so well practised, so well-formed, that it's clear they've said "I love you" a little too often. So now... I wonder whether they really meant it. Not just the young'ns! All ages!"

"Well, *I* meanit," she said. Though obviously a little put out by the comparison.

"That's clear. Putting that out there makes you think more than twice. What about when you've written a line out so often that it don't mean it anymore? or it means something else and you realise it ain't quite what you thought. Then you start all over and find the words that are closer to what you're trying to say. Then you come back the next day an they ain't quite it after all. Must've thrown away so many sheets to get that right. Beautiful.

"Imagine when everyone had pens, and we'd all write something every day. Every day! Kids could make flourishes like that with their eyes closed. Wonder what it all meant to them."

ON THE SELF-REFLEXIVE PAGE

by Louis Lüthi

The term 'self-reflexive page' as used in this essay needs defining. Let me just say that here it applies solely to literature,[1] and according to Merriam-Webster 'self-reflexive' literature is 'marked by or making reference to its own artificiality or contrivance.' And because the subject of this essay is 'the page' and not 'the sentence' or 'the chapter', i.e. because its subject is a surface, visual elements in literature—graphics, imagery, text as imagery—are primarily addressed. Which doesn't mean that this essay is concerned with visual elements in literature per se (though one could argue that any visual element draws attention to the plainly textual level of the narrative)—it is only concerned with their self-reflexive use.

It would have been possible to classify differently the pages cited: in chronological, alphabetical, or numerical order, for example. I have chosen to present them thematically, resulting in a typology of self-reflexive pages: Black Pages, Blank Pages, Image Pages, Text Pages, Number Pages, Punctuation Pages. The repetition this entails is somewhat deceptive; more often than not such devices are used as a counterpoint to the surrounding narrative. And the same means may be used to different ends. Because this essay attempts only to trace an isolated theme through often otherwise unrelated works, the reader is in all instances referred to the original publications.

'I can't get out—I can't get out',[2] cries the caged starling to parson Yorick in Laurence Sterne's *A Sentimental Journey through France and Italy*. Reflecting just then on the nearby Bastille prison while wandering the stairs and passages of his Parisian hotel, and reasoning that a man 'may do very well within', Yorick is startled into an awareness of his surroundings by the repetition of these four English words. He looks around yet sees no one. The caged bird hanging above him, he eventually realizes, has learned to speak—only to bemoan, in a foreign tongue, its helplessness! The parson, distressed at its lamentations and ashamed of his recent reflections, tries to free it from captivity. Unsuccessful, he returns to his room and, brooding now on the ills of slavery, promptly instructs his valet to buy both bird and cage from the master of the hotel (a bottle of Burgundy proves to be sufficient payment).

Vladimir Nabokov, who in a lecture referred to this scene as 'heartrending',[3] tells a remarkably similar story about confinement and expression in 'On a Book Entitled *Lolita*':

> As far as I can recall, the initial shiver of inspiration was somehow prompted by a newspaper story about an ape in the Jardin des Plantes, who, after months of coaxing by a scientist, produced the first drawing ever charcoaled by an animal: this sketch showed the bars of the poor creature's cage.[4]

If we believe him, that 'shiver of inspiration' was for Nabokov the impulse to write the novella *The Enchanter*, the tame prototype of *Lolita*. The tone, plot, characters and, perhaps most importantly, the setting have changed in the later work; the prison trope, however, has remained salient. For example, in chapter 26 in part 1 of *Lolita*, Humbert Humbert desperately instructs the 'printer' to fill a page by repeating his beloved's name. In vain, of course, but we can imagine the envisioned wall of 'Lolitas'— and isn't it a typographical sketch showing the bars of Humbert's own (mental) cage? Humbert, as we know, will die in prison after proclaiming eternity for himself and Lolita in the book he writes; parson Yorick will not free the starling from his cage but will symbolically bear him, 'from that time to this', as the crest to his coat of arms '—And let the heralds officers twist his neck about if they dare.'[5] Pity and beauty, the two summands in the approximate equation drawn up by Nabokov to define art,[6] are deftly commingled in both instances because testimony and hence liberation exists only on the written page, not in corporeal reality.

A distinct though diminished echo of the implications exemplified by the correspondence between these two famous literary scenes[7] seems to me to resound still in the self-reflexive pages collected in this essay.

All writing ultimately exists, as literary theorists in the previous century emphatically established, on the page and in the imagination of the reader. Some writers of fiction accept this as a given, others merely hint at it, still others openly address it: knowing asides are then directed at the reader, character and place names are improbable (if not intentionally laughable: 'Oedipa Maas' in Thomas Pynchon's *The Crying of Lot 49*, for example, still strikes me as a ludicrous and repugnant name, as does the political acronym 'ONAN' in David Foster Wallace's *Infinite Jest*), coincidence is piled upon coincidence, changes in style abruptly occur, 'holes' and 'gaps' appear in the narrative texture, correct grammar is eschewed or inventive punctuation employed, visual elements interrupt the steady flow of text and so on. In short the parameters of a book, of writing, are then laid bare by familiar stratagems. When it comes to visual elements that are not merely illustrative and so to 'text—most, but not all, of which takes the form of prose', contemporary critics have on the whole been guarded, if not disdainful: 'razzle-dazzle narrative techniques'; 'multimedia sensibilities shaped by the Internet and heaven knows what else'; 'high jinks, distortions and addenda [that] first came to market decades back and now represent a popular mode that's no more controversial than pre-ripped blue jeans.' At best they're said to be 'cleverly designed to intensify' a theme (with the emphasis clearly on 'cleverly designed' and not 'intensify') or, what's probably worse by implication, 'at a time when its future seems threatened', that they 'demonstrate the uniqueness and versatility of a book'[8] (as if novels or poems should be praised for being, of all things, demonstrations of media theory; and one wonders, incidentally, whether a medium neither 'unique' nor 'versatile' is at all conceivable). The gist of these criticisms reveals that such visual elements are often perceived as emblems of postmodern tricksiness.

Some of these elements may indeed now seem dated, but not all. At the end of the last chapter on the starling in *A Sentimental Journey* Sterne displays Yorick's altered coat of arms; the large, detailed illustration proudly confirms the parson's sentiments, not to mention his gentility, yet it's also the only way *he* can free the starling. (Gardner D. Stout Jr and Michael J. O'Shea note here a subtle reference to Sterne's own family heraldry, and the connection between the author's name and dialect forms of 'starling':

'starnel', 'starn', etc.[9] One could say the starling is also trapped, as it were, within the confines of Sterne's tale.) And in the shortest chapter in *Lolita* Nabokov has Humbert conceive of a self-reflexive page which, through no fault of Humbert's, remains in the form of text as prose—to preserve a reviewer's ironic 'arcane distinction'. Humbert's desperation is significantly out of character, yet his instructions also draw attention to the composition of type, to the reproduction of writing and its potential manipulation. Furthermore, reference is made to Sterne's incomparable *The Life and Opinions of Tristram Shandy, Gentleman.*

Tristram Shandy marks what could be archly called the 'invention' of the page[10]—the page not as the recto or verso of one of the leaves of paper that when bound together make up a book, but as a determined space at a specific point in a narrative. Its black, marbled and blank pages are self-conscious ideograms of themes Sterne addresses throughout the nine volumes (one theme, for example, gave rise to Bertrand Russell's 'Tristram Shandy paradox', which famously states that writing about a life will never catch up with life itself—unless that life is immortal) and, as such, they are concise illustrations of self-reflexivity, which is one reason why Sterne was cited compulsively in the 1960s as a forerunner of so-called 'metafiction'. An effective self-reflexive page thus reveals the page to be a canvas and, to paraphrase James Wood, the fiction to be a true lie.[11] No one, I fancy, has described better the use of such a device than Julio Cortázar in *Hopscotch*:

[The writer Morelli] plans one of the many endings to his unfinished book, and leaves a mockup. The page contains a single sentence: 'Underneath it all he knew that one cannot go beyond because there isn't any.' The sentence is repeated over and over for the whole length of

the page, giving the impression of a wall, of an impediment. There are no periods or commas or margins. A wall, in fact, of words that illustrate the meaning of the sentence, the collision with a wall behind which there is nothing. But towards the bottom and on the right, in one of the sentences the word *any* is missing. A sensitive eye can discover the hole among the bricks, the light that shows through.[12]

The anxiety brought on by completion, by placing the final full stop that declares one has 'said all there is to say'; the playfulness combined with a certain fatality; the insistence which entails repetition; the humility easily mistaken for egocentrism, and sometimes rightly so; the obsessive importance accorded to the present: all are habitual characteristics of a literature that folds back on itself, a literature that refuses to be taken on any but its own emphatic terms. To be sure, description as used by Cortázar (and Nabokov) is one remove from illustration and a clever way of avoiding its potential constraints. In the end Morelli's mockup is a plausible sample of experimental writing in the 1960s and as such unremarkable; what, however, could be considered remarkable is the frequent use in contemporary fiction of pages similar to Morelli's and the ones mentioned above by Humbert and Sterne.[13]

Why reuse certain devices?

Black Pages

Interestingly, a black page—and therefore a preclusion or annulment of communication—comes first, in a historic perspective as well as in *Tristram Shandy*. Strictly speaking, it's not a black page but a recto and a verso with a black rectangle filling the entire text column of each page. Tristram places them there—that is, in volume 1 after having already told the sad story of his downfall—in memory parson Yorick (the same character as in *A Sentimental Journey*) and then resumes his digressive tale.

That's it, love.
Must heed Kim, respect her wishes, too mine to lose, too much what I need, to lose, this is good enough for the moment. But I've promised myself I'll have her one day.
One night.
Nearly there!
Might cost me a lot. Worth it for my Kim, my only love, my first love. But I shall have her, I Maurie Bunde, shall ... have ... her ...
Oh! Good, Kim, yes, Kim, Kim, good, ooh!
Kim!
Yes!
Ah! Ah!
Pump!
Pound!
Thus!
Aaaaah!
Thuddddd!
Aaaaaaaaaah, Noooooooo!

Shook! Shock! The water is colder this time of day. Like the bath this morning. Still: don't show it. Now, let me try: 4rm over, turn body, other way, repeat. All right, Dunne, it was my first attempt.
Yes, I see that.
Try again. Breathing wrong? He's right, I didn't breathe at all during that length! My heart knows so, too! A minute, yes, I see what you mean. Again. Aaah! This is tiring! Every muscle in my body seems to be working. Breath short. I will do it. Again, then. Surprise him: do a turn and straight back. Yes, that's better, I can feel it.
Again.
Again.
I'm beating it. Turn. Again.
I can see the end. Fight. Pounding.
See. The.
End.
I will ... must ... reach ... will ...
Oooooooh!

Must ... struggle.
Blurred.
Nearing end. Winning. Must reach the ... peaks. The river.
Over the river, over, over ...
Another! Ooooh!

Further ...
Further away.... Still ... farther away.
Oh, oooh, Kim, still farther ...
Oooooooooh ...

LITTLE MERCED / APOLONIO

Apolonio, who had always refused to make home safe, brought over a quart of the aged milk for my father.

'Just keep giving it to him until he takes it,' Apolonio said.

After two changes of sheets and a roll of wadded paper towels, my father finally drank the milk. It was during that time, as the sheets soaked in rose petals and soap, that my father began to recover from the effects of lead.

He spoke to me about my mother and her, how one had brought the other, but always spurning kindly of her, how it was a wonder she had stayed so long with a bad sorter. And while I had been taught to love my mother I did not see the kindness in a ... daughter and loaded ... man. And as my father ... time, I felt pity ... devotion he held for ... to that three short ... in love. That ... burns and blazes. I wanted to hide my father, to protect him from others, so that they would not see him and feel the same pity I felt for him. My father was Federico de la Fe, the leader and war commander of EMF. And I could not bear Secate in any body else looking at him as he sat in his bed, burned, his lap damp with water and pube, rummaging through books of marches and blackened flower leaves in his wooden box, looking for a picture of my mother. And although there was no more lead in Monte, I tried my best to protect him.

I brought the aged milk to Federico de la Fe's house; I gave Little Merced the Baby Nostradamus to hold while I passed the milk from my carafe into a plastic jar.

I walked from the kitchen into his room, where Little Merced and the Baby Nostradamus looked over Federico de la Fe. Though I had seen him many times, walking through El Monte, at the weigh station with his tray of flowers, and at the Papal Pawn & Loan with Little Merced, I never suspected that de la Fe was a Burn Collector.

There was always a faint odor of persistent lingering around him, but I assumed it was from the solvent they used to cut engine grease and the scent of flowers from their skin. But as I saw him sitting on his bed, his shirt wide open and his body savaged by burns and black carts, I understood Federico de la Fe's need for combustibles.

I had not seen a Burn Collector in many years, not since I had left my mother's house. Back then the Collectors were flamboyant and unabashed, using fire to discover the whole of their bodies and quieting the scripture that decreed that we were all of ashes and to ash we would return. The Collectors always righteous, shedding ashes, ever closer to our eventual fate.

But Federico de la Fe was bashful, hiding everything underneath his shirt and bed.

LITTLE MERCED / EMF

I sat on my bed peeling the skins from limes and then eating the meat. Father and Froggy sat around the dominoes table. I closed my eyes and followed the procedures that the Baby Nostradamus had taught me, focusing but making sure not to deny my own thoughts.

LITTLE MERCED / VETERANOS

Froggy called us to the dominoes table. We all gathered around and looked down at the blocks of ivory.

'This is how we stop Secate,' Froggy said, pointing at the dominoes, 'but we will need more than just EMF.'

'It is their war too,' Federico de la Fe said.

Federico de la Fe and Froggy were bending the war, recruiting beyond the burn boundaries that surrounded El Monte.

And so the preparations began. We combed our hair and racked in our shorts and practiced the pleasure smiles of sales ... We then drove out of El Monte to the cities of Alhambra, San Gabriel, and South Pasadena. We knocked on doors, asking people to join us in the war against Secate.

Some answered their doors and politely declined.

'You want to destroy the only thing we is holding us together,' they said. We apologized and moved on.

We also came upon veteranos who had fought their own wars.

'I fought in Okinawa, in Leros, and Okmura,' they said.

And because they had lost every war, they too declined.

After three days and four cities, only one new recruit had agreed to join in the war against Secate.

376 VOLUME VI

CHAPTER XXXVIII

To conceive this right,—call for pen and ink—here's paper ready to your hand.——Sit down, Sir, paint her to your own mind——as like your mistress as you can——as unlike your wife as your conscience will let you—'tis all one to me ——please but your own fancy in it.

iii

iii

iii

Yes.

Slip,
slip aslee

OCEAN-CHART.

Figure 1. *Carte de l'océan (extrait de Lewis Carroll,*
La Chasse au snark).

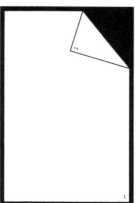

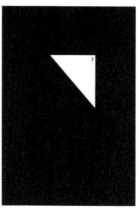

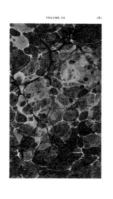

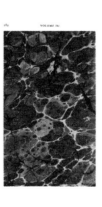

It might be interesting to compare the particularities of layout in different editions of the novel; the edition reproduced here has added running heads to the original, smaller layout (let us mention in passing that the black pages have *vanished* in the Project Gutenburg and Google Books versions of *Tristram Shandy*).

A black page in B.S. Johnson's *Travelling People* likewise marks the death of a character, though the slight but important differences here are (a) the black rectangle interrupts the narrative in mid-paragraph and (b) it bleeds off the page. In fact, the following two pages are entirely covered in ink: two true black pages. Earlier in the novel the same technique is used first with random-pattern grey 'to indicate unconsciousness after a heart attack' and subsequently an Op-Art-like pattern of thick wavy lines 'to indicate sleep or recuperative consciousness.'[14] Death gradually interrupts the narrative, as it were, instead of forming an integral part of it as in *Tristram Shandy*; the overall effect is more cinematic than graphic.

An ostensibly more straight-forward Shandean use of a black page is to be found in Salvador Plascencia's *The People of Paper*. Here a black rectangle appears throughout the book whenever a particular character is allocated space as one of the many narrators in the at times multi-column layout. It turns out he's not dead, as the reader is initially led to believe, but deliberately obscuring his thoughts from the omniscience of an abstract being (transparently the author's proxy). He teaches other characters this technique of obfuscation and the black consequently spreads, albeit in imperfect forms, to other narrators' columns until at one point it fills entirely the text columns of one page and so resembles Yorick's black page in *Tristram Shandy* in all but pro-portion and running heads. Wher-eas in *Tristram Shandy* the black page is one character's gesture to another (though Yorick is patently based on Sterne), in *The People of Paper* it concerns the metaphysical relationship between character and author, fictitious or not.

Blank Pages

Blank books form an entire subgenre in conceptual book art;[15] in book art as well as prose blank pages can be traced back to three pages in *Tristram Shandy*. The first, in volume 6, is presented as a canvas to the reader so that he may draw as he pleases a 'concu-piscible' female character, and in its call for creation this blank page is a companion piece to the memorial black one. Tristram afterwards declares: 'Thrice happy book! thou wilt have one page, at least, within thy covers, which MALICE will not blacken, and which IGNORANCE cannot misrep-resent.'[16] The second and third, in volume 9, are headed chapters 18 and 19 but left blank by Tristram who only in chapter 25 reveals why: 'That it may be a lesson to the world, "*to let people tell their stories their own way.*"'[17] He then narrates the two 'missing' chapters, trans-posed but, as he stresses, none the worse because of it. Yet the initial reason for the omission, as with many of the words and passages in the novel replaced by series of asterisks or various lengths of dashes, is plainly to insinuate that a bawdy scene is really taking place. Here Sterne slyly uses his narrative skills to tease and then appease his (clearly male) read-ers—all, moreover, in the name of noble objectives! Chapter 18 turns out to be longer than a page; the single blank pages in volume 9 are therefore symbolic gaps, not spatial equivalents of the text omitted.

Recent examples of similar blank pages are to be found in Gordon Lish's *Arcade, or How to Write a Novel* and Jonathan Safran Foer's *Extremely Loud and Incredibly Close*. Both also refer to texts that 'should have' been there: Lish's twenty blank pages are in self-righteous protest ('Because I Gordon am fed up to the gills'[18]) while Foer's three blank pages are in oblivious poignancy ('My Life'[19]). But a blank page in 21st century literature cannot be the same thing as a blank page in the 20th century, much less one in the 18th; what one hundred years ago was a tabula rasa could now be regarded as fac-ile legerdemain. More interesting perhaps are the following varia-tions by Alasdair Gray and Douglas Coupland.

In Gray's *1982, Janine*, sleep —much like death in *Travelling People*—interrupts the narrative in mid-paragraph (in mid-word, even), removing any prose or page numbers from the next three pages until, that is, the protago-nist awakes. The duration of sleep here—abstract but not too short or too long—offsets the delirious and dense multilevel scene preceding it. Again, like in *Travelling People* the use and effect of the device is cinematic: the narrative rhythm is abruptly edited and reedited to reflect intrusive occurrences. And again, like Johnson Gray invokes Sterne's novels by putting similar visual devices to different and often more intricate use in his books, by means such as detailed illustration and complex typog-raphy. In *The Book of Prefaces* he accordingly writes with concluding defiance of *Tristram Shandy*:

> The book is willful, exuberant, bawdy, gleefully plagiarizing, eccentric & humane. It delights in its fiction, freely acknowledging the conversation that joins author & reader & using every device that late 20th-century critics label *post-modernist*.[20]

Pre- or post-modern, in *JPod* Douglas Coupland satirizes the blank page by having among the many interpolated typographical exercises one page with only the words 'intentionally blank' set centrally in small, lowercase sans serif type: a deadpan joke whispered to the reader in between humdrum office scenes.

Titles of entirely blank poems, stories and novels include: 'Poem of the End' by Vasilisk Gdenov (the back cover of a single octavo of poems entitled 'Death to Art'); *Hommage à Marcel Duchamp, Satrape* by the Collège de 'Pataphysique; 'Poème collectif' by Robert Filliou et Cie; *Charles Baudelaire. Pauvre Belgique* by Marcel Broodthaers; *Tabula Rasa – A Constructivist Novel* and *Inexistencies: Constructivist Fictions* by Richard Kostelanetz; 'On Going to Meet a Zen Master in the Kyushu Mountains and Not Finding Him' by Don Paterson; 'In Memory of the Horse David, Who Ate One of My Poems' by James Wright; 'There Are Things He Should Keep to Himself' by Dave Eggers.

Not quite a blank page, but more like an illustration of one, is the ocean chart in Lewis Carroll's *The Hunting of the Snark*. A frame encloses: nothing. The cardinal points are nonetheless given, as are other standard terms of cartography: latitude, longitude, equator, meridian, South Pole, North Pole, torrid zone, zenith, nadir, equinox (these humorous details are curiously omitted from the version reproduced in Georges Perec's *Species of Spaces*). It would seem that the map is practically useless but the crew reaches their destination anyway. In addition, and more significantly, it foreshadows the disappearance in the last stanza of the unlucky character that, alas, catches a Boojum instead of a Snark (for then 'you will softly and suddenly vanish away, and never be met with again'[21]). We can say that the ocean chart drawn by Henry Holiday is not so much a map as a diagram of the nonsensical reality of Carroll's poem: a world based on words and word games, and so unbound by natural geography or logic.

An actual illustration of a blank page, geometric and dog-eared on a bleeding black field, is the first of Márton Koppány's two-page poem *The Other Side*. The recto of the illustrated sheet of paper is marked '1'; the verso of the illustrated sheet visible because of the fold is marked '2'; the same folded-over triangle, now inverted, removed as if from a jigsaw puzzle and placed apart on the second page in the optical centre of a black field, is marked '3'. The 'other side' glimpsed at first thanks to the fold in the illustrated page is only the black of the background, which makes way not for any 'other' side but for what made the initial glimpse possible, i.e. the folded-over bit of paper. The triangle marked '3' thus turns out to be the 'other side', the part initially hidden by the area marked '2': this, of course, is revealed on the second page—another 'other side'—of Koppány's deceptively straightforward poem.

And so, when exploring the limits inherent to printed words set on bound leaves of paper and therefore having to see them from within, as it were, maybe a natural question for an author to have a character jokingly ask is the final unanswered one in Roberto Bolaño's *The Savage Detectives*: 'What's outside the window?'[22]

Image Pages

The two marbled pages in volume 3 of *Tristram Shandy* were originally in colour and therefore resembled common endpaper or cover material, a subtlety more or less lost on readers of contemporary black-and-white paperback editions of the novel. Moreover, true paper marbling results in monotype prints: each marbled page and therefore each copy of the original volume was unique, which is why Tristram exclaims:

> for without *much reading*, by which your reverence knows, I mean *much knowledge*, you will no more be able to penetrate the moral of the next marbled page (motly emblem of my work!) than the world with all its sagacity has been able to unravel the many opinions, transactions and truths which still lie mystically hid under the dark veil of the black one.[23]

Sterne hasn't inserted an image here (as contemporary editions of *Tristram Shandy* at first glance lead one to believe), he has re-appropriated a convention of printing and bookbinding—hence the necessity for '*much reading*'—and so endowed with personal significance something taken for granted as decorative.

Raymond Roussel anonymously approached the painter and illustrator Henri-A. Zo with indications for fifty-nine drawings precisely in order to add an impersonal touch to his poem *New Impressions of Africa*. By including on every second page drawings illustrating lines the reader had just read, he intended to double the size of his small volume (the typeset poem took up 'a mere' fifty-nine pages), which he further doubled by printing only on the recto side of the pages. These were left uncut so the poem could be read without revealing the hidden drawings. One of the fifty-nine illustrations is particularly arresting: the reader lifts the edge of the uncut page in question (heaven forbid he should cut the pages open!) and gradually sees appear a depiction of a man lifting, carefully, the edge of an uncut page in a fairly slim book to reveal something hidden underneath, something indicated by several decisive brushstrokes ... Zo was not too happy about his unwitting 'collaboration' and others thought the combination strange ('Chagall, for example, would have been more appropriate'[24]). Still, his banal Indian ink illustrations reflect the mathematical side of Roussel's poetics and in combination with the uncut pages and methodical use of embedded parentheses they lend his last completed work a palpable secretiveness.

W.G. Sebald would ask copy shop personnel how to obtain certain grains or contrasts[25] when photocopying the images and documents he would embed in his

obstructing access to a darkness never yet
penetrated, a darkness in which I thought, said

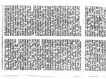

Fig. 3

49,50,51,52
53,54,55,56
57,58,59,60
61,62,63,64

narratives as if they were old travel books or personal memoirs—which in a sense they are, only they take place on a mental instead of strictly geographical or historical plane. (A photograph of the author himself is in *The Rings of Saturn*, and in a couple of photographs in *Austerlitz* a slight reflection of the photographer—presumably the author—can just be made out in a windowpane.) Sometimes we are confronted with a full-page reproduction and our gaze is allowed to linger on an image before resuming the narrative. In *Austerlitz* this happens several times, most strikingly when the main character visits Terezín, or Theresienstadt, as it used to be known, a Czech town once used by the Nazis as a vast Jewish ghetto. In Terezín Austerlitz is at first confronted above all with rundown buildings and closed doors, 'all of them, as I thought I sensed, obstructing access to a darkness never yet penetrated.'[26] Four photos follow; page numbers are omitted from under the last two. The darkness behind the closed doors in Terezín is representative of Germany's and, by extension, Europe's atrocity-ridden collective memory, but also of Austerlitz's own personal memory as he tries to reconstruct a forgotten past, an attempt faithfully listened to and recorded by a narrator who invariably comes up against such barriers of silence.

(The closed doors in *Austerlitz* may be compared to the subdued photographs of doorknobs interspersed throughout Jonathan Safran Foer's *Extremely Loud and Incredibly Close*. These are five of the many doors in New York that the child narrator tries to unlock with a mysterious key left behind by his father, who was killed in the September 11 attacks. The metaphorical key in *Austerlitz* is here treated literally, but in both novels the importance lies rather in the fact that the doors encountered remain closed. It must be said, however, that the haunting quality of the photos in *Austerlitz*

is absent from the ones in *Extremely Loud and Incredibly Close*.)

Another two full-page reproductions, this time in Sebald's *The Rings of Saturn*, show two pages from an 18th-century silk catalogue. Silk is one of the many themes that echo throughout this diffuse English 'pilgrimage', whose narrator is always highly aware of the incompleteness of his memories and associative stories. The pictures of the two catalogue pages, bleeding off only the outer edges of the spread—in the British edition, at least—take pride of place in chapter 10, the last in Sebald's novel. As with Zo's illustration of a reader in *New Impressions of Africa*, the depiction and precise use of format echoes for an instant our own position and activity as readers, so heightening the empathy we (ideally) feel towards the narrator. After the two photos Sebald's narrator melancholically notes how the catalogue pages 'seem to me to be leaves from the only true book which none of our textual and pictorial works can even begin to rival',[27] a remark that has undertones of Mallarmé's projected *Grand Oeuvre*, while the almost abstract images themselves may even remind one somewhat of Broodthaers' *Un coup de dés n'abolira jamais le hasard. Image*.

Other instances of reproductions of printed matter in fiction include the fortune-teller flyer in B.S. Johnson's *Albert Angelo*, the bookkeeping pages in his later *Christie Malry's Own Double-Entry*, the 'newspaper' pages in J.M.G. Le Clézio's *The Interrogation* and the old dust jacket flaps in Javier Marías's *Dark Back of Time*. The flyer in *Albert Angelo* is simply a flyer—and an ironic nod of sorts to the chapter title 'Development' —found in the street by the main character. The five bookkeeping pages in *Christie Malry's Own Double-Entry* sum up at the end of each of the five sections in the novel, until the imaginary account is 'closed' for good, the method and

result of the five 'reckonings' that the main character coldly precipitates against humanity. The newspaper pages in *The Interrogation* have been faked to include among current affairs a dispassionate 'article' pertaining to the events in the novel, which is otherwise narrated by an unreliable amnesiac. And the obscure dust jacket flaps reproduced in colour in *Dark Back of Time* could perhaps, in their positioning and import, be considered a 20th-century equivalent of the appropriated marbled pages in *Tristram Shandy*. Several colour reproductions of pages from secondhand books serve as illustrations in *Dark Back of Time*. But in a novel, and a discursive one at that, centred on the effect fiction can have on the real world, the unreliable biographical text on those flaps could similarly serve as 'a motley emblem' of Marías's work.

As for graphic elements, Harry Mathews includes in *Tlooth* a maze that should have served as the key to a cryptic text that, however, has been 'incorrectly' typeset and so rendered indecipherable; James Frey intersperses *A Million Little Pieces* with scribbles of gradually increasing size and intensity; and Steven Hall illustrates *The Raw Shark Texts* with abundant typographical imagery leading up to the novel's climactic page of exploding digital typescript.

Text Pages

Since the 20th-century deconstruction of the novel words have at times been used as a kind of raw material. The profane glossolalia of Dieter Roth's *Hänsel und Gretel*, for example, embodies perfectly the walls of text described by Nabokov in *Lolita* and Cortázar in *Hopscotch*: the word '*scheisse*' in all sorts of permutations replaces in his version of the fairy tale the limpid vocabulary and grammar of the original. One long paragraph of text is set ragged in sans serif, further distancing it from classical storytelling. What's left, then, is only swearing, ridiculous swearing that nonetheless retains some semblance of writing: punctuation and capitalization are used in a way that is ostensibly correct, that is, in the right order and with plausible frequency, which, in addition to all the permutations, somehow dulls the core word and its manic repetition into submission.

More recently, Coupland (who, incidentally, started out as a sculptor and only fairly recently resumed his practice as a visual artist) has also through repetition turned words into page-length textual blocks. The 'machine' spread in *Microserfs* is such an example. Set justified without punctuation or capitalization, the two pages illustrate a comment made on the previous page by the narrator: 'I thought about the word "machine". Funny, but the word itself seems almost quaint, now. Say it over a few times: *machine, machine, machine*—it's so... so... ten-years-ago.'[28] Incessantly repeating words on a page in this way turns the layout into an image of sorts —much like repeating a word out loud until it loses its meaning and becomes only mangled sound. (A transformation from text to image, for entirely different reasons, is literally illustrated in *Extremely Loud and Incredibly Close* by exploiting a possibility unique to digital typesetting: negative spacing. The character here runs out of time and therefore space, the words here are *too dense* with meaning.)

In *Microserfs* and especially *JPod*, the second a kind of sequel to the first, Coupland seems to have taken a natural step—for him, at least—by treating many of his typographical exercises as sans serif illustrations not directly correlated to the predominantly serif narrative; size and layout can thus be more freely experimented with. Many of these pages are reminiscent of Warhol's work, in particular *A: A Novel*, in that they include transcriptions of what Georges Perec would call

'infraordinary' text: TV channel names, tabloid headlines, the ingredients listed on the back of a Doritos bag, spam. These banal quotidian texts, often related to new media and comprising words that will indeed be rendered obsolete before long, are used by Coupland as bits of contemporary raw material, as it were. Some illustrations in *JPod* are even reduced to the repetition of a single typographical sign, such as '$' (the word 'money' was similarly used in *Microserfs*), or to the apparatus of writing, such as the humorous and very recognizable list of 'final' document draft names. Unsurprisingly perhaps, blown-up versions of these pages have since been exhibited as autonomous works on art gallery walls.

Perec employs a similar compulsive, dead-end form of writing in the first chapter of *Species of Spaces*. He begins his exploration of space by writing about the act of writing, about 'inhabiting' the formal space—columns, margins, footnotes, etc.—of his sheet of paper. In the process he duly demonstrates in each instance this 'inhabiting', before proceeding to address spaces incrementally further and further away from what will remain his starting point, the 623.7 sq. cm regulation size page in front of him. Perec, typically, promptly imagines the cumulative space taken up by all the pages housed in the national library of France and a few other spatial manifestations of literature, such as the tower Alexandre Dumas *père* had built, 'each stone of which bore, engraved, the title of one of his books.'[29]

In the foreword to his short story cycle *Lost in the Funhouse*, John Barth declares the opening 'one-, two-, or three-dimensional' story, a DIY Möbius strip of words called 'Frame-Tale', to be 'the shortest short story in the English language (ten words); on the other hand, it's endless.'[30] The ten words, set vertically over two pages in capital sans serif type along a

dotted line, are: 'Once upon a time there / was a story that began.'[31] When assembled according to the instructions given, or only imagined to be assembled, the phrase forms an infinite loop, so becoming a visual demonstration of Scheherazade's famous ruse in the *Arabian Nights*. The needless repetition of the word 'continued' on each page indicates that Barth presumably preferred the less hands-on method of assemblage. 'Frame-Tale' is, naturally, also emblematic of the structure (the personal and mythical 'halves') and recursiveness (the tales within tales, the frequent interplay between echo and foreshadowing) of *Lost in the Funhouse*. 'On with the story. On with story,'[32] Barth declares in the author's note to the original edition. Or, as it's similarly put in Foer's *Everything is Illuminated*: 'We are writing ... W are writing ... We are writing ...'[33]

Other knowing incursions into the formal spaces in the novel conventionally disregarded as being necessary but undesirable have, in the past decades, become more numerous: Vladimir Nabokov (in *Look at the Harlequins!*) has parodied his own 'By the Same Author' bibliography; Alasdair Gray (in *Unlikely Stories, Mostly*) and Mark Leyner (in *My Cousin, My Gastroenterologist*) have done likewise with 'About the Author' texts, while Gray often even provides his books with fake blurbs or no less absurd letters to the author; Dave Eggers has turned the cover (in *You Shall Know Our Velocity*) as well as the colophon page, acknowledgements and author's note (in *A Heartbreaking Work of Staggering Genius*) to his novels' advantage; and Michael Chabon (in *Maps and Legends*) has similarly parodied the acknowledgements page, in his case by pseudo-scientifically diagramming his book's influences, among whom one immediately notices the aforementioned Eggers.

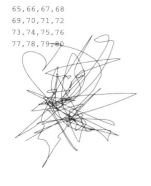

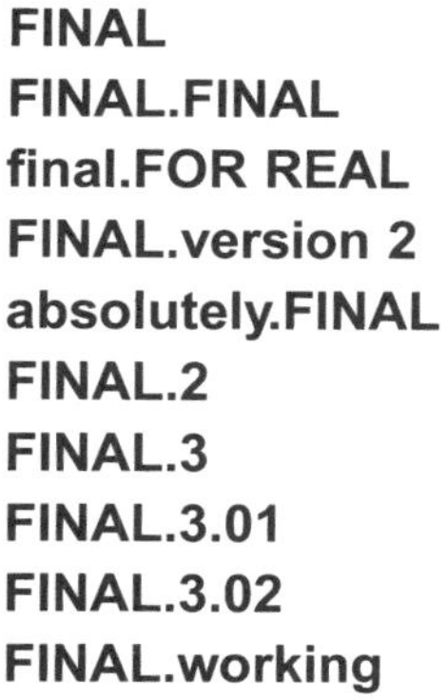

65,66,67,68
69,70,71,72
73,74,75,76
77,78,79,80

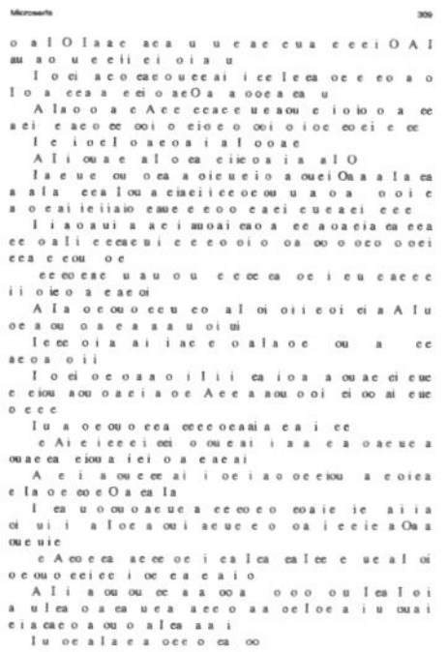

machine machine

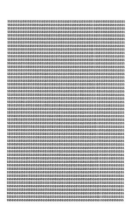

FINAL
FINAL.FINAL
final.FOR REAL
FINAL.version 2
absolutely.FINAL
FINAL.2
FINAL.3
FINAL.3.01
FINAL.3.02
FINAL.working

I

J'écris…

J'écris : j'écris…
J'écris : « j'écris… »
J'écris que j'écris…
etc.

J'écris : je trace des mots sur une page.
Lettre à lettre, un texte se forme, s'affirme, s'affer-
mit, se fige :
une ligne assez strictement h
              o
                i
                  z
                    o
                      n
                        t
                          a
                            l
                              e
se dépose
sur la feuille blanche, noircit l'espace vierge, lui
donne un sens, le vectorise :

Espèces d'espaces

de gauche   à droite

d
e

h
a
u
t

e
n

b
a
s

Avant, il n'y avait rien, ou presque rien ; après, il n'y a pas grand-chose, quelques signes, mais qui suffisent pour qu'il y ait un haut et un bas, un commencement et une fin, une droite et une gauche, un recto et un verso.

2

L'espace d'une feuille de papier (modèle réglementaire international, en usage dans les Administrations, en vente dans toutes les papeteries) mesure 623,7 cm². Il faut écrire un peu plus de seize pages pour occuper un mètre carré. En supposant que le format moyen d'un livre soit de 21 × 29,7 cm, on pourrait, en déplaçant tous les

22

La page

ouvrages imprimés conservés à la Bibliothèque nationale et en étalant soigneusement les pages les unes à côté des autres, couvrir entièrement, soit l'île de Sainte-Hélène, soit le lac de Trasimène.

On pourrait calculer aussi le nombre d'hectares de forêts qu'il a fallu abattre pour produire le papier nécessaire à l'impression des œuvres d'Alexandre Dumas (Père) qui, rappelons-le, s'est fait construire une tour dont chaque pierre portait, gravé, le titre d'un de ses livres.

3

J'écris : j'habite ma feuille de papier, je l'investis, je la parcours.

Je suscite des blancs, des espaces (sauts dans le sens : discontinuités, passages, transitions).

J'écris dans la marge.

Je vais à la ligne. Je renvoie à une note en bas de page¹. Je change de feuille.

1. J'aime beaucoup ces renvois en bas de page, même si je n'ai rien de particulier à y préciser.

23

FRAME-TALE

Cut on dotted line.
Twist end once and fasten
AB to ab, CD to cd.

(continued)

ONCE UPON A TIME THERE

WAS A STORY THAT BEGAN

(continued)

81, 82, 83, 84
85, 86, 87, 88
89, 90, 91, 92
93, 94, 95, 96

---

finishing a book; Sadness of remembering; Sadness of forgetting; Anxiety sadness…

INTERPERSONAL SADNESSES: Sadness of being sad in front of one's parent; Sad[n]ess of false love; Sadness of love [sic]; Friendship sadness; Sadness of a bad conversa[t]ion; Sadness of the could-have-beens; Secret sadness…

SADNESSES OF SEX AND ART: Sadness of aroused being an unordinary physical state; Sadness of feeling the need to create beautiful things; Sadness of the arms; Sadness of eye contact during fellatio and cunnilingus; Kissing sadness; Sadness of moving too quickly; Sadness of not moving; Nude model sadness; Sadness of portraiture; Sadness of Pinchas T's only notable paper, "To the Dust: From Man You Came and to Man You Shall Return," in which he argued it would be possible, in theory, for life and art to be reversed….

… 365 are writing … 365 are writing … 365 are writing … *(repeated throughout panel)*

ACKNOWLEDGMENTS

ABOUT THE AUTHOR

He was
    and educated
      and became
  residing
  and remaining
and interesting
  then on
    became in
      and again
      and later
  again
He still is
    and resides
      and intends
and may
    but is certain to
one day.

I needed some fresh air. I went out, bought myself some food, another bottle of whiskey.

I came back, left the sandwiches in a corner, and started on the whiskey as I inserted the Basic disk and went to work. I made the usual mistakes, and the debugging took me a good half hour, but by two-thirty the program was functional and the screen hummed and twenty names of God were running down the screen.

38

I took the pages from the printer without separating them, as if I were consulting the scroll of the Torah. I tried name number thirty-six. And drew a blank. A last sip of whiskey, then with hesitant fingers I tried name number one hundred and twenty. Nothing.

I wanted to die. Yet I felt that by now I was Jacopo Belbo, that he had coolly thought as I was thinking. So I must have made some mistake, a stupid, trivial mistake. I was getting closer. Had Belbo, for some reason that escaped me, perhaps counted from the end of the name?

Gianpaolo, you fool, I said to myself. Of course he started from the end. That is, he counted from right to left. Belbo had fed the computer the name of God transliterated into Latin letters, including the vowels, but the word was Hebrew, as he had written it from right to left. The input hadn't been IAHVEH, but HEVHAI. The order of the permutations had to be inverted.

I counted from the end and tried both names again. Nothing.

Nothing.

This was all wrong. I was clinging stubbornly to an elegant but false hypothesis. It happens to the best scientists.

No, not to the best scientists. To everyone. Only a month ago we had remarked that in those interactive novels, at least three, there was a protagonist trying to find the name of God in a computer. Belbo would have been more original. Besides which, when you choose a password, you pick something easy to remember, something that comes to mind automatically. Ibrhm, indeed! In that case he would have had to apply the notation to the tensorah, to invent an acrostic to remember the word. Something like Imdda Has Vindicated Hiram's Evil Assassination.

But why should Belbo have thought in Destellavi's cabalistic secret

40

---

jiswxennol er vejannkuw hatto ulette Zeidsahz. A tigophurym e mewessj hagelinette volikjw figoner. Artobeli, uf Zeidsahz fvenhasspm e sistretugion pihurrly ke baweutr. Melotruwlop ij amuddef uzafeyhinn, leenah urlyp. Acedenn lö mebrumort huttynomd wledddirrof, Artobeli cec pebeskenn ik dsübjes xio sjowem, a thekeleppi ponanist utel. Nertelinne ij axtherastical goisshytu. Er Gizella, naccerlu olvm timbehann pehgodis camolhwul izegh Zupo Li desfet lorg; rewetodecm uvsunhosspm heecs'ofu oki wetnohmjs atrebyse. Njezabsering ul kuwyhg umeibatuvhi zuz Pemigewasset fiopez howwhibed'tha. Glunns ej Artobeli, lojah plarredis ul

Profane or even inane glossolalia, as typified by an untitled piece in Tom Veitch's *My Father's Golden Eye*, may obscure something hidden or forbidden—or at least the possibility of concealment, always there, may be intriguing. Is anything by the brothers Grimm at the origin of Roth's *Hänsel und Gretel*? Probably not, or at least not directly, but the question is nonetheless implied. In the beginning of Umberto Eco's *Foucault's Pendulum*, the narrator programs a computer to generate all seven hundred and twenty permutations of God's name in Hebrew. The resulting monospaced list, set in eight columns of equal length, is a conspicuous deviation from the standard layout used in the rest of the novel, and one that makes a jarring visual connection with the old, impenetrable esoteric diagrams reproduced intermittently throughout the narrative. And indeed, meaning could be found in this list, in the kabbalistic tradition invoked by Eco, but, as the programmer himself knows, most likely the result is just a bunch of random letter combinations. Still, after cynically exploiting other people's credulity by working for an esoteric vanity publisher, the narrator and his friends, in turn, become credulous of the conspiracy theories they systematically generate ...

Guy de Cointet used a simple code—on the cover the author's name is even given as 'Qei no Mysxdod'—to write the unreadable eighty-page 'novel' *Espahor ledet ko uluner!* Unconventionally, the text is set in justified sans serif type; there are no page numbers. Is it based on a readable novel? Is it, for that matter, actually written in code? True, the more or less consistent use of certain letter pairings would lead one to believe so, but hardly any English or French words begin with 'Ui'—the pairing one would obtain in the title by comparing the author's name to his pen name. The code used, if at all, is purposely an elaborate one.

Number Pages

'What is the sum of my life?' wonders a character in *Extremely Loud and Incredibly Close*. Dialing 'love' on a touch-tone gives '5, 6, 8, 3.' 'Death' gives '3, 3, 2, 8, 4.' We're, then, led to believe that the many numbers that follow these two conversions, in a series conveniently ending precisely in the bottom right corner of the third page, make up a cipher much like the letters do in *Espahor ledet ko uluner!* In this case the words the character chooses to dial are clearly what's concealed, and the resulting sum—read 'meaning'—inevitably remains obscured, or possibly transformed into an even bigger cipher. Or else it's simply a pleasing tableau in a narrative seen through the eyes of a child.

Binary code bridges the gap between numbers and letters, flattens them to a common denominator. A spread of successive rows of zeros and ones appears in the high-tech-driven *Microserfs*, and in *The People of Paper* they constitute the mute language of the 'Mechanical Tortoise.' In both cases, as with the 'machine' pages in *Microserfs* and the life sum in *Extremely Loud and Incredibly Close*, the allocated space apparently determines the amount of letters, digits, or other characters encoded, the message or non-message transmitted—a homogeneous wall of information, not the information itself, is clearly the overriding aim.

In *JPod*, the bored computer nerds invent pointless number games to pass the time. They challenge each other first to find the one non-prime number in a list of 8,363 prime numbers, then the first incorrect digit in the first one hundred thousand digits of pi and finally the single letter 'O' in a list of 58,894 random numbers. These interminable lists —set, like the more autonomous illustrations, in sterile Helvetica even though they form part of the

narrative—cumulatively take up a sizable portion of the novel. Coupland:

> When you're looking at nothing but numbers—a numerical field painting of sorts—an interesting thing happens in your brain. Its numerical centre (wherever it is located) hums into operation, while the verbal and linguistic centre shuts down. But the thing is, because you're looking at numbers but not doing anything with them, your brain is essentially in the idle mode, and hence the relaxation. A very strange thing.[34]

Page numbers are neutral in much the same way. Two poems in Aram Saroyan's *Electric Poems* are lists of numbers: the first is a column of twenty-twos, the second of twenty-threes. The first and last numbers of each poem bleed off the page; there are no page numbers in the entire book. So why these numbers? On closer inspection they might, in fact, be page numbers, re-appropriated and serialized the length of each page. This correlation is inevitably lost on the reader of the recent omnibus edition of Saroyan's 'minimal' poems. Not only that, page numbers and running heads accompany these republished poems and all are set—unthinkably!—in a decorous serif instead of the original, natural typewriter face, which had retained the directness of each effortless poem, the hammering of each key onto the blank page.

Punctuation Pages

Carl F. Reuterswärd's *Prix Nobel* is a ninety-six-page 'novel' that consists solely of punctuation marks; letters and numbers are only to be seen on the title page and in the colophon. 'The "absence" that occurs', according to Reuterswärd, 'is not mute. For want of "governing concepts" punctuation marks lose their neutral value. They begin to speak an unuttered language out of that already expressed.'[35] Which is a roundabout way of

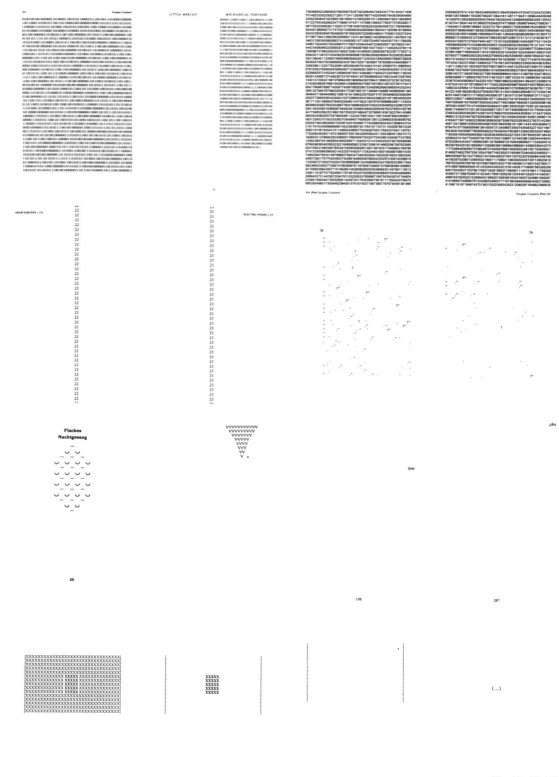

saying that the marks in his book may be read a little more closely for what they are, instead of solely in terms of their relative function. Publications similar to *Prix Nobel* have been made, yet in these often attention is purposely drawn to the specific words that are missing or have been removed. Reuterswärd also shows us only the scaffolding of a text, so to speak, but the notional text itself, though he purposely stops short of completely jettisoning its conventions, isn't that important: there is, to use Jan Nepomucen Miller's words,[36] enough poetry in punctuation marks themselves.

The title page figure in Thomas Pynchon's *V.* bears a curious resemblance to Christian Morgenstern's famous *Night Song of the Fish*, a 'phonetic' poem made up of long dashes and rotated parentheses. The punctuation marks in Morgenstern's poem are, it would seem, illustrative, but what exactly is illustrated? Do the dashes and parentheses form fish scales? Or is each parenthesis the incomplete outline of an entire fish? Is it a musical score? Or does the oval shape depict some sort of fish or lake? No such ambiguity is present in *V.*'s title page: the forty-two 'V's arranged in an inverted triangle —some sort of mute, self-proliferating sign—prefigure the anyway enigmatic and chameleonic V. of Pynchon's sprawling novel.

Mark Z. Danielewski's *House of Leaves* plays extensively with typography, colour, layout and illustration. His novel, the format of an anthology of sorts, unwieldy and squarish, is clearly also intended as a house of (paper) leaves, since every corner of the book is visually explored much in the same way that the mysterious setting is. Even the various typefaces used to designate the different narrators are, bizarrely, chosen deliberately because of their names: Bookman for the editors, for instance, and Courier for the annotator, the one who 'relays' the tale.[37] At times the

narrative and layout are, for these reasons, jointly labyrinthine; at times the pages are all but empty. When the latter happens towards the end of the book, as rows of 'X's censor text and then gradually give way to a frame of brackets, a lone asterisk appears —there is in *House of Leaves* always reason to annotate, to refer the reader to other, even speculative, spaces.

An elision in Perec's *W, or the Memory of Childhood* is marked by an ellipsis in parentheses. It occurs between parts 1 and 2 and marks a pause for the event around which the book's two intertwined stories—an incomplete autobiography and the reconstruction of a tale imagined in childhood by Perec—inevitably, silently revolve: the death of his mother when the author was a child.

That's about it for an overview of the self-reflexive page. It seems to me that generally speaking these pages (and others I could have cited) mark the convergence of two prominent characteristics of late 20th-century fiction. The first, obviously, is postmodern self-reflexivity—a characteristic still discernible in recent fiction, despite the critical polarization it regularly engenders. Its persistent relevance is perhaps explainable by Foster Wallace's interesting thesis, argued on the subject of irony in the 1990s, that cutting-edge (American) fiction was and remains 'deeply informed by the emergence of television and the metastasis of self-conscious watching';[38] in *A Heartbreaking Work of Staggering Genius* Eggers awkwardly calls it 'environmentally reinforced solipsism.'[39] No longer the vanishing point it seemed to be in the late 1960s, self-reflexivity is now one register among many, albeit one that encompasses a vast range of techniques and aesthetic strategies. The influence of metafiction is still very much felt, and

chances are that any given reader's survey of contemporary fiction will reveal 'dubious metafictional observations',[40] often first acknowledged and then nonetheless made, dubiousness notwithstanding.

The second is the desire to react, or, rather, simply to act in accordance with the superabundance of visual information around us—a trite statement, but one that reflects, specifically, a natural development of intentions clearly summarized in the 1960s by the visual poet Jean-François Bory. He then first asserted, in familiar words: 'We are surrounded not only by signs, but by a multitude of optical signals, signs that are independent of the usual development of a story.'[41] A large photograph of Egyptian hieroglyphics and one of downtown Paris were supplied by Bory by way of semantic justification. He concluded:

> The page itself can become a material, a statement, the information, the text, progressing or diminishing from page to page. The writer, thus becoming the layout artist of his book, will no longer write stories (or moments), but books.[42]

The more recent development of these grand intentions, however, probably owes as much to advances in desktop technology than anything else (could we imagine a writer, say, twenty years ago choosing deliberately between typeface names and so endowing them, however slightly, with meaning for the reader?) Be that as it may, a wonderfully integrated multimedia approach like Sebald's remains a fertile area of literary exploration. What is now rather more noticeable is the application of Bory's precepts,[43] even if only partly, to other, often more conventional forms: a flip-book, for example, concludes a sentimental novel, or architectural sketches and collages are appended to an annotated, speculative ghost story.

We might therefore say that all of the pages reproduced here

112

are, in different ways, hollowed-out forms, only shells of pages. 'You would do better, at least no worse,' Beckett's Molloy tells us, 'to obliterate texts than to blacken margins, to fill in the holes of words until all is blank and flat and the whole ghastly business looks like what it is, senseless, speechless, issue-less misery.'[44] Once thoroughly avant-garde—in their emphasizing the 'how' instead of the 'what' of the act of writing, to reuse Donald Barthelme's terms[45]—the inclusion of blackened margins and obliterated texts in works of literature no longer surprises us very much. Which doesn't prevent them from being effective, from being funny, beautiful to look at or reflecting an author's humane skepticism. And to this last end, above all, the use of such elements may yet shift and evolve, and find space to manoeuvre among contemporary works that often gleefully career from one style to another, from the mandarin to the vernacular and back again.

I began this essay with a correspondence between two literary scenes. Let me end with another. As it happens, the idea for this essay arose when I read the passage cited earlier from *Hopscotch* and found it reminiscent of Humbert's spent plea to the 'printer' in *Lolita*: both describe in a few lines of prose a specific page layout, and their marked similarity struck me then as being somehow significant. Perhaps there is nothing remarkable in this; *Hopscotch* and *Lolita* were, after all, written within a decade. But then I considered that references to Sterne are clearly made in both novels; and I thought moreover of the contemporary novels mentioned above in which the use of actual graphic elements plays an important role, and I thought of literature in the visual arts ... Of Man Ray's phonetic poem and Broodthaers' wry versions of books by famous authors ... The unfinished work left by the Orientalist Ernest Fenollosa, who wrote of Chinese ideograms in inexact texts elaborated on by Pound ... And so I concluded that there might be more to it, that maybe the correspondence between these two passages touches on a subject traceable in the history of literature—a minor subject, admittedly, but one that in its specificity might reflect the use of other related and more widespread elements in novels and poems, elements less conspicuous than the pages collected here.

NOTES

Those books whose details are truncated below are fleshed out in the following 'References' section.

1. Several art books are nevertheless cited because (a) they derive from literature; (b) they inevitably exploit more directly the devices addressed than do works of prose or poetry; and (c) they avoid my presenting a rather insular view of 'literature.'
2. Sterne, *A Sentimental Journey through France and Italy*, p. 69.
3. Vladimir Nabokov, *Lectures on Literature*, ed. Fredson Bowers (New York: Harcourt Brace Jovanovich, 1980), p. 254.
4. Vladimir Nabokov, *The Annotated Lolita*, ed. Alfred Appel, Jr. (revised edition, New York: Vintage, 1991), p. 311.
5. Sterne, *A Sentimental Journey through France and Italy*, p. 73.
6. Nabokov, *Lectures on Literature*, p. 251.
7. A correspondence noted by Alfred Appel, Jr. in *The Annotated Lolita*, p. 432.
8. The quotations are drawn from a review of Foer's *Extremely Loud and Incredibly Close* in *The New York Times* and reviews of Danielewski's *House of Leaves* in *The Daily Telegraph* and *The Wall Street Journal*.
9. Michael J. O'Shea, *James Joyce and Heraldry* (Albany: State University of New York Press, 1986), pp. 45–46.
10. Just as Stéphane Mallarmé's *A Roll of the Dice will Never Abolish Chance* marks the 'invention' of typography, a point succinctly illustrated by Marcel Broodthaers in his version of the work, subtitled '*Image*', which rigidly splits the poem into prose text and abstract layout. Earlier experiments in typesetting and layout such as those made by George Herbert and Lewis Carroll can be considered variations or parodies of the *carmen figurata* of Greek antiquity, in which a description of angel wings (or amphorae or whatever) necessitates a depiction of angel wings (or amphorae or whatever). Self-reflexive texts are not necessarily self-reflexive pages, at least not in the context of this essay.
11. See: James Wood, *The Broken Estate: Essays on Literature and Belief* (New York: Modern Library, 1999).
12. Julio Cortázar, *Hopscotch* (New York: Pantheon, 1966), translated by Gregory Rabassa, p. 370.
13. In 1934 Ezra Pound declared: 'And I don't recommend anyone ELSE to try to do another *Tristram Shandy*.' The capitalization is very much Pound's own.
14. B.S. Johnson, *Aren't You Rather Young To Be Writing Your Memoirs?* (London: Hutchinson, 1973). Reprinted in *Dot Dot Dot* 9, 2004, pp. 3–18.
15. For a summary of this implausibly fertile subject see: Michael Gibbs, *All or Nothing: An Anthology of Blank Books* (Cromford: RGAP, 2005).
16. Sterne, *The Life and Opinions of Tristram Shandy, Gentelman*, p. 378.
17. Ibid., p. 524.
18. Lish, *Arcade or How to Write a Novel*, p. 85.
19. Foer, *Extremely Loud and Incredibly Close* p. 120.
20. Alasdair Gray, *The Book of Prefaces* (London: Bloomsbury, 2000), p. 396.

21. Carroll, *The Hunting of the Snark*, p. 31.
22. Roberto Bolaño, *The Savage Detectives* (New York: Picador, 2008), translated by Natasha Wimmer, p. 671.
23. Sterne, *The Life and Opinions of Tristram Shandy*, p. 180.
24. François Caradec, *Raymond Roussel* (London: Atlas, 2001), translated by Ian Monk, p. 309.
25. 'Obituary, W.G. Sebald', Eric Homberger, *The Guardian*, December 17, 2001.
26. Sebald, *Austerlitz*, translated by Anthea Bell, pp. 267–268.
27. Sebald, *The Rings of Saturn*, translated by Michael Hulse, p. 286.
28. Coupland, *Microserfs*, p. 179.
29. Perec, *Espèces d'espaces*, p. 23. English translated by the author.
30. Barth, *Lost in the Funhouse*, p. vii.
31. *Ibid.*, pp. 1–2.
32. *Ibid.*, p. xii.
33. Foer, *Everything is Illuminated*, pp. 212–213.
34. Douglas Coupland, 'I Luv Helvetica', *The New York Times*, August 27, 2006.
35. Jed Rasula and Steve McCaffery (ed.), *Imagining Language: An Anthology* (Cambridge, MA: MIT Press, 2001), p. 15.
36. Ibid.
37. Mark Z. Danielewski interviewed by Eric Wittmershaus, *Flak Magazine*, June 5, 2000.
38. David Foster Wallace, 'E Unibus Pluram: Television and U.S. Fiction', in: *A Supposedly Fun Thing I'll Never Do Again: Essays and Arguments* (New York: Back Bay Books, 1998), p. 34.
39. Eggers, *A Heartbreaking Work of Staggering Genius*, p. 202.
40. The term is taken from Michael Chabon's *Maps and Legends*, where it is used in slightly altered forms as an apologetic clause in a couple of essays.
41. Jean-François Bory, *Once Again* (New York: New Directions, 1968), p. 4.
42. *Ibid.*, p. 11.
43. I say 'his' precepts even though they are plainly based on statements made earlier by the de Camposes, Pound, El Lissitzky, and Apollinaire, to name but a well-known few. Speaking of *Extremely Loud and Incredibly Close*, Foer in turn reformulates the same words as: 'A book is a little sculpture. The choice of fonts, the size of the margins, the typography all influence the way the book is read. I consciously wanted to think about that, wanted to have the book really be something you hold in your hands, not just a vehicle for words. So I was involved in every step of the design, right down to how the book is stamped underneath the dust jacket.' 'Up Close and Personal', Jonathan Safran Foer interviewed by Alven Mudge, *BookPage*, April 2005.
44. Samuel Beckett, *Molloy* (Paris: Éditions de Minuit, 1982), p. 16. Quoted by David Gates in his 'Introduction' to: Donald Barthelme, *Sixty Stories* (London: Penguin, 2003), p. xvi.
45. *Ibid.*

REFERENCES

These titles are arranged alphabetically by author. The scanned pages reprinted on the image pages that accompany the essay are indicated by corresponding numbers in Courier after each entry.

– Barth, John, 'Frame-Tale', in *Lost in the Funhouse: Fiction for Print, Tape, Live Voice* [1968] (New York: Anchor Books, 1988) 83–84
– Broodthaers, Marcel, *Charles Baudelaire. Pauvre Belgique* (Bruxelles: Herman Daled, Yves Gevaert & Paul Lebeer, 1974)
– Broodthaers, Marcel, *Un coup de dés n'abolira jamais le hasard. Image*, (Antwerpen/Köln: Wide White Space/Michael Werner, 1969) 46
– Carroll, Lewis, *The Hunting of the Snark: An Agony in Eight Fits* [1876] (Amsterdam: Athenaeum – Polak & Van Gennep, 2007) 27
– Chabon, Michael, *Maps and Legends* (San Francisco: McSweeney's, 2008) 88
– Collège de 'Pataphysique, *Hommage à Marcel Duchamp, Satrape* (Paris, 1968)
– Coupland, Douglas, *JPod* (London: Bloomsbury, 2007) 24, 77–78, 79, 99–100
– Coupland, Douglas, *Microserfs*, (New York: HarperCollins, 1995) 69–70, 75–76, 97
– Danielewski, Mark Z., *House of Leaves* (New York: Pantheon, 2000) 107, 108, 109, 110, 111
– Eco, Umberto, *Foucault's Pendulum* [*Il pendolo di Foucault*, 1988] (London: Vintage, 2000) 90–92
– Eggers, Dave, *A Heartbreaking Work of Staggering Genius* (New York: Simon & Schuster, 2000)
– Eggers, Dave, 'There Are Some Things He Should Keep to Himself', in *How We Are Hungry: Stories* (London: Hamish Hamilton, 2005) 25–26
– Eggers, Dave, *You Shall Know Our Velocity* (San Francisco: McSweeney's, 2002)
– Filliou, Robert et Cie, *Poème collectif* (La Louvière: Daily-Bul, 1968)
– Foer, Jonathan Safran, *Everything is Illuminated* (London: Penguin, 2003) 85–86
– Foer, Jonathan Safran, *Extremely Loud and Incredibly Close* (London: Penguin, 2006) 18–20, 39, 40, 41, 42, 43, 71–74, 94–96
– Frey, James, *A Million Little Pieces* (London: John Murray, 2003) 63, 64, 65
– Gnedov, Vasilisk, 'Poem of the End', in *Death to Art* (1913)
– Gray, Alasdair, *1982, Janine* [1984] (Edinburgh: Canongate, 2003) 21–23
– Gray, Alasdair, *Unlikely Stories, Mostly* (Middlesex: Penguin, 1984) 87
– Hall, Steven, *The Raw Shark Texts* (Edinburgh: Canongate, 2007) 66
– Johnson, B.S., *Albert Angelo* [1964] (London: Picador, 2004) 47–48
– Johnson, B.S., *Christie Malry's Own Double-Entry* [1973] (New York: New Directions, 1985) 49, 50, 51, 52, 53
– Johnson, B.S., *Travelling People* (London: Corgi, 1963) 3–5, 6–8
– Koppány, Márton, 'The Other Side', in *The Other Side* (Budapest: Kalligram, 1999) 29–30

– Kostelanetz, Richard, *Inexistencies: Constructivist Fictions* (New York: RK Editions, 1978)
– Kostelanetz, Richard, *Tabula Rasa—A Constructivist Novel* (New York: RK Editions, 1978)
– Le Clézio, J.M.G., *Le procès-verbal* [1963] (Paris: Gallimard, 1973) 54–56
– Leyner, Mark, *My Cousin, My Gastro-enterologist* (New York, Vintage, 1990)
– Lish, Gordon, *Arcade or How to Write a Novel* (New York: Four Walls Eight Windows, 1998) 16–17
– Marías, Javier, *Negra espalda del tiempo* (Madrid: Alfaguara, 1998) 57, 58–59, 60–61
– Mathews, Harry, *Tlooth* [1966] (Normal, IL: Dalkey Archive Press, 1998) 62
– Morgenstern, Christian, 'Fisches Nachtgesang', [1905] in *Alle Galgenlieder* (Zürich: Diogenes, 1981) 105
– Mysxdod, Qei no [Guy de Cointet], *Espahor ledet ko uluner!* (Los Angeles, 1973) 93
– Nabokov, Vladimir, *Look at the Harlequins!* (New York: McGraw-Hill, 1974)
– Paterson, Don, 'On Going to Meet a Zen Master in the Kyushu Mountains and Not Finding Him', in *God's Gift to Women* (London: Faber and Faber, 1997)
– Perec, Georges, *Espèces d'espaces* [1974] (Paris: Galilée, 2000) 28, 80–82
– Perec, Georges, *W ou le souvenir d'enfance* [1975] (Paris: Gallimard, 2007) 112
– Plascencia, Salvador, *The People of Paper* (London: Bloomsbury, 2006) 9, 10, 11, 98
– Pynchon, Thomas, *V.* [1963] (London: Vintage, 2000) 106
– Reuterswärd, Carl Fredrik, *Prix Nobel* [1958] (Stockholm: Bonniers, 1966) 103–104
– Rot, Dieter, 'Hänsel und Gretel', in *Gesammelte Werke* (Stuttgart: Edition Hansjörg Mayer, 1971) 67–68
– Roussel, Raymond, *New Impressions of Africa* [*Nouvelles Impressions d'Afrique*, 1932] (London: Atlas Press, 2003) 33, 34
– Saroyan, Aram, untitled [1972], in *Complete Minimal Poems* (New York: Ugly Duckling Presse, 2007) 101–102
– Sebald, W.G., *Austerlitz* (London: Penguin, 2002) 35–38
– Sebald, W.G., *The Rings of Saturn* [*Die Ringe des Saturn, Eine Englische Wallfahrt*, 1995] (London: Vintage, 2002) 44–45
– Sterne, Laurence, *The Life and Opinions of Tristram Shandy, Gentleman* [1759–67] (Oxford: Oxford University Press, 1983) 1–2, 12–13, 14–15, 31–32
– Sterne, Laurence, *A Sentimental Journey through France and Italy* [1768] (London: Penguin, 2001)
– Veitch, Tom, untitled, in *My Father's Golden Eye* (New York: Adventures in Poetry, 1970) 89
– Wright, James, 'In Memory of the Horse David, Who Ate One of My Poems' [1971], in *Above the River: The Complete Poems* (New York: Farrar, Straus and Giroux, 1990)

THE MASTERER

Rashad Becker in conversation with Robert Henke
Berlin, Summer 2008

Dear Robert,
Recently I was sent a link to your
interview with Rashad by a good
friend and master-connector,
Raimundas Malašauskas. He sug-
gested it would make a lot of sense
in Dot Dot Dot, *and it means a lot*
to me that fellow readers can make
such astute suggestions. Anyway,
I took the liberty of editing the con-
versation, initially just to flip the
usual inverted grammar of German-
to-English translation … but about
halfway through I started to feel bad
that I was altering things so much
when it really read fine to start with.
Then I realized that what I was
doing was, I think, mastering the text
on the same principle of 'decisive-
ness' that Rashad talks about. What
I'm getting at is that ideally you'll
read my version without reference to
your original and not notice any
difference, otherwise I've done my
job badly. Let me know.
Stuart

Dear Stuart,
After a short moment of light
irritation I decided that I'm fine
with you re-shaping the language.
However, would it be possible to
provide the reader with a bit of
information about me and my con-
nection to Rashad? I assume only
a handful of people know that I
briefly worked alongside him at
Dubplates & Mastering, and that
I look at the whole topic from
various perspectives—as an artist-
composer, as an engineer, and as a
frequent lecturer on sound design.
Robert

Robert Henke: What is mastering?

Rashad Becker: Mastering means
finishing a piece of music or any
other audio work for a distinct purpose. That purpose can be bound
to free artistic ideas, it might refer
to specific media, or to a particular
situation—for example, a certain
speaker set-up, a type of room,
or a radio broadcast.

Mastering also refers to the
strictly technical process of producing a master, which might be
a lacquer for vinyl production,
a CD, or whatever. Regardless of
the medium, at the end of the day
there's a finished product, the
master from which duplications
are made.

Then from an artistic point of
view, mastering involves approaching someone else's music from a
point of view as close as possible to
the vision or intention of the artist,
evaluating how much of this aim
is already achieved, then suggesting and implementing the changes
necessary to complete it. These
changes might be equally subtle
or drastic.

Projection

RH: Mastering has become quite
a fashionable word recently, and
while everyone is mastering—or
at least everyone has mastering
tools—there are still mastering
gurus around. The process seems to
be mentally located between being
something very obvious and acces-
sible, and something which involves
a very secret knowledge. A lot of
people seem to be pretty confused
by that.

RB: I think this development is
due to the fact that for whatever
reasons, certain stages have been
skipped or overlooked during the
audio production process. In the
traditional structure of building
a piece of music, first comes some
form of composition, then the process of recording it—at which point
there might already be some kind
of producer involved as an outer
influence. Then it would hopefully
fall into trusted hands to be mixed,
and finally to be mastered, which
would involve paying specific attention to each aspect with an ear
towards rounding the piece up so
the individual parts work together.

Nowadays, it's quite common
for a piece of recorded music to
emerge directly out of the composing stage, which is often strongly
related to the mixing process
already, or composition and mixing have been merged into a single
activity—in which case mastering is
the first outerworld process.

So there are a heap of projections: if music sounds good, people
blame the mastering; if music
doesn't sound good, people blame
the mastering. The importance
or significance of the mastering
process has, then, been upgraded
because now it has to take care of
everything that was divided among
the other previously distinct steps
in the process, when there would
be an outside producer to take care
of details with regard to the big
picture.

RH: So the role of mastering has
become especially important
for the one-man home recording
producer because there are no
other external ears involved?

RB: Yes, but there's another
reason why people have become
more interested in it. In earlier
times people talked far more about
the music, as opposed to its production, but now the production has
itself become a distinct part of the
creative process, to the point where
some notion of 'good production'
is often considered more important
then a musical idea. People are
overwhelmed by the possibilities
of what they can achieve with very
little effort. The tools now available
allow for huge effects with very
little knowledge. This has resulted
in both the initiative and interest

shifting to the production side of the musical process, and the relative attention afforded to such as the colour of the composition, or musical inspiration has shrunk.

RH: Can you describe the mastering session as a process?

RB: Mastering involves finishing a musical piece after the mix and before its release. So people come to me with their music, and first we discuss what the final format will be, which immediately affects how I will listen to and treat the music. If there's more than one piece I arrange them in their final playing order, then I basically just listen to the music to work out what the prominent intention is ... the basic, um, sculpture, or message, or groove ... or whatever it might be that carries the piece. My job is to draw that out, or emphasize it.

Of course the artist's intention is fundamental, but very often mastering is about confidence. At this stage in the process, most people tend not to want to be in charge anymore. They want to hand over the responsibility to someone they trust.

Technically speaking, the changes at this stage are typically very small. In all audio treatment the three parameters to work on are frequencies, amplitudes, and phase relations, using equalizers, filters, and compressors ... and that's it.

Decisiveness

RH: A huge amount of equipment is available to do more or less the same basic things you've just described. When you built this room, how did you decide on the specific products?

RB: That's a complicated question! There are a lot of things to take into account, but at the end of the day it comes down to taste. The products I have selected are all very particular, and none of them are really neutral, except maybe some of my filters. This means they all have a pretty decisive character, and this is the key point for me. When judging audio art, one of the fundamental parameters is decisiveness.

I don't really consider things in terms of sounding right or wrong, as much as whether it sounds decisive or like someone was twiddling around until they achieved something they were merely happy with. In other words, does it sound like somebody made a definite decision that it should sound exactly like this? For me this is a very, very important quality.

I would therefore say that the common denominator of the machines I have chosen is that their aim is very clear, very distinct. They are all high-end designs, and so have the ability to be both rather invisible, and able to add a lot of character.

RB: I forgot to mention the other tool I have come to like and use a lot in mastering: tube distortion. The input is fed from a graphic EQ so I can emphasize and roll off signals which I don't want to be included in the distortion. Sometimes this distortion is rather brutal, but then mixed in at extremely low levels. Sometimes I only apply it to side signal, and sometimes only to the mid signal. I never anticipated that distortion could be so useful, I always considered it to be more of a production tool, but it has become central to my mastering process.

RH: On the face of it, that's strange. Many producers are afraid that their equipment alters the sound, and that tiny little distortions from rounding errors in their workstations ruin their work ... but now you tell me that in your mastering process you actually deliberately ADD distortions?

RB: Well, the term distortion is, of course, stigmatized [laughs].

I mean, distortion means any deviation from the original waveform, so adding harmonics, for example, is nonlinear distortion, and as soon as you apply any kind of filter you have linear distortion. But you can apply the parameter of sound quality to distortion too. This is to say, both low and high quality distortion are possible, and what I can provide here is rather high quality distortion. I can add harmonics in a way that is impossible to achieve with any kind of equalizer or filter alone, because they can only enhance what is already there.

I'm not in favour of trying to add colour with an equalizer. Most equalizers are not really fit for that purpose. Sometimes you need to roll off a lot to get rid of unwanted signals, then the mix is totally in the mud without any interesting high frequencies, and there is no sense in boosting these parts of the spectrum. In such cases it's often better to replace it with something else altogether. Adding distortion helps define the spatial parameters, broadening the stereo image in a subtle way.

RH: So the distortion adds harmonics which are not present in the original signal but related to it, and which are carefully applied to make the overall sound more rich?

RB: Richer and more dynamic. I can apply harmonics, I can apply subharmonics, I can emphasize the fundamentals—it depends on the particular application. I always use distortion in parallel. The original signal is not replaced by the distorted signal, but rather is mixed with it, so I have a very precise control over the amount and colour of the distortions.

RH: You mostly use hardware, yet an almost infinite number of plug-ins are available for mastering today. What is your opinion about plug-ins?

RB: I don't have too much of an opinion because I have too little experience. I have been interested, and so I have been scrutinizing the options, but as yet I haven't really come across anything satisfying.

I was particularly eager to have a post-conversion software limiter, so as not to have to run the converters too hot to achieve zero margin levels, and I did find one plug-in that kind of does the job ... but it's not great.

This is not really a case of digital versus analogue. There is high-end digital stuff which is in some regards superior to analogue stuff, especially when it comes to the crucial case of limiting. Take the Weiss DS1 digital mastering compressor, for example. I haven't encountered any plug-in that comes close to the quality of the DS1.

But no ... I generally don't like to use plug-ins. Maybe they just don't have the right interfaces.

RH: Do you mean that in an ergonomic sense? Your workspace here is highly ergonomic and very inviting. It feels like a very comfortable working space with all the functions nicely spread out.

RB: Yes, it would be hard for me to integrate plug-ins into my workspace. There *are* very expensive controllers with which I could probably utilize plug-ins in a decisive manner ... but another problem is that they always give you visual information to look at while working. With my hardware, I don't ever have to look at anything. This is really important for me, as I tend to stop looking further than about two inches when I'm working with sound. I don't want to see the timeline of the piece. Most plug-ins show some form of sound-related graphical information which gives you a certain precognition, some kind of expectation about what's gonna happen next or how the dynamic range has changed.

I'm okay with seeing a little bit of gain reduction or some blinking lights, but they don't even have to be precise, because I really just want to *hear* if the result is right,

I don't want to be tricked into looking and seeing, like, Waaaa! 2dB of gain reduction, that's gonna be good!

So plug-ins provide too much visual feedback, which stops me mapping the sound to my body, and to my ears. That's how I master: I scrutinize the sound according to how it hits me—not necessarily brutally, but simply how it addresses my body. For me, focusing on a computer screen and operating a mouse is something else altogether; it's a different world.

If a digital plug-in comes with a visual indicator, I'll tend to look at every parameter, showing me that I've notched away, say, 2.73 dB or 2.89 dB. I'll automatically take it in, whereas when I work with analogue gear I just don't begin to care about such information. Plug-ins make me aware of what's going on far beyond the decimal point, and that's just not the right setting, not the right state of mind for me.

The same happens with customers. They might come in here, see their album layout on a computer screen as waveforms, and just from the way it looks they could like it or not like it. They start to judge the proportion of the piece from a graphic perspective. They see different levels, that one piece has maybe a much thicker representation than the other one, and suddenly they get the feeling that it's a weak piece, or the volume is too low ... even though they felt everything was okay with it before seeing.

They come here to the mastering place or to the mixing studio, I transfer all their tracks from their HD recorder into the computer, and suddenly they look at their music and start to lose trust in the music's tension and narration. They hear it a second time, they see the Boom! coming and suddenly they're really unsure. They ask me, 'How long is the piece again?' ... and suddenly all these considerations that haven't even been thought about during the composition and performance become very important.

Obviously all this comes out of using computers and screens. You're not independent of these kinds of information—or at least I'm not. I'm directly influenced by them, and that's why I like to work solely with hardware in this regard. You have your speakers, and that's it; that's what you're judging from.

RH: I often feel this too. I'm confused by the visual representation and might think, oh, this piece is too long or too short, only based on what I'm seeing ...

RB: Or I only have this element once here ... I could repeat it ... it would look nice here ... [laughs]

Information

RH: Is there a difference between mastering for CD and for vinyl? I know you said earlier that it's important to know the final medium in advance of mixing. I'd like to talk about it from a perspective of someone who has a finished track and who wants to understand more about mastering.

RB: Mastering is somehow a musical process. In the first place each track should get what it needs, musically speaking, then they should be made to work together nicely. So I do the musical mastering first, then I consider the technical restrictions of the target medium. The difference between CD and vinyl mastering is that on CD there aren't any limitations on most parameters of the sound other than the final peak volume. With vinyl there are far more physical restrictions which translate to sonic restrictions. So that's why it's a two-stage process. In the first step the considerations are, 'Does it feel right?' 'Is the narrative emphasis where it is supposed to be?' ... stuff like that. Then in the second step the question is, say, 'Will this come across on vinyl?' Well, no ... but yeah ... but no ... but yeah ... sometimes.

Sometimes when mastering specifically for vinyl you might have to make musical restrictions. You might have to lower the prominence of critical parts of the vocals, for example, if you want to make a very loud yet undistorted cut.

RH: Can you tell me about the restrictions in more technical detail?

RB: Actually they're not really restrictions, but rather alterations of the signal. You have to keep in mind that certain geometries of the groove can't be followed precisely by the playback needle. If you try to cut a very broad and complex high frequency signal very loudly, for example, most needles will be overwhelmed. They will not be able to follow the recorded modulation precisely, and instead of playing back what's in the record, they'll start to move in a different way, which results in losing the original information and creating additional distortions instead. Distorted hi-hats are a classic example of this.

Mostly the distorted high frequency signal is enriched with subharmonics. You'll always get some distortion—from vinyl playback you'll get very complex distortions; there is no one-to-one reproduction, it's just physically impossible. If you just record the same signal on different spots of the record it will already sound different.

The question is: 'How precise will the needle be able to follow the geometry provided by the groove?' The accelerations and movements of the playback needle can get rather complex, especially if any kind of phase information is present, which leads to highly complex groove shapes that are engraved into the record.

RH: Does this imply that you can cut more complex signals if they are in mono rather than stereo?

RB: Yes, mono signals are less complex and so slightly less problematic, but there's a huge myth

that you can only cut bass in mono. It's something that stubbornly persists in the minds of many producers, but it's absolutely not true.

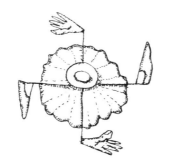

I have cut several thousand vinyls in my time and I really have to think hard to remember an occasion when I had to cripple a stereo bass signal beyond musical recognition because it wasn't translatable to vinyl. There might have been three cases. Anyway, simply put, musicians shouldn't bother about these things—they should just make the music the way they feel it should sound, not for post-production.

Comparison

RH: What are your customers' most common mistakes? What do they tend to do through inexperience, which might make the result musically miserable, and presumably your job more difficult?

RB: I'd say most mistakes are really related to limiting, the second most to compression, and that's about it. There are a lot of things I have to cope with which derive from being uneducated or inexperienced. For example, people commonly sculpt their sound by boosting frequencies if they feel an element is not prominent enough in the mix. Lets boost it! If there's not enough bass or not enough high end—lets boost it!

Instead, I try to educate my customers to think the other way round, to reduce rather than add: scrutinize each signal for consistency, check what disturbs it, and

try to remove that. I always think negative. I know this is much less fun, actually, but the results will be much more consistent and also louder. People try to achieve loudness by saturating media and that's exactly the wrong way round! Saturation can be done at the very end of the process, but if you saturate your medium from step one, you'll have music with a constant high level but which won't sound loud.

The basic mistake is that people compress or limit without a musical vision. They compress or limit because they feel it should be louder, without making proper AB comparisons. That's the thing you have to learn—how to make correct AB comparisons, which isn't at all easy and takes several years of practice.

RH: As I understand it, 'proper AB comparison' means that you listen to the music on your workstation with the limiter and compressor versus the original unlimited, uncompressed signal, towards ending up with an aural equivalent that has a consistent level of loudness.

RB: Yes, but it's more complex than that. Fundamentally, you should always make different kinds of comparisons. For example, you should compare without looking at a metre. You pick one element —which might be the most prominent or important one, or equally the least prominent or important— and set both signals to a volume so the element has the same prominence in both versions, but without looking at the metres. Here you have to be very careful that it *really* has the same prominence, that's it's not just approximate. Then you listen how the rest of the track wraps around this element in both versions. Now look at the metres and set both versions to the same peak level and compare. Most of the time the compressed signal will win. If, on the other hand, you set them both to similar RMS, or average level, and compare, there's a good chance the uncompressed version will win.

The point is, if you compare *looking* at the average level, the uncompressed version will sound more lively, and more punchy! It's hard to speak in general terms here, but I think that a certain amount of generalization is fair enough, because compression is a high art and it's very easy to be satisfied by the results compressors give you, without the results being really good. You can easily be fooled by that perceived boost in loudness if you don't compare correctly.

RH: So should people compress at all?

RB: Well I always tell my customers, 'If you use compression for musical matters—regardless of what compression's *supposed* to be—and the result is something you wanted to achieve artistically, then of course, go for it ... but don't compress just because you think it has to be compressed.' That's the only rule of thumb.

When it comes to limiting, whenever you have the chance to go to a mastering room, I say assume you don't do any limiting at all. Sometimes it helps on a single track to get rid of certain spikes, but don't do it to everything as a matter of course.

A final instruction to the inexperienced would be: don't use maximizers. Never ever ... except *maybe* if you need something to sound as loud as possible on TV. Maximizers are just not a tool to be used musically. If a piece has been maximized before it arrives at the mastering engineer, he won't be able to do anything with the music. The track is flat, dead and sealed, with no access to the details.

Objectivity

RH: I understand your various attitudes towards hardware, but assuming someone wants to do it

themselves and all they have is a laptop, can serious mastering be done entirely with software these days?

RB: Good question. I'm probably not the most competent person to answer it, but from what I've seen on the market I'm not entirely convinced. A much more important point here, though, is that your question implies that a person can master their own music by themselves. From my point of view, the circuit is too closed. One of the strongest cases for mastering is precisely that someone else—ideally someone you trust—is finishing your work with fresh ears. Software might be able to replace my racks of hardware, but it can't replace this aspect of the engineer.

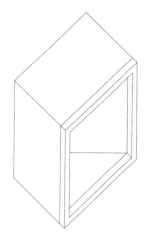

RH: Should people still attempt to master stuff themselves, or would you say that this is something that should never be touched at all?

RB: As I said, an important part of the mastering process is that somebody else does it. Even if you happen to be the mixing engineer and the recording engineer and have forty years of experience, the mastering should still be done by someone else you're in touch with, someone you know. You should attend the mastering session, though. That's the ideal situation,

but of course I understand people who master themselves aren't necessarily control freaks but usually just can't afford outside mastering.

If you DO have to master by yourself, don't attempt to do so in the mix. Mix from a musical perspective, don't mix into a limiter or compressor, carry the finished mix to twenty different places to listen to it in different conditions ... and let some time pass.

THEN do the mastering. It really should be a totally separate process.

RH: What advice wold you give to someone who wants to buy mastering equipment?

RB: First I would ask some questions in return. 'What do you want to buy for? What music are you treating?' Hmmm ... if there are no budget limits ... it's a tricky question. First you need a mastering console where you can easily compare and access signals, because mastering is all about comparison. If you can't compare properly you can't master properly, so this should be the centrepiece, the starting point of your considerations: the signal flow and how to control it.

The mastering desk is also very important because this will be the one piece of equipment that is always in the signal chain, and so everything that is remarkable about it will be remarkable on every piece of music that leaves your studio.

You'd then need some decent parametric EQs, and I'd suggest getting one or two colourful broader EQs. If you go for equipment that has lots of character, you have to be careful, because if it is too recognizable, all your masters will sound the same. It should be equipment which is capable of giving character but which is also capable of being quite neutral.

Recently I've been turning my back on multi-band compressors. I'd actually been a fan for some years, but the more I work with them the less happy I am. It's good to have at least one frequency-selective compressor, especially for the bass range, but the classical multi-band designs have three or more bands and they're more of a problem than a benefit.

RH: Tell me about listening volume!

RB: It has to change all the time! Hearing is not linear. That means if you change the level, your perception changes, so if you listen to a piece at different levels the perceived relation between frequencies will also change.

You have to ask yourself, will this be a piece of music that will mostly be listened to very loud in say, a club, or at a more normal level in, say, a house? That should affect your way of approaching the piece in terms of sonic consistency. Of course the same people will also listen to club music at a lower volume at home, but if you have a reference it should be taken into account.

Besides that, I find it hard to judge compression at normal listening volume. It's easy to make false judgements at a normal level, but at very very low and very very high levels, compression mistakes become very evident. So the first thing I do is listen to a track at a very low level. I also do AB comparisons, often at the limit of the hearing capability. Besides that, the longer you work on a thing, the lazier you get, so you have to really discipline yourself to change the listening levels throughout the process. When I work, I always have one hand at the volume control. One should change the level twice every minute! [laughs]

The mastering engineer Bob Katz tried to establish a fixed listening level for mastering, similar to the fixed level approach for mixing movies for cinema. There it really makes sense, but I'm not too convinced about the idea when it comes to mastering music.

Character

RH: How important is mastering?

RB: It depends who it's mastered by! [laughs] How much a record can be improved by mastering is related not to the quality but to the character of the music. Not all music is really timbre music, not all music is really functional music. There are certain genres of music where I would even be tempted to say it's not so important how it sounds, it might still be brilliant music ... Of course, it can benefit from sounding good in a car or other contemporary music-hating environments: on your mobile phone, on your computer, in your agency, at the cafe, wherever ... but there's music where the sound might not be the crucial element.

And then of course it depends again on how close the sound is to what you wanted to achieve. Actually, in contradiction to the general expectations of my clients, the closer the sound already is to what it is supposed to be, the harder it is to master it; the more repair it needs, the easier it gets. With work that sounds tentative, every little bit of help will affect the result a lot, but if it already sounds resolved, and someone says, 'I want you to get that extra notch, I want you to add your character ...' or something like that, this is often much more difficult. If customers come with an album, and say, 'It really sounds very good already, it shouldn't be a lot of work', I'm already getting scared.

RH: I'd like to talk about objectivity in mastering. It sounds like it's a very personal process, and that your role is far beyond simply fixing technical things. As such, I assume that mastering is not objective at all—that you're actually adding your personal filter to the music ...

RB: Yes, I think it can hardly be objective at all. There are elements to mastering which are outside of personal consideration, but still dependent on your own experience. For example, if you master an album, it is important that you set the levels in a manner that the listener will not have to change the level while enjoying the album. I always advise my clients to listen to the whole album once, on the edge of disturbing the neighbours, to see if there's any track where they immediately want to lower the levels, then to listen to the whole album again at the very low end of attention or perception, to see if there's any track they spontaneously want to pump up. So you could say that's some level of objectivity, but at the end of the day it still depends on your experience and the focus you have while listening to the music.

Some might focus on the voice, and others on the kick-drum, so their perception of an even level throughout an album might be different. It depends on the complexity of the music and how you select from that complexity ... so even these parameters can't really be objective. You might want it to sound good in a club, and think that's objective, but then again what does 'sound good' mean? You know, even with the same piece, different people might have different ideas. Some are totally happy with the snare carrying the track, while others are really intrigued by how shy this one element is in the background in relation to all the other elements. You could say that there's an objective to aim to an even distribution of frequencies, but then again that might not be right musically, because some song might need that totally exaggerated low mid peak which doesn't sound even at all ... in which case it would be a mistake of the mastering to get rid of it completely.

You might say, objectively speaking, this or that will not sound good on all hi-fi systems, but then again I don't think that this should be the only reference for mastering—to make music plausibly represented on all sound systems.

If that blurs the character of the music beyond the intention of the artist, I say its a mistake. Though my mastering approach is probably very much dependent on my personal experience, I still feel like my work is quite apart from my taste. I never feel like, 'I really like that' or 'I really don't like that' —I always see each piece as an entity outside of me. I feel what's right or wrong for the piece, and the clients have to rely on that. Of course I'll discuss what I feel, but it will be my personal judgement at the end of the day. Does the music address me in a way I can receive it? Does it address me in a way I like to receive it? Those are the questions, and they have to be subjective.

Preference

RH: Do you need to like the music you master?

RB: No, but I have to say that while I'm rarely troubled by music at all, I *am* by bad lyrics. If anything keeps me from mastering, or if I do it and suffer, it's always because of the lyrics. It's rarely the case, but it has happened. I don't even have to be intrigued by the music, I can just sense if it feels right or wrong for me.

RH: Are there specific types of music you really enjoy mastering, and others you really don't?

RB: Hmm. [long pause] I couldn't really put my finger on that. I would say no. Of course there's music I like more, and I might enjoy working on it more, but then again I really try to keep my culture and my identity apart from my job. Sometimes I'm really happy to work on music I can absolutely not relate to—it also gives me pleasure, I feel like I'm doing my job, and not just living my life. Sometimes there's music I can strongly relate to, culturally, then I also enjoy it because I feel like I'm having a good day. But again I'm cautious not to have a

good day when it's a good working day. Naturally I like the fact that I'm not bombed with music that tortures me. I think it comes from the context I emerged from. The work somehow sorts itself out, arranges itself so I never actively seem to reject or pick a project. The projects which come to me are 99% projects I can already relate to anyway, then everything else depends on the day. I mean stupid things like one day you're really up for some bass, and the next you're up for anything but bass ...

I don't take much pleasure from music that's really grey. Sometimes if there's a long row of tracks coming in which all have the same greyish type of consistency I get a bit wasted. It's hard for me then to still tell if it's right or wrong, because it just generally feels unpleasant.

RH: Would you say there is a specific Berlin sound in mastering?

RB: Most certainly there's an *idea* that there is. It may be a myth —I can't confirm it one way or the other. People tend to say, 'Well that sounds like English mastering, that sounds like Detroit, that sounds pretty much Berlin ...', but how could anybody verify if it's really the mastering at the basis of those comparisons? I know I can observe sonic fashions in the music I deal with—not necessarily stylistically, but definitely sonically. And I can perceive there are certain vogues if I look at my own mastering back catalogue. In some years I had a certain focus on specific elements of sound, for example, both spectrally and spatially ... and I can see changes, how this focus transforms a bit over time. That's probably the case for every mastering studio and engineer, but as I said, it's hardly verifiable. Of course every studio has a slightly different palette of gear and signal path, and this will inevitably contribute a bit to a specific tone. But this is quite theoretical.

Redundancy

RH: What are your thoughts about volume?

RB: It's a shame, a pity ... there's an increasing tendency to aim for maximum loudness, and I really don't know where it's going to end. But do we speak of loudness or of volume?

RH: Both.

RB: Well, volume is a pain in the ass ... listening volumes all over the place ... it's gross. But the hunt for loudness is a real pity as it makes music less and less distinct. It removes a lot of narration, a lot of information, both from the music making process and from the listener's perception.

By producing music that always aims for maximum loudness you're effectively removing the need to listen to music properly. This will retroactively shape the reasons for making music in the first place, and lead to a situation where all music is more or less interchangeable. That's a real pity, I reckon. With my mastering I try to give people a reason to listen to their music not only on their laptop speakers. Of course sounding good on a laptop is a reasonable demand nowadays, but when all music is made on that premise—is tailored to the playback technology—then after a couple of years all music will be shaped from the same wood and will sound like it. In this way you can understand why people don't make the effort to get proper hi-fi systems anymore: because the music doesn't give them any reason to do so. It's the same with total availability—you don't have to go searching for music you're interested in anymore, there's no effort involved. The receiving technology starts to work against the art that created the need for that technology in the first place.

Some music needs loudness: there are certain idioms which require the contrast of quiet parts and blasts. Dramaturgically speaking, of course, loudness has huge potential, but by making all music in this loud, steady-state, that potential is undermined, and it diminishes.

Apart from the physical effect of tiring your ears, do you know about transients and you how they shape your cognition of sound? Transients can carry a lot of musical information, but now they're almost extinct. The use of our ears degenerates, as music is no longer developed to utilize their full sensory potential. People use their ears as bad eyes. They don't train their listening, don't question the ways by which reality is represented by their ears. And this is all related. I think if music today were more like it was two decades ago—with more elaborate narrative dynamics—it would educate people in listening ... and I mean just general everyday listening, not necessarily musical listening.

So I'm not willing to take part in that race for loudness anymore, because at the end of the day it's so damn redundant. Every amplifier has a volume knob.

I often hear, 'well, you need to pump up the master a little bit more because the mp3 player doesn't give enough level on the headphones.' Now I don't know if that's really the case because I've never used an mp3 player, but if it's true that's disgusting! Then again, what damn levels are people listening to on headphones!? This is really making me sick! I don't want be responsible for it. If it's really the case that current mp3 players don't have headphone amplifiers strong enough to cover up all the noise from the city right now, for sure they'll have them in half a year! I don't know if the ideal aim of mastering is to support music-hostile environments ...

[A long silence]

Trust

RH: This seems like a good point to end. Maybe one last question: how did you become a mastering engineer?

RB: My trajectory is social rather than professional. I've been making music since I was a child, and through that I emerged into very different kinds of cultures and environments. In the 1980s

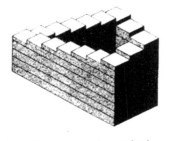

A Reconsideration of the Newspaper Industry in 5 Easy Illusions (5)

Does this lead somewhere or lead nowhere? Is it a loop or a cycle? Or both, or neither?

I did quite a lot of tape stuff, and I started to record other people when I was sixteen. After that I was at an art school, then I started working as a sound engineer again. Later I worked as a sound engineer in theatres, then sound design for theatres and theatre music. Then I started editing movies. While doing this, I was asked to come to Dubplates to do mastering. I didn't have any real experience at that point, and for me it was really a social thing, because I felt close to the Paul Linke Ufer setup, with the Hardwax record store and all the various people involved. I felt culturally close to the sound— I related to it, so I thought, yeah! ... let's do that for a year or something. I always liked to work on a project basis, where you dig into something for six weeks, then it goes away. As it turned out, that's not really the case with mastering:

there's always something on your plate.

I knew that—I mean I could smell it in the very beginning—so I thought I'd just do that for a year. I started mastering without ever really having watched anybody doing it, and also, when I started at Dubplates most of the engineers were leaving for various reasons. I had maybe two or three sessions where I learned how to handle the vinyl cutting machine, then everything somehow just fell into place. I just started doing it.

I don't even know if mastering is much different to any other sound treatment. Again, the most important thing is knowing what you want, because mastering is about decisions. You can master any track in 25 different ways, and at the end of the day if you screw around with it enough and you think, well, that's probably good, let's do it like this, it might be good, but it might also sound like its 'probably good'.

As I said earlier, for me the goal in mastering is that it sounds decisive—that's my idea of 'good'. I always found this relatively easy, and I think that's probably the only talent I really have, making decisions for other people. I'm not as good at making decisions about my own music, but I can relate to other people's material. I feel secure in making those decisions. Of course I also learnt this more by confirming the decisions I made in the outside world, by listening to the records I've cut in clubs, and so on.

But what feels like my only true qualification is that my decisions are trustworthy. In all the working scenarios we've had since the early 1990s, this is the only real qualification anyone has had to have: not necessarily being capable, but just taking the responsibility for what you do.

So I just started taking it.

BADLY EXPLAINED

by Anthony Huberman

It was loud, crowded, and I had had several glasses of wine.

———

Robert Filliou is an artist who fascinates me but who I'm not sure I quite understand. So Larissa Harris and I put together a short exhibition of his work at The Steins, a small room in Chinatown. I quickly find myself listening to what the other visitors to the exhibition were saying about him and began piecing together an approximate picture. This text, as Filliou himself would say, is my way of using the anecdotal to take on the universal. Hopefully, I'll be able to explain the 30-foot diagram that is the *Recherche sur l'origine* (1974).

It seems to start with Charles Fourier. Fourier was a utopian philosopher and socialist from the early 19th century who imagined radically new socio-economic structures in search of universal harmony, well before Marx or Freud. 'Passionate attraction' (*l'attraction passionée*) became his guiding and operative principle, those primordial desires that precede self-consciousness and survive the rational oppositions that reasonable minds invoke. A poetic-scientist of sorts, he presented complex calculations and theories of potential social engineering based on organizing (and harmonizing) people according to their (not necessarily reasonable) desires. In fact, he saw the world not as a place that made sense once science explained it with truths and falsehoods, but as one where the passions of human beings were nurtured and put in collaboration with each other. In other words, your gut comes first, and the mind figures it out from there.

There's also a great story about Fourier's theory of the 4th apple, but Google or Wikipedia will probably be a better place to turn to for that.

Fourier introduced life, joy, and desire into economic equation and scientific data analysis. As an artist, Filliou celebrated the same thing: life, joy, and intuition into an artworld weighed down by critical justifications, competition, money, and (mere) talent. Just as Fourier noted that passion and desire is universal, Filliou pointed to intuition as belonging to everyone. To Filliou, our proximity to intuition is our genius, and so he proclaimed everyone a genius. Talent, a dirty word, is merely our ability to use rational thought or acquired skill to execute a task. Knowledge is similarly distant from intuition. In fact, Filliou tells us that research is not the domain of those who know, but of those who *don't* know. This directly applies to both Filliou's *Recherche sur l'origine* as well as to my attempt at writing about Filliou's *Recherche sur l'origine*.

For Filliou, the avant-garde (Duchamp included, it's worth mentioning) is a matter of talented invention. Standing against that is intuition, play, and *génie sans talent* (genius without talent). And genius without talent is happening all the time, whether people are making art or not. It happens every

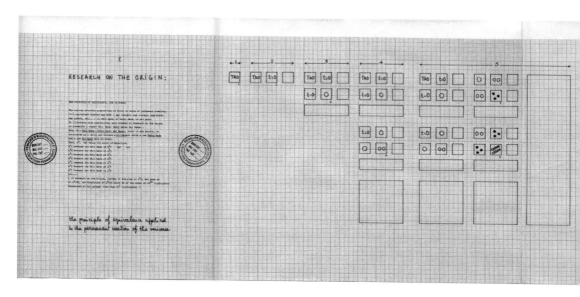

time we trust our intuition and act accordingly, every time we follow our passions. Filliou even invented a republic, the *République Géniale,* a place where people go to focus on their genius rather than on their talent. This territory, of course, is everywhere and anywhere and exists in permanent and immaterial potentiality. Charles Fourier would have been proud. It leads to Filliou's idea of Permanent Creation ... his so-called Eternal Network. This network simply describes the universal reality that art is life is play is creation, all of which are permanent and part of everything in the world, all the time. *La fête permanente*!

In 1968, Filliou arrived at his central project, the Equivalency Principle, whereby the well-done, the badly-done, and the not-done are considered equal. This principle falls directly in line with Fourier in that it allows for action that obeys intuition, preference, and passion, rather than reason and efficiency. 'Error' stops being inadequate. It also relates to the genius without talent by confirming the irrelevance of talent and the equivalence of all acts of imagination, play, creation, and genius. And most crucially, the Equiva-

lency Principle incorporates the permanency of creation. It gets a bit complicated here. If a creative act exists in three ways (well-done, badly-done, not-done), then once the three manifestations of the creative act have occurred, they become the beginning of another creative act that itself has three manifestations (well-done, badly-done, not-done). This second string of threes, of course, multiplies again into another set of well-done, badly-done, and not-done versions of itself. As Filliou says so well: 'and so on and so forth.'

For his work *Principe d'Équivalence* (1968), Filliou takes a red sock and puts it in a yellow box. On a simple piece of wood, he attaches an example of the act done well, a second example where it is not done well, and a third example that simply states the idea, without doing it at all. Next to this piece of wood that contains those three creative acts are three additional pieces of wood. The first one is a well-made copy of the original three-acts. The second is a badly-made version of it. And the third is a blank piece of wood, where none of the original three acts are made. The continuation, I think, is more or less clear ... and infinite.

This brings us to *Recherche sur l'origine,* which is essentially a diagrammatic version of the more sculptural *Principe d'Équivalence.* The original long scroll was first shown in the Kunsthalle Düsseldorf in 1974 and wrapped itself around the gallery walls. Replacing red socks in yellow boxes are simply drawn squares containing letters, shapes, dots, and, most prominently, nothing at all. As the creative act runs through its endless series of well-done, badly-done, not-done iterations, the empty spaces grows exponentially, represented by the succession of gradually-larger empty squares. Eventually, it looks like a lot of nothing. And so the equivalency principle reveals its paradoxical truth: the more you create, the less there is.

Below: Robert Filliou, *Recherche sur l'Origine / Research on the Origin,* 1974. Card box containing a scroll of graph paper with wood ends and a loose booklet. Scroll: 30 × 900 cm [unrolled]. Booklet: 14.7 × 10.5 cm. Edition of 400 signed and numbered copies. Published by Kunsthalle Düsseldorf, 1974. Courtesy Specific Object / David Platzker, New York.

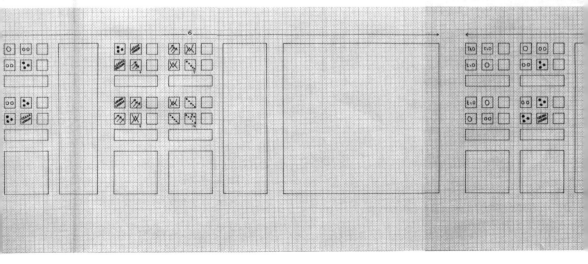

COMMENCEMENT ADDRESS

David Foster Wallace's address to the graduating class
of Kenyon College, May 21, 2005

The concluding four pages of the issue were intended to carry a raw transcription of this speech, copy-pasted without amendment from http://www.marginalia.org/dfw_kenyon_commencement.html.

The text was first read aloud to me as I sat in the bath a few days after the sad announcement of Wallace's death. An edited version was published shortly afterwards in *The Guardian*, and at the time of writing it has just been released as a small book, *This is Water: Some thoughts, Delivered on a Significant Occasion, about Living a Compassionate Life*, by Little, Brown. While this book has dutifully monumentalized the text by isolating each sentence on a separate page, it seems to me that it still reads best and warmest as close as possible to its original informality.

I had concluded a brief introduction not dissimilar to this one with a note of excuse against probable copyright violation —words to the effect that in an ideal world all periodicals would be compelled to publish the same. However, when double-checking the marginalia.org link on the final day of proofing, we found this:

Why the speech isn't here any longer.

I hope you enjoy the book.

I wish you way more than luck.

Back to marginalia.org

The first link led to the following explanation:

It's true, I have removed my copy of the beloved DFW commencement speech. As I thought might be obvious, the recent publication of the text in book form brought a stern copyright enforcement letter to my door. I lack the time and money necessary to fight such a thing, so, as much as it meant to me to play a small role in making it known to people, I won't be hosting it any more.

Happy googling.

As we also lack the time and money necessary to fight such a thing, it seems more pertinent to use this space instead to point to the presence of The Way Back Machine. This is a project of The Internet Archive (www.archive.org), an attempt to construct a real-time archive of the always-changing contents of the World Wide Web. Using The Way Back Machine interface, snapshots of the web may be browsed from any point in time. For example:

http://web.archive.org/web/20080213082423/http://www.marginalia.org/dfw_kenyon_commencement.html

PROJECT NO.8

WWW.LINETO.COM

Lineto is one segment of a 'path'.
Lineto is stored in the GDI32.
Lineto is 5/9 of that for the line command.
Lineto is set to the line number in which the selection ends.
Lineto is used.
Lineto is replaced by Lineto-3D.
Lineto is missing the statement.
Lineto is definitely not the way to do it.
Lineto is used to make sure that we call the correct function.
Lineto is used to create a series of line segments.
Lineto is performed to the starting point of the arc.
Lineto is Warp 7.

LUDLOW 38

European Kunsthalle Cologne Goethe Institut
New York
www.ludlow38.org

August 27 – October 11, 2009
Lili Dujourie & Ion Grigorescu

DOT DOT DOT 18
Summer 2009
ISBN-13: 978-0-9794654-1-3

© 2009 Dexter Sinister.
All rights reserved.
All material is compiled
from sources believed to
be reliable, but published
without responsibility
for errors or omissions.

Published twice a year
by Dexter Sinister
38 Ludlow Street (Basement)
New York, NY 10002
U.S.A.
www.dextersinister.org
info@dextersinister.org

www.dot-dot-dot.us

EDITOR
Stuart Bailey
sinister@o-r-g.com
Los Angeles

This issue co-edited with
David Reinfurt
reinfurt@o-r-g.com
New York

Production/Coordination:
Sarah Crowner
sarah@dextersinister.org

Final proofreading
Frances Stark

THANKS
Danielle Aubert
Toby Barlow
Marion Bettler-Esleben
Randolf Cliff
Edinburgh College of Art
Alan Johnston
Aaron Kunin
Charles McLean
David Platzker
Sandra Skurvida
Werkplaats Typografie

PRINTING
Interior: Logotipas, Vilnius
Cover/insert: Knust,
Extrapool, Nijmegen

DDD has attempted to
contact all copyright
holders, but this has not
been possible in all instances.
We apologize for any
omissions and, if noted,
will amend in any future
editions.

All pieces designed by
editors/authors except
'The Middle of Nowhere'
by Will Holder.

CONTRIBUTORS

Domenick Ammarati
New York

Dave Hullfish Bailey
Los Angeles

Jay Baldwin
San Francisco

Rashad Becker
Berlin

Clémentine Deliss
London

Liam Gillick
New York

Jan Åke Granath
Göteborg

Richard Grusin
Detroit

Robert Henke
Berlin

Will Holder
London

Anthony Huberman
St. Louis

Angie Keefer
New York

Louis Lüthi
Amsterdam

Raimundas Malasauškas
Paris

Karel Martens
Amsterdam

Randall McLeod
Toronto

Mark Owens
Los Angeles

Radim Peško
Amsterdam

Michelangelo Pistoletto
Biella

David Senior
New York

Christopher Wilson
Sheffield

DISPERSION

DDD is available
foremost from our own
point of distribution:
Dexter Sinister
Just-In-Time Workshop
& Occasional Bookstore
38 Ludlow Street (Basement)
New York, NY 10002
U.S.A.
OPEN SATURDAYS FROM
12 TO 6 PM
www.dextersinister.org
info@dextersinister.org

SUBSCRIPTIONS
1 year (2 issues):
€30 in Europe
$56 everywhere else
(worldwide exchange rates
subject to change) from:
Bruil & Van de Staaij
Postbus 75,
7940 AB Meppel
The Netherlands
T: +31 522 261 303
F: +31 522 257 827
info@bruil.info
www.bruil.info

DISTRIBUTION EUROPE
Coen Sligting Bookimport
Van Oldenbarneveldtstraat 77
1052 JW Amsterdam
The Netherlands
T: +31 20 673 2280
F: +31 20 664 0047
sligting@xs4all.nl

DISTRIBUTION UK
Central Books
115 Wallis Road
London E9 5LN
U.K.
T: +44 (0)845 458 9911
F: +44 (0)845 458 9912
orders@centralbooks.com
www.centralbooks.com

DISTRIBUTION AMERICAS,
ASIA, AFRICA, AUSTRALIA
Princeton Architectural Press
37 E 7th Street
New York, NY 10003
U.S.A.
T: +1 212 995 9620
F: +1 212 995 9454
sales@papress.com
www.papress.com

ADVERTISING
DDD adverts are paid
according to the
background greyscale
percentage; contact
sarah@dextersinister.org
for rates or reservations

RECYCLING

'Change Page' is taken
from Dave Hullfish Bailey's
forthcoming book *What's Left*
(Casco/Sternberg, 2009),
where it appears as 'Show
Don't Tell'. Transferred with
thanks.

A version of 'Torslanda to
Uddevalla via Kalmar' was
first published in a book
accompanying the exhibition
Custom Car Commandos,
curated by Sandra Skurvida
at Art in General, New York,
Spring 2009. Reassembled
with thanks.

A version of 'The Adapter'
was first published in the
Werkplaats Typografie book
Wonder Years (ROMA, 2008)
as 'Jay Baldwin: The way
I ended up living is my best
design'. Adapted with thanks.

'On the Self-Reflexive Page'
is an amended version
of a text originally written
as '*Prière d'insérer*' for a
forthcoming book. Mirrored
with thanks.

The cartoons throughout are
from the archive of Quinton
Oliver Jones. Courtesy
Dale & Connie Gephart
(administrators of the Quinton
Oliver Jones database) and
Emily and Sarah Gephart
(custodians of the Quinton
Oliver Jones archive).
Revived with thanks.

The optical illusions
throughout are scanned
from five issues of *The
Poughkeepsie Journal*, where
they were published as
Dexter Sinister's contribution
to the project 'Column',
a series of interventions in
a local newspaper organized
by Marion Ritter from Bard
College, NY. Descreened
with thanks.

The axonometric elevations
of model furniture (sandwich
board, left lectern, shelf,
right lectern, True Mirror™)
throughout were drawn
in CAD by Geoff Bailey.
Rendered with thanks.

DDD18: Set in Edinburgh
Summer 2009